NINE SIDES
OF THE
DIAMOND

NINE
SIDES
OF THE
DIAMOND

BASEBALL'S GREAT GLOVE MEN

ON THE FINE ART

OF DEFENSE

David Falkner

Library of Congress Cataloging-in-Publication Data
Falkner, David. Nine sides of the diamond : baseball's
great glove men on the fine art of defense / by
David Falkner. p. cm.
ISBN 0-8129-1806-1
1. Fielding (Baseball) 2. Baseball—United States—
History. 3. Baseball—United States—
Defense. I. Title. GV870.F35 1990
796.357'24—dc20 89-40191

Manufactured in the United States of America

Book design by Mina Greenstein
Photo layout design by J. Vandeventer

2 4 6 8 9 7 5 3

First Edition

This copyright page is continued on pages 371–72.

TO JENNY

Contents

Introduction

Out Where the Wild Things Are: **WILLIE MAYS** *about to make his
historic catch in the 1954 World Series. The fact that it became quite
so historic bothered Mays. He believed he made better ones.*
AP/WIDE WORLD PHOTOS

THE PHOTOGRAPHS SHOW sunlight that day. Thirty-seven years old and snowy with time, the images are as permanent in our memory as if they were recorded yesterday. The box score says that there were 52,751 actual witnesses on September 29, 1954, at the Polo Grounds for the opening game of that year's World Series between the Giants and the Indians, but the number of people who remember, freeze frame by freeze frame, what is referred to now simply as the Catch probably includes every baseball fan on earth.

There are one to four frames that bind our memories. The first shows Willie Mays, his white-shirted number 24, his back to the world, running out of room at the far end of the longest outfield in baseball, his hands up, his head slightly back, a blob of white clearly in his glove. That is almost enough in itself. Who ever has made a catch like that, out where the wild things are, 450 feet from home plate?

But now take frame two. The ball is no longer in sight. The hands held initially at head level are parallel with the chest, and the slight twist of the body to the left in the act of extending for the catch has disappeared. There is more of Mays's back now. It appears he is actually tilting backward except that his right leg is extended out straight as a ramrod. But it is not a ramrod at all.

Frame three shows exactly what has happened. Simultaneous with the Catch, number 24 has already prepared for the Throw. In this frame, Mays's hat has flown free from his head, his body is twisted left again, but now he is in a crouch, his hands almost at his waist, his head looking back toward the infield—even from a mile away, you can see the glare of concentration in his eyes.

His right leg is firmly planted, the left curled at the knee, his shoulder pointed to the target.

Frame four is Mays releasing his throw. His head is twisted left, the left shoulder is down, his right arm, fully extended, is high above his other shoulder, and the ball is a blur of white just off his fingertips. The right leg, still behind him, is no longer planted. The heel of the foot is slightly raised and it is the striding-forward left foot that is now planted—almost. The frame, which arrests Mays at the midpoint of his weight shift, shows even more dramatically the titanic effort involved in the throw.

But there is something missing. There is no fifth frame showing what followed, and the consequences of the Catch and the Throw were, if anything, even more dramatic. The game was in the eighth inning with the score tied, 2–2. The Indians had just gotten their first two men on base, had driven Sal Maglie, the Giants' starter, from the mound, and were clearly in position to win the game. This was the effect of what Mays did: The runner on second, Larry Doby, who might have been able to advance two bases and score if he had anticipated a catch being made at so deep a point in the park, was able to move up only one base. The runner on first, caught in between and equally disoriented, merely retreated to first. Instead of the Indians' claiming a lead with another runner in scoring position, the tie was preserved, an out recorded, the possibility of a double play kept alive.

I have always thought that this play defined what defense in baseball is all about. There was nothing defensive in it. It was not only a game winner, it was game, match, and series. The Indians subsequently were swept in four games, and it takes little imagination to believe that these young Cleveland players, victims of the play, must have wondered afterward whether or not the man who made it was real. Upstairs in the radio booth, what Mays did was described as an optical illusion. Vic Wertz, the player who hit the ball to Mays, a ball that almost anywhere else would have been one of the longest homers in Series history, said a few years before his death that he felt a kind of lasting pride to be

associated with the Catch. "I look at it this way," he said. "If it had been a home run or a triple would people have remembered it? Not very likely."

Great defense has always seemed to have that effect: It snatched away not only games but spirit as well, deflating, sometimes hypnotizing one's opponents, while elevating one's teammates. Think of these leaping, diving, acrobatic, behind-the-back, tumbling, upside-down, hat-flying, gravity-defying disappearing and appearing acts, where you are faced with arms stronger than javelin throwers', legs and feet trickier than tap dancers', hands as fast as three-card-monte dealers'. If you are an impartial witness you may share with sportswriter Jimmy Cannon the sense that baseball is a higher art than ballet because the artistry of baseball is not aided by choreography.

In any sport other than baseball, the relationship between defense and winning is obvious. Put the Chicago Bears of the early 1980s in their 4-6 and watch their opponents die; let the New York Giants hire a Lawrence Taylor, the Buffalo Bills deal for a Cornelius Bennett, and watch those franchises live. The same is true in basketball. The "bad boy" Pistons smother their opponents with defense. Don't ask what the Philadelphia Flyers do. And in football, basketball, hockey, soccer, volleyball, lacrosse, water polo, even quoits and curling, the defense that wins, everyone knows, need not be eye-catching to also be headline-grabbing. Routine is big, bad, blue, and bruising enough. It doesn't quite come off the same way in baseball. Great fielding plays—though they occur with relative infrequency—are usually what many fans think of as great defense in baseball. Yet ask any insider and he will tell you that routine play is the heart and soul of any sound defense. As Mike Schmidt, the Phillies' ten-time Gold Glove third baseman, who retired last season, puts it, "Show me a great fielder and I'll show you a fielder who makes the routine play."

There are certain consequences that flow from a game so arranged, not the least being that defense may be honored more

in word than in deed. Regardless, this word *defense* remains with us, apart from all other defenses in sport, elusive, obvious, and mysterious, whether in great or routine play.

To go back to the Catch: The obvious part was Mays's sheer athletic ability. Lesser athletes would simply not have been able to make such a play. It is surely elusive and mysterious that only a few among us are the recipients of superior physical gifts, but even more wondrous is the thinking, imagination, instinct, decision making—all that produced frame five—that allowed Mays to be where he was, when he was, and to know, in a split second of time, precisely what to do once he got there. In the end, it was not sheer athleticism that allowed him to make the play. There was a kind of intelligence beyond hand-eye coordination, a summoning of powers and procedures older than Mays or any individual player at any given time. The play was really the collective possession of all players.

WE DATE BASEBALL from Alexander Cartwright, but its skills go back almost to the dawn of creation, to the first use of clubs and stones. Almost every culture in the world (particularly now that baseball has become so international) lays some sort of finder's claim to the game. Robert Henderson and Harold Peterson have examined some of the claims. In his book *The Man Who Invented Baseball,* Peterson has traced baseball-like games far back in history—and far afield. Long before cricket and rounders came anywhere near the playing fields of Eton, the Slavs, the Lapps, the Danes, the Swedes, the Finns, the Goths, and the Berbers had their batting and fielding games. Peterson locates in the Domesday Book of 1086 reference to a game called "bittle battle" (the Saxon word *bittle* means "bat"); an illuminated manuscript from 1344, he notes, includes an illustration of a woman throwing a ball to a man holding a bat with others, possibly fielders, standing by. The Berbers played a game called *"om el mahag,"* with teams of batsmen (called "marksmen") and fielders ("hunters"). The marksmen struck a ball similar in size to an American baseball,

then moved between five irregularly arranged bases. Outs were recorded by catching a ball in the air or throwing at and striking a runner. Scandanavians, centuries and thousands of miles apart, with no possible contact with the Berbers, played a similar game called "longball" (unrelated to Reggie's game).

"Every bit of anthropological evidence," Peterson writes,

> says that these games go back to uttermost antiquity, back to the first fertility rites . . . The Berbers call the runner's base "mother"; some Slavs carried this further and called the captain of the fielding team "mother," even when male. Eugen Piasecki, preeminent scholar of Slavic games, feels sure that the original contests were between a "father's" side—the batters—and a "mother's" side—the catchers.

Citing an abundance of anthropological literature, Peterson notes the magical and ritualistic associations of bat and ball. The spherical shape of a ball, for example, was a magical representation of everything from a seed to an egg to the womb of the earth mother herself. To the Berbers the ball may have represented raindrops falling from the sky, necessary to draw life from parched ground. To Europeans, "*Ball* is so old and basic that it originally seems to have meant almost any globular clump of anything." *Bale* of hay, *bole* of a tree, *bullet, bubble, ballad, ballet,* all have specific associations with *ball*.

> Have you ever wondered why a dance should be called a "ball" or a "ballet" and a song a "ballad"? Ballet derives from some of the same early ball games we have been discussing. A ball would be thrown about, gracefully, in pagan fertility rites. Only thereafter did the ballplaying become a dance. Eventually music was added and singing. At last the ball itself disappeared.

In America, baseball developed right out of these old games. In 1845, when Alexander Cartwright "invented" baseball, what he really did was alter and adapt older, prevailing popular games,

particularly "town ball," which was widely played in the Northeast. Town ball, unlike cricket but like rounders, "one old cat," and those old Berber and Norse games, used multiple bases and recorded outs either by catching balls on the bound or fly or by striking runners with the ball as they moved between bases. As in cricket, however, a ball could be struck anywhere. With no foul territory, defenders had to concern themselves as much with a tick off the bat as with a ball dispatched to a pasture in the next township. Position playing could be anywhere between here and China and, true to the name of the game, any and all townsmen who showed up, nine, ten, fifteen, or more to a side, got to play. (A game popular in Connecticut, wicket, had as many as thirty players or more in the no-foul field.)

Most significant as far as the development of baseball was concerned was that a town-ball field, whether laid out on a hillside or in a pasture, with or without obstructing trees in the middle of the playing area, employed four "bases"—with a separate place for hitting—in a boxlike design. Cartwright's first, primitive diamond is just the old town-ball box at a tilt.

What this tilt did was stand the game on its head, civilizing what had been a recreational vestige of a primitive rite. Gone was the disorder of balls being hit anywhere and players being drilled on any part of their anatomy. Instead, there came rules of law and decent divisions of labor. Foul lines separated balls in and out of play, throwing or tagging runners out at each base replaced the high hard one to vulnerable body parts. Skills, old as they were, were refined accordingly. Modern position play came into being.

While it took a couple of decades to settle on the exact number of players permitted in the new game, the positions of the field as we now know them became quickly fixed. By the time of the first professional teams in the late 1860s, though dimensions between mound and plate and rules governing balls and strikes were still to be fiddled with, what fielders did would be quite recognizable to us today. An anonymous member of the 1869

Cincinnati Red Stockings, baseball's first super team (they went a season and a half without being defeated), wrote a paean to his club. Nothing is said in the poem about hitting, though the Red Stockings regularly scored twenty, thirty, forty, fifty runs a game. Little is said in the poem about pitching, though opponents were often held to single-digit scores. But everything was said about the men at their positions—that was where the game really was.

With the field newly designed and rules still not settled, the game clearly favored hitters, and there was a need to emphasize the work of the defense. In those early years, for example, pitchers did not yet throw overhand; until 1887, a batter was entitled to call for a high or low pitch; it wasn't until 1888 that a batter once and for all was entitled to only three strikes (though fouls were not then counted as strikes); and it wasn't until the following year that hitters were limited to four balls per plate appearance. Amidst all this, the stout-hearted men of the field enacted their rituals of defense with little or no protection. The first gloves did not appear until the 1870s (and those were pads used merely to protect already broken fingers), and the first catcher's mask (players were accused of being "babyish" for donning them) dated from the same period. There is little wonder, then, that long before "Casey at the Bat," songs were sung to the men of the field.

In newspaper accounts of the era, it was not uncommon for a story of a shutout—or even a no-hitter—to make more of the defense than of the pitching. Three straight shutout wins by the St. Louis Browns over the Hartford Blues in 1876, culminating in the first no-hit game in National League history, made for rivers of purple in the St. Louis press:

> The GLOBE DEMOCRAT yesterday morning announced the fact that the St. Louis Base Ball Club intended accomplishing the greatest feat in the annals of the game, if sharp play could bring about the result prayed for, which was nothing less than the white-

washing of the famous Hartford nine for the third consecutive time.
They did it, and thereby covered themselves with glory and sent
their admirers into ecstasies. . . . Bradley's pitching, and the magnificent backing given it by the fielders, won the day for St. Louis. For
the first time in the annals of the League, nine innings were played
without a single base hit being placed.

There have been enormous changes in the game since it
emerged from the dead-ball era. The mound has been adjusted
and readjusted, equipment has been changed, as have the size,
weight, and shape of balls and bats, ballparks have been altered
and destroyed, playing surfaces have been transformed. The com-
panions of Alexander Cartwright would have a hard time recog-
nizing their modern millionaire counterparts in spandex double
knits today, but what is required from each of the nine positions
of the defense is not terribly different now from the time of the
Red Stockings. The gift of baseball is the positions. Put a diamond in the wilderness and everything will grow up around it
like nothing else in Tennessee. Over here will be a first baseman,
there a shortstop, behind him a left fielder. These men will enact
over and over again the rituals of their beginnings, each in his
precise way, as though the moves, thoughts, and emotions powering them were not so much coached as biologically transmitted
so that we might see in the present, in the players of the tube and
the nightly news, in the men who spit and paw the ground and
scratch themselves, the very first ground ball, the first diving
catch, the first play at the plate, the first midair pirouette on a ball
slowly chopped toward third.

Willie Mays was a center fielder, as much a man defined by
his territory as George Washington or Peter the Great. But he
was also Frank Lloyd Wright, creator of spaces. He played center
but what he did speaks to all fielders everywhere from the first
hunter to Billy Hunter.

One thing more. From the time he made the Catch to the
present, Mays has always shrugged off the play. For many years,

he argued that other outfielders regularly made better ones. More recently, in his 1988 autobiography, *Say Hey,* possibly because the chorus of praise has, if anything, grown with the years, Mays once again sought to downplay his accomplishment—but this time not so much by a modest denial but by an explanation of situation baseball:

Doby led off with a walk. Rosen beat out an infield hit. First and second, none out, and Vic Wertz was up. He was 3 for 3 against Maglie—a triple in the first, a single in the fourth, single in the sixth. He was a left-handed power hitter. Leo had seen enough, and he called for Don Liddle, a left-handed pitcher, to relieve Maglie and face Wertz.

I played Wertz to pull the ball slightly. He had been getting around well all day, and in this situation, two runners on, I figured he'd be likely to hit behind them so they could advance. Also, I knew that most hitters like to swing at a relief pitcher's first pitch, and that crossed my mind as Liddle was warming up.

And that's what happened. He swung at Liddle's first pitch. I saw it clearly. As soon as I picked it up in the sky, I knew I had to get over toward straightaway centerfield. I turned and ran at full speed toward center with my back to the plate. But even as I was running, I realized I had to be in stride if I was going to catch it, so about 450 feet away from the plate I looked up over my left shoulder and spotted the ball. I timed it perfectly and it dropped into my glove maybe 10 or 15 feet from the bleacher wall. At that same moment, I wheeled and threw in one motion and fell to the ground. I must have looked like a corkscrew. I could feel my hat flying off, but I saw the ball heading straight to Davey Williams on second. Davey grabbed the relay and threw home. Doby had tagged up at second after the catch. That held Doby to third base, while Rosen had to get back to first very quickly.

Was it the greatest catch I ever made? Some people think it was the greatest catch anyone ever made, but I think that's because it was in a World Series and seen by so many people on television. Also, there is a famous action sequence of the catch by a photographer and it is pretty dramatic.

There are little hints in this account (such as the distances covered, the fact that relay man Davey Williams was standing *at second base* rather than in medium center field) that will always keep things in perspective, but Mays's principal point is that he was able to make his play because he knew the situation so well. He later lists other catches he made during his career that he felt were more difficult—and perhaps they were—but nothing lends more grace to this particular play than his unspoken assumption that the sort of intelligence he brought to bear was, well, part of the job. Of course, he was absolutely right—and that is the whole point. Great fielding, first and last, is geared to situation.

Any ballplayer says that what the game is about is winning. But the desire to win is a kind of blank slate, to be filled in by a player's hold on the situation. This requires imagination, which counts even more than the desire to win because it determines what you do to win—and even how you deal with losing.

Willie Mays says that he learned to walk at six months by tottering after baseballs his father set out for him on different chairs. "See the ball, see the ball," Mays remembers his father saying to him—until he could let go of one chair and get to another completely on his own. When Mays went to elementary school, he carried a rubber ball with him at all times. He played catch on the way to and from school, and when he was by himself he bounced balls off sidewalks, off stoops. "When I try to remember events as a kid, in my memories somehow, a ball always winds up in my hands."

Willie Mays, as special as he was, wasn't special at all. He was a fielder from the start. That is, his childhood imagination was peculiarly engaged by fielding. It is frequently that way with great fielders. Most baseball-loving children are attracted to games that focus on hitting and pitching—stickball (which came later for Mays), tee ball, cork ball, half ball, and so forth. Mark McGwire, the huge home-run-hitting first baseman of the Oakland Athletics, played a childhood game in his backyard in which he closed in a circular area with a makeshift fence and then, warming up for the future, whacked Whiffle balls clear out of his park. But

with child fielders, the games have always been a little different. Since such play generally required no partners, the dreams and imaginations of the young fielders often seem rooted in privacy and solitude.

Willie Kamm, a great defensive third baseman with the White Sox and Indians during the twenties and thirties, spent a lot of his childhood time alone. His parents, strict German immigrants, neither approved nor even understood his early appetite for baseball. "I was always nuts about baseball," he told Lawrence S. Ritter in *The Glory of Their Times*. "I couldn't play enough. It was always that way, far back as I can remember. There were three cemeteries near our house when I was a kid, and I remember throwing balls, or stones, up against the walls of those cemeteries for hour after hour. All by myself, hour after hour."

Brooks Robinson, arguably the greatest third baseman in history and a gregarious, cheerful man, as much in love with the game today as when he played it, remembers spending hours by himself when he was a child in front of his home, which had a five-step stoop in front. Brooks, of course, had a ball in his hand.

"I used to fire a rubber ball off this stoop," he says, "off each step because the ball came back differently from each of the steps. I can't believe how much time I spent doing that and all the while I had only one dream, which was to be a major league ballplayer. I never wanted to do anything else. It was with me every second of every day in everything I did."

Ditto for Al Kaline, the Hall of Fame outfielder for the Tigers who, even as a skinny, frightened, 150-pound rookie, knew he could throw a ball farther, harder, and more accurately than others.

"I played every day as a kid, that's all I did. I was a great stone thrower," Kaline remembers. "I used to live on the railroad tracks and when trains went by, I'd throw at them, try to hit them, try to hit targets. I knew what times the trains went by every day and I'd go get my stones and rocks and I'd fire at them, right at the O in the B&O on the sides of the trains."

Ray Dandridge, the old Negro League third baseman and also a Hall of Famer, used to follow the sun of a baseball season with a glove tied to his belt. He had a game he played by himself, as he went.

"I used to hold a ball in my palm," Dandridge, diminutive and bent with age, recalls, "then I'd slap the heel of my palm with my other hand, knocking the ball up in the air. Soon as the ball went up, I'd close my eyes and swipe at it. Trick was to take it out of midair without looking. I did it over and over again; I don't know how many hours and years of my life I spent doing that."

Fielders today are no different. Mike Schmidt grew up bouncing golf balls off walls from a couple of feet away. Frank White used to make balls he could toss in the house by stuffing the heads of his sisters' old dolls with paper. Tony Fernandez, like other Dominican children, grew up in an environment of dire poverty and little open space. He fashioned a fielding glove from cardboard and fired rubber balls off stones, stoops, walls, sometimes by himself, sometimes with friends who would turn into base runners and first basemen between this rock and that. And, of course, Ozzie Smith, as a child, was already dabbling in magic: "When I was about ten or eleven, I used to lie in my room, alone, on my back, on the floor. I used to toss balls at the ceiling. Just as the ball reached its height," he says, "I closed my eyes and put out my hands to see if I could catch it."

The fielders who leave these games of childhood behind take with them improved coordination, softer hands, quicker feet. But there is a carryover in habit of mind as well. The imagination of a solitary youngster with a ball is still a powerful tool for mature hunters in the field.

Willie Mays says one of the reasons his catch was not so special was that he got "a good jump on the ball." Think on that a moment. In this casual "good jump" of his, he was able to move into the moment before it happened, knowing who was hitting, who was pitching, how the ball was coming off the bat, what the

score was, who was on base, what park he was playing in. Twenty years and thousands of plays after his father first set him loose between two chairs, the inchoate lure of a ball had become a precisely honed, though still powerfully instinctive ability to sniff out perfectly what he had to do. As is the case with any master hunter, this "good jump" came from the ability to anticipate. The art—as opposed to the mechanics—of fielding begins with this.

Branch Rickey, that Buckminster Fuller of baseball invention, was once reported to have told a fledgling scout that the way to watch a game was to watch players at their positions. "Watch one portion of the field at a time," the old mahatma was supposed to have said, urging the scout to avoid the natural inclination simply to follow the flight of the ball from play to play.

If we follow this instruction, we see players in their private moments of anticipation. At first glance, nothing may seem to be happening. But look again. It is a little like observing a pond, still on the surface, but pulsing with submerged life. Before every pitch, the players are caught in small, idiosyncratic movements: two steps and a tiny jump, a funny little three-step crab walk, a sudden hiking of the britches accompanied by something that looks like a cross between a deep knee bend and a sharp gas pain. Players will thrust their gloves to the ground, dangle them at knee level, spit in them, punch-punch-punch them before each pitch.

The problem is that anticipation does not show up in the box score and that when it is spoken about it is usually in terms of getting that "good jump," a phrase that probably does more to obscure than explain what happens.

The ability to anticipate varies with the player and where he is playing. Imagine, for a moment, a newly acquired but inexperienced third baseman, chunky, a little slow-footed, but brave as a lion, a shortstop or pitcher in high school but who became a third baseman after he was drafted because Team X knew he was a bit slow but because of his big bat wanted to keep him in the lineup. This player probably has come to take fielding seriously.

He has turned in his hours in the minors, has listened to his coaches. In a late-inning, bases-loaded situation, he is playing somewhere between even to a few steps behind the bag and not too far off the line. He knows who's hitting, who's pitching, and he's an aggressive sort—he's thinking, "Hit it to me, hit it to me." He has anticipated that his pitcher, predominantly a breaking-ball pitcher, has a good chance to induce a ground ball. He has already decided before the ball is struck that if it comes his way and he has time he will, as his coaches have trained him, go to second for the force or the beginning of a double play.

In just this situation at a recent season-opening game between the Yankees and the Twins, Gary Gaetti, the Twins' Gold Glove third baseman, started an around-the-horn *triple* play by first stepping on third and then going to second. "I was *looking* for a triple play," he said afterward. "To me, when there are men on base and no one out, you get yourself into triple-play position." The difference between double- or triple-play position for Gaetti turned out not to be a matter of where he stationed himself—which was a step or two in and closer to the bag—but in the game going on in his head, where all of the elements of the situation, even the reading of a batter's face from in close and the look and feel of the strike zone isolated through a kind of tunnel vision he had learned to develop, led to a readiness in which decisions still to be made were already poised on the edge of doing.

Sometimes this sense of anticipation comes close to actual clairvoyance. In the celebrated sixth game of the 1975 World Series, won by Carlton Fisk's body-English home run in the twelfth inning, Dwight Evans, the Red Sox right fielder, made a game-saving catch in the eleventh by diving into the stands to take a home run away from the Reds' Joe Morgan.

"Just before the pitch," Evans says, "I was going over in my mind what I would do if the ball went into the stands. I saw the ball going in and myself diving after it—and then it really happened."

If ballplayers anticipate differently, each depending on the peculiar imaginative powers he brings with him, it is also true that players anticipate differently at different positions. As specific as the physical skills are at a given position, there is a different kind of mental engagement as well. It is almost impossible, for example, to imagine Gary Gaetti having the luxury of the extended prevision Dwight Evans had in right field, any more than the jumpy, hair-trigger mental preparations of Gaetti would suit Evans—or any other outfielder.

Paul Molitor of the Brewers is one of an increasing number of ballplayers who play more than one position. It is as though he needs a different thinking cap for each position.

"I came up originally as a shortstop," Molitor says. "I was used to having time to think about how I wanted to play a ball. The same was true at second except everything seemed backwards: the angles and spin of the ball coming at you, making the double play blind, realizing that things happened with your back to the play. Third base was much more reactive. There was no time to think whole thoughts—everything's so close, right on top of you. When I went to the outfield, it was a shock. You're a lot more isolated, separated from your teammates. In high school, the fences are two hundred and fifty feet away, in the pros it's three hundred fifty to four hundred feet. The look of the game out there makes you feel lonely and it's harder to concentrate."

More than anything, anticipation suggests just how much the game in the field is decided by what takes place in a player's mind. Several seasons ago, Clete Boyer, then a coach on the Oakland A's and who had been as fine a fielding third baseman in his time as anyone, was watching a young infielder on his team take ground balls. "The thing about the game at this level is that there really is very little difference in physical skills between players; the real difference between them is upstairs. No one will ever have more tools than that kid," he said, continuing to keep an eye on the fielder, "but so what? The other day, he made a great play in the field, the kind you just don't make without great hands and

feet, and you know what he does? He comes to me and says, 'Did I do it right?' Can you believe that, asks me if he did it right!" Boyer shook his head disbelievingly. "That question," he said, "has to be out of the way long before you ever get here—you can't play at this level with that in your head—it's just a different game up here."

But the game Boyer was talking about was beyond crises of identity and self-esteem. It was about the Catch, not *The Catcher in the Rye*.

This mental game in the field, something easy to exaggerate but hard to pin down, is nowhere better illustrated than in the career of Mark Belanger, the Orioles' shortstop during the glory years of Earl Weaver. Belanger, by his own and everyone else's admission, was a good-field, no-hit player. The difference between him and batallions of others similarly tagged was that his career lasted. Belanger spent eighteen years in the majors, eighteen years compiling a lifetime .228 batting average along with the third-highest career fielding average for shortstops ever.

Like a lot of other "born" fielders, Belanger had his childhood games. Growing up in Pittsfield, Massachusetts, he drove his parents to distraction, blackening the white clapboard of the family house with his ball games. He began at about age eleven, he says, and had a routine. Initially throwing at a distance of around one hundred feet, he would move closer and closer so the re-bounding ball would come at him faster and faster. There was an area of brick between the ground and clapboard, and when the ball struck there, it would ricochet more sharply.

But the chief feature of this game, which ended ten to fifteen feet from the house with the child hurling wall-shaking bolos, was that it was geared always to make-believe game situations.

"I never threw a ball without imagining a game situation," says Belanger, now middle-aged, with scars from old spike wounds on both legs and with a son who has grown up blackening the sides of *his* house. "Our backyard was on a slope, the grass was always kept pretty short, so the ball was always flying at me.

I'd get it to come back at different angles—the height would be different, the look of it different, I'd throw it one way so I could backhand it, another way so I could extend for it, and all the while the whole thing would be 'runner on first, one out, two—two game,' or 'second and third, nobody out, we're up by one.' . . . I'd be doing this so close the ball would literally come rocketing back at me. I know for sure I improved my quickness and my hands doing this, but I also improved my thinking. You improve your thinking not so much by thinking as by repetition in specific situations. Even today, when I give clinics, that's what I teach. If you take enough ground balls in enough situations, you'll eventually get to a point where it's like you're remembering plays rather than waiting for them to happen."

But when Belanger came up he was not nearly so sure of himself. He was surrounded by a cast of characters on the Orioles who tore down fences for a living and nourished themselves on the meat and bones of pitchers. Belanger's diet was more modest. He was not even certain he belonged at the banquet table. The task, however, just because of that, was clear-cut.

"When I got to the majors, I knew the only way I was ever going to survive in baseball was if I did my job defensively," he says. "Because of my offensive disabilities, I worked very, very hard at my defensive skills—even though I had good hands and a lot of ability."

Working very, very hard at his game involved, first, a physical regimen. Belanger made a virtual science out of the different mechanical moves shortstops were called on to make. Taking infield practice for him was time in the lab. "It was never just taking infield for me," he says; it was a process in which he took anywhere from sixty to one hundred balls on a daily basis so the correct body positions on any conceivable play were committed to memory. But, even more than that, he worked so that he could take the field knowing he had as much to contribute as any of the heavy hitters who played alongside him. This didn't involve numbing himself with prayer but instead constantly learning

what he had to do to stay one step ahead of the game. Just because his situation on the Orioles was so uniquely defined, he came to articulate, perhaps as well as any fielder ever has, just how and why defense wins games.

"I didn't know this right away," Belanger says. "It took time, but eventually I learned that in almost every game there were hidden plays in the field, usually just one, on which the whole game turned. It could be anything—a catch made over the wall, a great throw—but more often than not it was something smaller, done in a split second of time—successfully executing a relay throw, completing a double play."

Belanger became almost like a man possessed in his quest to find these inner keys. Slowly his skills became wedded to a ripened sense of on-field situation. Every ball hit, every fielding play to be made was different depending on what was happening at the moment. Aggressiveness for Belanger was the ability to use his baseball instincts, honed through repetition until they became second nature.

"Words like *aggressiveness* and *instinct* were never mysterious to me," Belanger says, "because I always regarded them as part of a process of adjustment and readjustment within split seconds of time—which is the lifeblood of any game."

Belanger still looks as though he has never dined on meat. He is as blade thin as in his playing days, but his hair is flecked with gray and there are crows' feet around his eyes from all the years in the sun, from the thousands of plays whose only residue are line entries in the record books and Belanger's settled sense of the way things should be done.

"You're in a situation," he explains, choosing his words carefully, but still sounding, for all the years that have slipped away, like the boy working the clapboard of his parents' house, "a ball is hit to you, you know exactly what you have to do with it—but then, just like that, something else happens. You better have the hands and you better have the head. Here's a perfect example: Bases loaded, guy hits a ball between the outfielders. Okay, as a

shortstop, I run out there, look around, and see a runner just hitting third. I'm about to receive the ball, telling myself, 'home, home.' Then I drop the ball; I can't make that play. So in three fifths of a second, I have to do something else, and it has to be right. I may wind up getting an error on that play but I still may wind up having done something to help win a ball game if my next move is right. You never let up; you never stop looking for that advantage."

THE BASEBALL HISTORIAN Emil H. Rothe says that among all phases of the game, "fielding plays tend to be more quickly forgotten than batting or pitching accomplishments." Great plays are surely applauded, he notes, but the applause seems to survive only a short while beyond the play—unless, of course, photography manages to preserve what our eyes catch only briefly.

There are a variety of possible reasons for this. The art of the field may be too obscured by routine for most people to fully appreciate what superlative skills support it. It may also be that statistics, which so enticingly augment our appreciation of hitting and pitching, don't offer that much when it comes to fielding. Fielding numbers are notoriously opaque and even more notoriously tricky.

What are we to make of something as seemingly elemental as fielding average, for example? Numbers guru Bill James and several other observers have sensibly pointed out that fielding averages differ radically from position to position. A fielding average of .980 at shortstop is considered excellent but at first base is considered excellent reason for finding another first baseman. But even when focusing on one single position, the numbers deceive.

The career leader in fielding average among shortstops, for instance, is Larry Bowa—not Ozzie Smith, Mark Belanger, Luis Aparicio, Marty Marion, or any of many shortstops going back to Honus Wagner and Dickey Pearce. Bowa happened to be an excellent shortstop. He had good hands, an aggressive playing style, and a strong accompanying cast (which, for many seasons,

included Mike Schmidt and Manny Trillo on either side of him, Gary Maddox in center field, Bob Boone catching, and a pitching staff anchored by left-handed Steve Carlton). On top of that, all home games, and a portion of others, were played on Astroturf, where the bounce was as true as the grass was false. Bowa's great skill was that he made the routine play with relentless consistency. But he clearly is not the best fielding shortstop who ever played.

The other standard fielding categories—errors, assists, putouts, total chances, chances per game—are also relative rather than absolute. The number of putouts made by a first baseman is important, but the number made by any outfielder says more about what kind of fielding skills *might* be involved. Assists at second base may seem like an excellent barometer of range. But before any conclusions are drawn it is almost mandatory to look at the number of double plays initiated by the team's shortstop— *his* range may have contributed heavily to the number of assists made by the second baseman.

Errors also can whisper lies like truth—and vice versa. Check your *Baseball Encyclopedia* and you will find that Steve Garvey, a very good first baseman, was the only player in the history of the position to go through an entire season without making a single error (Keith Hernandez and George Sisler never did); check the all-time single-season marks for outfield and catcher. Next to each category, the *Encyclopedia* has this entry: "Many players tied with . . . 1.000." To add to the confusion, also consider that *great* defensive players frequently go through seasons where they make a lot of errors. In the days before gloves were used and then, afterward, when little lumps of finger leather covered the hand, all fielders made lots of errors. Who was a better fielder, Larry Bowa or Herman Long? Long regularly made sixty to seventy-five errors a year back in the 1890s—and was considered an *outstanding* shortstop.

Even in our time, where high-tech gloves often look more like Venus flytraps, good players can pile up errors. The Cards' third baseman Terry Pendleton led the league in errors in 1987,

one of two Gold Glove seasons; Harold Reynolds, who won the first of two disputed Gold Gloves from Frank White at second base in 1988, also was a league leader in errors at the position that year. The fact of the matter is that errors sometimes occur because players get to balls other players would never get to—and sometimes occur because butchery has been performed. The numbers do not make a distinction.

In more recent times, with the advent of computers and, possibly, with a glut of unemployed mathematicians turning to baseball for solace, numbers games have grown far more sophisticated. It is possible now to peer into the inner workings of the game and see things, statistically speaking, that were unseen or only dimly perceived before. There are intriguing mathematical models now to measure almost every aspect of the game. But again, when it comes to fielding, the computer hacker has run into the same problem as the pencil pusher.

The most frequently used of the new categories for fielding is "range factor" (total chances minus errors successfully made per game). Actually, according to John Thorn and Pete Palmer in *The Hidden Game of Baseball,* the category was used and abandoned earlier. If it has not taken general hold now, it is probably because, as in the past, it is too hard to make meaningful sense of the numbers.

The goal of this category is simple: to show a fielder's range. The reasoning behind the criteria is also relatively simple: A fielder with good range will make more plays than a fielder whose range is limited. Hence, it becomes theoretically possible to distinguish between a player who has a good fielding average but poor range and one who makes errors but gets to far more balls.

A major problem with range factor is that it is pegged to chances per game rather than to innings played. A player who enters the game in the late innings as a defensive specialist will not have a range factor that will statistically read very well, even though the player—theoretically—may have better range than anyone who ever lived. He will have been charged with a game

played even though his presence on the field will have covered only an inning or two—not enough time to handle a significant number of chances. Same for a player who has to leave a game with an injury or who moves from one position to another in the same game, as frequently happens today.

Just as muddying are the usual variables. A left-side infielder playing on a team with predominantly right-handed power pitchers will almost certainly see less action than players on the right side of the field. If a particular pitcher tends to induce ground balls, infielders, regardless of their range, will see more action than outfielders—just as they will make fewer plays, again with no reference to their range, if a fly-ball pitcher is on the mound.

There have been many attempts to get past the obvious objections to range factor, to refine measurements of defensive play, but all have seemed as burdened in one way or another as any of the older categories. The point is not that fielding numbers are useless; it is just that their use requires, in Bill James's words, "sensitive mental calipers." They will help in some instances, not in others. And in any case, we are still left with trying to puzzle out precisely how fielders, those old sleight-of-hand artists, do what they do.

Another interesting, if useless and unanswerable question, is whether present-day fielders are better than fielders of the past. The question is only useless and unanswerable because, lacking statistical models that are absolute and eyewitnesses who have lived that long, what happens in one era of the game is largely lost or romanticized in following eras. But the question is nevertheless important because traditions and skills are passed from generation to generation. The way the game changes also changes the way the game is played. Changes in equipment, in stadium construction, in types of playing surfaces, profoundly change the nature of what happens on the field, of the kinds of skills players learn—or forget.

Take the matter of stadiums. Over the last thirty years, only five old ballparks, Fenway, Wrigley Field, Tiger Stadium, Munic-

ipal Stadium, and Comiskey Park (scheduled for demolition in late 1989), have survived the wrecking ball. The newer parks have all but eliminated the lopsided distances, the special nooks and crannies that made play quirky and uniquely demanding. Gone is Braves Field, which at one time had a center-field marker 550 feet from home plate, gone is Crosley Field, with its three-foot embankment in left, gone is Ebbets Field, with its concrete and concave wall in right, gone are Forbes Field's menacing left-field scoreboard and the funny three-step stoops along League Park's left-field wall, which also, unaccountably, had holes in it large enough to accommodate hopping baseballs. And gone, too, is the Polo Grounds, where Willie Mays played.

It is also a fact that in ten of today's twenty-six major league parks, there is artificial turf to go with uniform dimensions and outfield barriers that are made of all sorts of softened and collapsible materials. What all this means, beyond economics, is a fundamental adjustment of skills on the field.

Speed is the absolute, not at all unknown in the past, but here raw, Olympic-venue speed. The finesse and artistry that might accompany it is never sneered at but never a substitute for a basic set of Pratt-Whitneys. The requirement to play nooks and crannies—except in the five old parks—has been severely reduced, as has the fear of walls (and thus, perhaps, a certain skill in playing them). A recent bonus from Lawrence Ritter is a gorgeous photo album featuring Babe Ruth, *The Babe: A Life in Pictures*. There, on a page nearly as large as a television screen, is a photo of the Babe lying unconscious on the grass—no warning track—next to a concrete wall in Washington's old Griffith Stadium. The Babe lies there serenely, three men working over him, one cradling his sleeping head, placing it beneath the cushion of his tiny mitt, while rows of straw-hatted fans lean over the barrier just a few feet away. The point is not that Ruth was an inept outfielder, but that, as a matter of everyday skill, he played those killer walls.

Changes in gloves have also meant changes in skill. It is one thing to train the hand to deal with a rocketing baseball, quite

another to let a large glove do the work. The movement of hands, wrist, forearm, finally the whole body, change according to the size, weight, and flexibility of the glove being worn.

Rules changes have also wrought palpable effects on the field. Certainly the decision made in 1887 to take away a batter's right to call for a high or low pitch had an immediate effect on both offense and defense. Likewise the decision changing the distance between mound and plate, or that which finally permitted pitchers to throw overhand, or any of the subsequent changes in the height of the mound and the size of the strike zone. The designated hitter, introduced in 1973, had a tremendous impact on strategy and positioning. The recent but unofficial reduction of team rosters from twenty-five to twenty-four players may even have had a greater impact upon defense. The defensive specialist, the one-position player, has, with increasing frequency, been eclipsed by the multiposition player, the player who is a jack-of-all-trades but not necessarily a master of one.

All of this makes that unanswerable question about the relative skills of players in one generation compared to another worth considering, even if it is useless to do so, because at issue are learned—and sometimes forgotten—skills. What is the state of the art, anyway? Is it really flourishing, or is it, in subtle and curious ways, decaying without our even realizing it? Is that man with the flytrap glove really able to do more with his hands than that player from the daguerreotypes who wore blood and mud on his fingers?

There is a general consensus that players today are bigger, faster, stronger—are better athletes—than players of the past. "There's no question that fielding is better—it has to be," says Dallas Green, the ex-manager of the Yankees. "So many of the fields today have artificial surfaces, the parks are bigger, there's more ground to cover. Athletes have to play in these places. And because salaries are so much greater, they have to keep themselves in better condition."

But there are other opinions. Syd Thrift, ex–senior vice pres-

ident of the Yankees, agrees that defenders are better athletes but, he says, "what may be slipping away is that sense of artistry at the positions."

Harry Dalton, the Brewers' vice president and general manager, who was an architect of those old Orioles teams Belanger played for and who, like many in that organization, believed almost as matter of religious faith that games were won in the field, has still another view. "Years ago," Dalton says, "the game was built on pitching and defense. And the purist in me is still attached to that. But the executive in me knows something else: Offense is what puts bodies in the seats."

The money trail, unfortunately, raises just one more unanswerable question. Who can be quite so certain that money has corrupted—or spurred on—the skills of players? Has a whole generation of players, knowing that offense "puts bodies in the seats," neglected the defensive side of the game? Maybe. And maybe not. Someone in the game is paying Ozzie Smith $2 million a year.

More interesting, if just as puzzling, is what talent evaluators —executives, scouts, and others—are finding out there. "I'm not at all sure why—we may just be going through another one of those cycles," Harry Dalton says, "but one thing I've noticed is that kids coming up today don't seem to have the arm strength they used to. Again and again, you find players who just can't throw that well." This opinion, it turns out, is widely shared—as is the one that athletes today are bigger, faster, stronger.

Tom Borque, a scout for the Brewers, says one possible explanation is that young people probably play less than they used to. "Kids today, at an early age, are organized into teams; they do much less on their own," says Borque. "Beginning with Pee Wee League, they get uniforms, mitts, and bats, and they learn the proper way to hold their hands and feet, but you wonder how beneficial all that really is. When I was a kid, we went out in the morning and came home at night—we played all day whenever we could. Today kids will play two hours a day three times a

week and maybe in that time they'll be involved in a handful of plays because everybody else has to get their practice in too."

Borque's notion that there is a correspondence between level of skill and the number of games actually played is an elementary one. This is usually called experience, and surely when it comes to fielding, as with any other skilled labor, a talented person with that much more know-how will probably do better than someone equally talented but less experienced.

But more intriguing is Borque's belief that time by oneself, free time, is, for a young ballplayer, most valuable. "What regimentation into teams at too early an age does," Borque says, "is that it leaves no room for imagination. There's no time for kids to run and catch and hit, pretending they're this or that star in this or that situation."

Whether or not this is best left for sociologists is for someone else to say. But what seems unassailable—and most pertinent to what follows—is that fielding, great fielding, raised to the level of art, is composed as much of imagination as it is athletic ability. That was true when the game was called "bittle-battle" and it is just as true today.

FIRST BASE

In many a game we have played,
We've needed a First Base,
But now our opponents will find
The "basket" in its place.
And if you think he "muffs" the balls,
Sent into him red hot,
You'll soon be fooled by "Charlie Gould,"
And find he "muffs" them not.

—"The Cincinnati Baseball
Club Song," 1869

① **KEITH HERNANDEZ** *about to "release" from his holding position at first. Notice the turn of his forward right foot, allowing him to move in a direct line rather than sideways. In this, he is simultaneously "cheating" on runner Vince Coleman and taking more ground between first and second. Hernandez, like Sisler and Hal Chase, has been able to dominate a game from his position.*
© MARC S. LEVINE/THE NEW YORK METS

② **GEORGE SISLER** *played at a time when it was not the size of the mitt but the softness of hands and the speed of thought that counted.*
NATIONAL BASEBALL LIBRARY

③ **DON MATTINGLY,** *currently the American League's top first baseman, is ready for anything—except, possibly, a bunt. "You don't see too many bunts in the American League," Mattingly says.*
THE NEW YORK YANKEES

FROM THE MOMENT it was decided that putouts were to be recorded by means of a throw to first base, securely held by a fielder, first basemen have been guaranteed more action in the course of a game than all other position players save pitcher and catcher. That simple and elegant rule of outmaking established what the basic tasks of first basemen were: Catch the ball, regularly and adroitly, letting the best of them be baskets; and pick up the ball—any kind, but especially the red-hots.

The first baseman who does this today might get by, though it is almost certain that if his repertoire is not wider he will not be as celebrated as Charlie Gould.

Don Mattingly, the Yankees' Gold Glove perennial, amplifies:

"A good defensive first baseman is in the right place at the right time, he plays guys right, he knows when to play the lines and when not to, when to keep a runner close and when not to: When there are guys on first and second, he will think of what can be done to take the double steal away—you can jockey with that situation a little by the way you hold a runner at the bag, by cheating up the base paths with him a little, worrying him, keeping him a step back. You keep any base runner a step back and you give your catcher that much better chance of getting him on a steal, an outfielder that much better chance of nailing him if he takes the extra base—and you still have the double play in order. You're always in the right place for the cutoff. If you're at your position long enough, you get to read the runner coming around third, you teach yourself to check the coach at third when the guy's coming around, waving him in or stopping him. With the

crowd yelling you won't be able to count on hearing your team-mates yelling for you to cut it or let it go through. Above all, you need to make the plays, to have played enough and to be in the game enough to know what you are going to do with the ball when you get it, to know all the different options."

What is remarkable about this view of the position, delivered absolutely off the cuff by Mattingly one evening at his locker stall as he was going through a batch of mail, is its thoroughness and how it illustrates the continuity that exists between then and now.

More than songs, old pictures tell us about the game's first first basemen: They invariably show them hugging the bag, where indeed they stationed themselves with the sort of stolid immobility of armed guards at a bank door. But it was not long before first basemen figured out that they could do more. Two early players of the position illustrate the character and quality of that early change. To varying degrees, both of their markedly different styles are still around.

Adrian "Cap" Anson, anchor of the Chicago Colts' "Stone-wall Infield," dubbed by baseball historian William Akin as the game's "first great infield combination," perfected immobility at the bag. As Akin describes him,

> Anson learned the game when first basemen seldom ventured away from the bag. But in that tradition, he perfected all the plays. He made a big target, caught anything near him, and innovated the long stretch. At the end of the 1880's, Anson held career and season records for putouts, assists, and double plays, and had led the league in fielding five times.

And all of this, Akin might have pointed out, took place only a few years after the introduction of the game's first mitt, worn by sometime first baseman, Charlie Waitt. Waitt had probably injured himself somewhere along the line, and the mitt he intro-duced, a flesh-colored covering for the hand with an opening in the back to allow for ventilation, was a sort of Band-Aid, de-signed more for protection than production.

At about the same time Anson was perfecting his style of play in the National League, Charles Comiskey of the powerhouse St. Louis Browns was revolutionizing the position in the American Association. Comiskey, though not the first first baseman to play away from the bag, was the first to theorize about it. He believed in playing "deep" so that he could cover more ground, and he understood the relation of the line to the situation in a game, that different batters were played differently, and that the positioning of a first baseman could affect others on the field as well. Because he could cover substantial ground to his right, he probably allowed second basemen to play close to the middle of the diamond. He was almost certainly responsible for getting pitchers to cover first.

"In regard to first base, the position I played on the old St. Louis Browns," Comiskey said in an essay included in *The National Game,* "my opinions are set. I am a great believer in playing deep and depending on the pitcher to cover the bag in many instances. I always played my position ten or fifteen feet deeper than other first basemen, and the pitchers had to get over to cover the bag. They could not be sluggish and try to show me up. If I saw the pitcher was loafing on me I fielded the ball and threw to first whether anyone was there or not. Then the crowd saw who was to blame, and pretty soon the pitchers got in the habit of running over rapidly rather than be roasted."

When the image of a first baseman comes to mind today, it is remarkable how the picture still seems to divide between Anson, the immobile, big target, able to stretch, to "perfect the plays," and Comiskey, the smaller man, patrolling, prowling, testing, challenging, calculating; Anson, founding father to a whole line of large ones right down to Kent Hrbek and Andres Galarraga, and Comiskey, father of the gliders unto Mattingly and Keith Hernandez.

The imagery remains interesting in more than an abstract way because it raises the question of what the ideal physical type for first base is—and implies a reasonable answer: There is none. Or: Good and great first basemen come in all sizes and shapes.

Stuffy McInnis, a great early first baseman with the A's, Red Sox, and other teams, was five feet, nine and a half inches, about the same height as Steve Garvey—and Don Mattingly. Joe Judge, another early great, was even shorter than that, while Hal Chase, Frank Chance, Charlie Grimm, Lou Gehrig, and Jimmie Foxx were all six-footers—but only midsized models next to Hank Greenberg, Luke Easter, Mickey Vernon, Boog Powell, Mark McGwire. Larger first basemen—like McGwire—tend to be aware that their size makes them good targets, even when they are, as McGwire is not, somewhat stationary.

Regardless of size and mobility, what all good first basemen have always emphasized is skill with hands and feet, ability to receive throws and field what's hit—no matter how hard or slow, close or far from the bag.

According to turn-of-the-century Hall of Fame player and manager Hugh Jennings, who played first base for part of his career, first base was "one of the most difficult positions on a ball field to play properly." That was because catching a ball while keeping contact with the base involved more than anyone realized, certainly more than the uniformly one-handed styles of today's first basemen indicate:

"A first baseman must have natural talent for taking all kinds of pickups. He should be a sure catch *with either hand* [emphasis added]," Jennings wrote in *The National Game*. And why not, given the postage-stamp size of gloves when Jennings began playing?

When Paul Waner broke in as an outfielder with the Pittsburgh Pirates in 1926, he was sometimes shifted to first, but didn't know the position at all. He went to school, watching Stuffy McInnis, a teammate, and George Sisler. Waner, who was five eight and 150 pounds in his salad days, was assigned to room with McInnis that first year in Pittsburgh. McInnis was at the end of his career but Waner vividly remembered his skills, which McInnis tried to pass on to the younger player:

"When I joined the Pirates in 1926, Stuffy was there as a

substitute first baseman," Waner told Lawrence Ritter. "He must have been close to forty at the time, and I think that was his last year in baseball. He's been in the big leagues since 1910 or so. But he could still field that position like nobody's business, and he tried to teach me all he knew. I was his roommate in 1926 . . . and Stuffy would spend hours with me in the room showing me how to play first base, using a pillow as a base. Gee, even at that age, he was just a flow of motion out there on the field, just everywhere at once, making everything look so easy."

From early on, there has been a popular notion that first base is one of those places reserved for graceless lunks who can hit and therefore must play *somewhere*. Sometimes, with first basemen like Lou Gehrig and Jimmie Foxx, where iron, brawn, and bat so obviously color our impression of who they were, the other side —what they did with their hands and feet—is lost. And it is a real loss to us because beneath the brawn and iron they also possessed a kind of dancing skill required for the position they played if not for the durability of their lives.

Toward the end of his playing career, before he was cut down by illness, Lou Gehrig, the Iron Horse, had his hands X-rayed. Incredibly, there were seventeen different fractures in the bones, and no one, not even possibly Gehrig himself, had known it. Gehrig played through 2,130 consecutive games with all the battering such a streak inevitably exacts on body and soul. He was not the most graceful fielder, a fact still remembered with some sharpness by Babe Dahlgren, the man who finally replaced Gehrig at first base after the incredible streak was done (and whose own career in the interim was probably stunted as a result). Dahlgren, a smooth fielder who earlier in his career had been dealt to the minors by the Red Sox to make way for Jimmie Foxx, remembers Gehrig with bittersweetness. "Lou was an outstanding hitter but he was just an ordinary gloveman. If you look at the Hall of Fame, most guys in it are noted for their hitting, not their fielding," Dahlgren says.

"Gehrig was a sure-handed, dependable, durable first baseman

. . . and was considered very adequate as a defensive man on a championship team," wrote George Sisler, who was by all accounts one of the game's two or three great defenders at first. The numbers tell the story: Only two players in baseball history played more games at the position than Gehrig. Gehrig handled 20,790 total chances, eighth all-time, with a respectable .991 lifetime fielding average. In addition, he remains among career leaders in putouts and double plays, categories in which he was an individual league leader as well. But perhaps even Sisler didn't appreciate what Gehrig went through to perfect that side of his game. Paul Gallico, author of Gehrig's biography *Pride of the Yankees,* had an idea:

> Hustle all the time!
> That was the philosophy by which Lou Gehrig lived and died. I asked Ty Cobb for his definition of a "hustling" ball player. In his slow drawl he said . . . "A hustlin' ball player is a feller who never lets up for a minute, never gives his body a rest from trying. He's out there every second of the time playing as hard as he can, no matter how many runs he's ahead. He don' know what it means to take it easy and loaf along. He's ALWAYS working. Lou Gehrig was the hustlinest ball player I ever saw, and I admired him for it. When I first saw him break in the line-up as a rookie, I went and told him just that."

Gallico then described how Gehrig, with only collegiate and brief minor league experience, went about learning to be a major league first baseman. For a time, Miller Huggins, his manager, had him sit alongside him in the dugout and study hitters, each of whom presented slightly different problems of positioning. He was taught to watch his pitchers, to familiarize himself not only with what they were throwing but with their individual pitching strategies as well. Huggins deliberately kept Gehrig at his side rather than ship him to the minors because the art of hands and feet at the major league level, he knew, was powerfully joined to

a specific way of thinking. Then, one day—nothing special about it—Huggins sent him out to replace Wally Pipp, who was suffering the aftereffects of a recent beaning. Gehrig, we all know, remained where Huggins sent him for rest of his seventeen-year career. But his way in the field was not smooth.

"Then he set out to learn how to play first base," Gallico wrote.

> He was so anxious to learn, because he was such a clumsy Tanglefoot around that bag. He took advice from anyone and everyone, even Blind Tom . . . the ball players' charm-name for the umpire.
> Billy Evans, umpiring at First Base one time, noticed a serious flaw in Lou's play shortly after he broke into the lineup. Bill took a chance of drawing a rebuke, because ball players were pretty touchy where umpires are concerned, but he said . . . "Young fellow . . . you're putting the wrong foot back on the bag."
> Lou smiled at him and said . . . "Thanks, Mr. Evans. Watch me on the next play."
> He got the proper foot back, but had to hesitate and think before he could do it. The next morning at ten o'clock he had Charley O'Leary, the coach, out of bed and down to the field, practicing, until it became automatic.
> Poor O'Leary. Gehrig practiced him ragged. There was so much he had to learn about fielding his position. Day in and day out, he worked every morning from ten o'clock until game time. He was weak on balls thrown into the dirt. He made Charley throw balls at him into the dirt until O'Leary's tongue was hanging out. Lou did nothing naturally. Everything came the hard and tortuous way. Practice, practice, practice, until he did it right, and then practice some more to keep it right.

Extraordinary certainly applies to the way he threw himself at his fielding (he worked just as hard at hitting; there are similar stories of relentless early-morning batting practice rounds), but the skills he was learning were, for him, extraordinary as well. More recently, two Gold Glovers at other positions, George Brett

and Dwight Evans, have had extended playing time at first. Both men found the basic work of hands and feet to be as daunting as Gehrig did.

"Half the time, I don't know what I'm doing out there," Brett says. In more guarded moments with the press he's joked that the way of old third basemen was to be moved to first and from first to designated hitter. But in private he has other things to say. "Whoever says this is an easy position doesn't know what he's talking about. Just getting your hands and feet to work right is tough enough."

Dwight Evans, who spent the better part of a season and a half at first before being moved back to right field, talks about the hours he spent taking throws in the dirt and how hard it was simply to place his foot on the bag without having to look down to find it beforehand. "It took me months before I could trust my feet enough to find the base without looking," Evans says, "and then the hardest part was reaching a point where I could begin to play aggressively rather than defensively."

Bill White, the dominant fielding first baseman of the sixties, who believes that repetition of plays in the field is the surest of teaching tools, had trouble with his hands too, not at the bag or back in position but in handling relay throws. "I somehow would get the ball and drop it as I tried to transfer it to my throwing hand," he says. Early in his career with the Cardinals, White turned up in Florida during the off-season and each day for an extended period had coaches fire balls to him in near the mound, where he could repetitiously catch, plant, and throw until the movement became second nature.

The difficulty with hands and feet at the position is that in almost all the plays made by first basemen—taking throws in the dirt, reaching to one side of the bag or another, taking pickoff throws, handling relay throws, charging and disposing of bunts—quickness is required.

Consider for a moment the simplest of plays a first baseman makes: coming over to the bag, taking his stance and then the

throw for a putout. Because coordination is assumed, instructional writing—and the teaching behind it—can sometimes be tricky. A representative manual says that a first baseman

> finds the base with his feet, both heels touching the base. He faces the infielder who has fielded the ball. In this position he can shift to receive the throw. This is where quick feet come in.
>
> If the throw is to the right, he will shift so his left foot is on the base and he stretches out with his right. If it is to the left, he allows the right foot to remain on the base and stretches out with the left leg.

In practice, however, most first basemen today stretch with the rear foot opposite to the gloved hand. Dancing at first gives way to positioning at *different* parts of the bag, depending on where a fielded ball is thrown from. The latter is emphasized by Mickey Vernon, tall and as slick at his trade as anyone. He played even more games at first in his career than Lou Gehrig (only one first baseman in history, turn-of-the-century Hall of Famer Jake Beckley, played more games than Vernon):

"I never let myself get into fancy footwork," he says. "I got to the bag in a hurry and let the direction of the throw dictate what I'd do. Because I was a left-handed thrower, ninety-seven percent of the time I'd keep my left foot against the bag and stretch with my right. It's where on the bag you keep your foot that matters. If a ball went to the home-plate side of the bag, then naturally you'd take that corner; if it came from the second-base side, you'd take it from that corner."

The times he switched feet, Vernon says, were only when he had to—when there was a throw far off the base and into the dirt, when he had to go into the air on one side knowing that he would have to make a tag play and at the same time avoid a collision. What Vernon and a range of first basemen down to the present have done is make things simple so the catch and the out can be made. The play's the thing that will catch the conscience of any good first baseman.

While superior physical skills at any position are an advantage, they only partly account for great first basemen. The game at first, just because there is so much play-to-play involvement, is heady. The alertness, quickness, and anticipation on covering plays left and right, knowing when and when not to hug the line, when to charge, when to stay back, being correctly positioned to receive a cutoff or to back up a play, knowing how and when to hold runners, is all part of the repertoire and becomes vivid depending on the degree to which a first baseman is in command. An ordinary major league first baseman will make most of the plays. A great first baseman can wind up dominating a game. Early players like Hal Chase and George Sisler, who fielded bunts on the third-base side of the mound, and Fred Tenney, who may have been the first first baseman to pull off the 3-6-3 double play, had the ability to reverse the course of action anytime they were at their position.

Toward the end of his life, George Sisler was a scout and, according to Branch Rickey, as great an evaluator of talent as the game had. Sisler watched everyone and had ideas about every position on the field, most of which remain exemplary. His opinions about first base and first basemen are unusually valuable because they come from long experience both watching and playing. "I played against Hal Chase in an exhibition game once," Sisler wrote in his book *On Baseball*. "His name is proverbial as a first baseman." Sisler played against or saw other great first basemen, from Charlie Grimm and Bill Terry to a rookie named Gil Hodges, who, Sisler said, had "great hands and never misse[d] a ball thrown to him."

Sisler believed that to play first base really well, a player needed four fundamental qualities: good hands; quick feet and strong legs; speed in covering his position, particularly when it came to bunts; and, above all, "baseball sense," so he could anticipate, so he would always be ahead of rather than behind the action. In his time, Sisler defined the nature of aggressive defense. Here is his description of what "baseball sense" allowed him to

do on one bunt play in a game between the Browns and the Washington Senators in the 1920s:

> I remember one day in Washington when we were playing the Senators and anticipation paid big dividends. Sam Rice was on third base with one out and Joe Judge was at bat. The idea of a squeeze play was "in the air." Judge bunted the ball down toward me at first base. I anticipated the play, started in fast, had the ball before Judge had hardly left the plate. I tagged him and in the same motion threw to Hank Severeid, our catcher, who tagged Rice coming in, for a double play.

Sisler was schooled in winning in the days when players like Ty Cobb sharpened their spikes with files in enemy dugouts. Sisler, like Cobb, was a .400 hitter, but he also had a razorsharp sense of the importance of defense. He credits an appropriately named manager on the Browns, Fielder Jones, with instilling in him a "never-say-die spirit that wins games and makes for perfect defense." The rise and fall of Fielder Jones remained with Sisler as both a reminder and a sort of leavening long after his playing days ended.

> Jones managed one of the old St. Louis Browns teams when I was a member. Whenever we lost a game, he would not talk to anyone, hardly to his own family, until the next game rolled around and he had forgotten about the previous game and he could concentrate on winning the game at hand. One game in which I played and which we lost best illustrates Jones's psychology.
>
> We were playing the Washington Senators in St. Louis and were leading them 5 to 1 going into the ninth inning when they staged a rally and scored five runs. We were unable to score in the last of the ninth inning and they won from us 6 to 5. Fielder Jones walked out of Sportsman's Park, St. Louis, that day and I have never seen him since. After leaving the park, he packed up his family, and took off for the great Northwest, which was his home, and that was the last of Fielder Jones so far as baseball was concerned.

In our time, Keith Hernandez has been to first base what players like Chase and Sisler once were. In 1988, a year in which he spent a good part of the season on the disabled list, he won his eleventh consecutive Gold Glove. Anyone who has seen him play knows why. Hernandez makes "all the plays" and simply covers more ground than other first basemen. "First base is, what, one quarter of the infield?" Hernandez once said. "Okay, then my responsibility is one quarter of the infield." Logical. Except that others say it's crazy—first basemen can't cover that much ground. But Hernandez does—and not because he is particularly fast. He isn't. He takes chances—big ones—in positioning himself. Where other first basemen play fifteen feet wide of the line, he'll sometimes play thirty feet, forty feet wide, depending on the hitter. In late innings, he'll guard the lines because he's told to, because that's been baseball strategy since the time of Cap Anson, but he says that if he had his druthers he'd play wide because most balls are hit wide. Where other first basemen who are holding a base runner at first will get out three to five feet from the bag with the pitch, Hernandez gets out fifteen to seventeen. On bunt plays, Hernandez doesn't just charge, he will often perform a kamikaze raid on the hitter, sometimes hitting the smokestacks, always throwing the fear of God into the opposition. Keith is an impeccable model technically, and is even more impressive mentally.

Here is a play Hernandez made during the waning days of the 1989 pennant race in a game against the Cubs at Wrigley Field. It was the bottom of the fifth inning with the Mets leading 3–0, and the Cubs had gotten two runners on with none out. The next batter, left-hand-hitting Mark Grace, blooped a hit down the left-field line. One run scored and then another when the Mets' second baseman Gregg Jefferies let the throw from left field carom past him into short right-center field. With no Mets outfielder moving to back him up, with second base left unguarded and Grace, representing the tying run, looking to advance, Jefferies turned to pursue the ball. Suddenly, as though he

had been beamed there from another planet, Hernandez arrived on the scene, a hundred feet out of position, pursuing the ball and, at the same time, as though he were a traffic cop, pointing for Jefferies to return to second base. With the surprised Jefferies able to retreat to the bag, Hernandez scooped up the ball and threw it to him in time to catch the even more surprised runner, temporarily aborting the Cubs rally. Hernandez was able to make this rather otherworldly play not because he is endowed with special physical or metaphysical gifts but because his "baseball sense" is that sharp.

Though Hernandez says he always had "soft" hands, he insists that from the start he was something more than "a natural." Long before Keith was ready for Little League, his father, an ex–minor league player, took him over. John Hernandez was then a fireman with a work schedule that gave him ample time to devote to the baseball education of his sons—and others who played with them. It was common for him to organize two teams of an early Saturday morning, pitching for each side, until parents came to pick up their kids in the early evening.

John Hernandez was a first baseman and, Keith says, "a player who was noted for his fielding." The father passed on to the six-year-old son not only the tricks of the trade but the thinking that went with them. "What I got was professional instruction—and a real sense for the game," Keith Hernandez says. The father insisted that the players be well rounded. "He wouldn't let us hit unless we also worked on our fielding. By the time I got to Little League, I knew my position. I knew where to be on cutoffs, every possible situation . . . what to do, rundowns, backing up, the whole bit. A lot of kids now come up without real instincts for the game but have God-given talent. They don't really have base-ball instincts. My dad taught them to me—along with everything else—at a very young age."

To have any real appreciation of how much Hernandez does as a first baseman it is necessary to watch him work, and just as Branch Rickey suggested, to isolate him at his position in ordi-

nary circumstances. Among many recent opportunities was a midsummer game during the 1988 season between the Montreal Expos and the New York Mets, the second of the teams Hernandez has played for in his career. It will suffice to illustrate an ordinary workday for Hernandez (actually, it was something more—it marked the first time in fifty-four games that he was playing following a serious hamstring injury he had sustained that season). This game was also an opportunity to compare Hernandez with Andres Galarraga, the young but stylish right-handed first baseman of the Expos, who had been a runner-up to Hernandez in Gold Glove balloting the previous couple of seasons before winning one of his own in 1989.

Hernandez's usual procedure, aborted that evening because of late rain, is to take ten to fifteen minutes of grounders during batting practice in addition to the usual set round of fungoes prior to the game. On the road, he puts in more time because the commonsense objectives, always, are to study the way balls come off the bat and to be as familiar as possible with any oddities in the terrain he may encounter later. Even on easier-to-field turf surfaces he devotes the extra time to this because "the sponginess and texture are different enough to pay attention to. It's all part of preparation." On-field preparation that night was a little different. During the first innings of the game, Hernandez used his warm-up tosses to other infielders to get the feel of both the bag and the ground around it. He pawed and measured the dirt as though trying to determine whether his lair had been violated while he was out; he took the base gingerly but methodically, planting his foot on different parts of the bag from the outfield side to the infield side as he readied himself for incoming practice throws.

Preparation, it turns out, is as big a word for Hernandez as *remembering* is for Mark Belanger. Hernandez tends to ignore scouting reports on hitters. While other veteran players are similarly self-sufficient, he goes one step further by selectively resisting what is generally accepted as accurate intelligence. He relies on

charts for players he doesn't know, but once his own sense of a
hitter clicks in—after a series or two—he relies on himself.

"I know every veteran in this league. I'm not going to look at
the charts—and where he hit the ball in the last series," Hernandez says in that peculiar manner of his that allows him to impart
to a listener the sense that he or she is eavesdropping on a mono-
logue. "He may have done that in one series but he's not a pull
hitter—he's gonna have to show me."

For Hernandez, the number of hitters who consistently pull
or slice are few and far between. It hardly matters whether this is
actually the case; the fact is this relatively simple notion activates
his willingness to take risks in positioning.

"There just aren't that many dead, dead left-handed pull hitters," he says, "and very, very few right-handed hitters who hit
the ball down the right-field line, so what does that tell you? That
you're going to get beat more in the hole than down the line.
Therefore I'm gonna get out as much as possible."

Those present on this particular night and capable of doing
real damage—Tim Raines, Tim Wallach, Hubie Brooks, Andres
Galarraga—were neither dead left-handed pull hitters nor right-
handers with enough bat control (like the Cards' Ozzie Smith) to
exploit extra yards on the right side. The charts of the evening's
hitters were intact in Hernandez's head exactly as he had prepared
them long ago. His time on the DL notwithstanding, the Expos
were a team he was ready for.

On the other side of the field, Andres Galarraga, like most
younger players, prepared more traditionally. He listened carefully to that evening's preseries scouting report, a capsule review
of New York's personnel with additions covering recent games.
Positioning, Galarraga acknowledges, is still something he depends on the bench for. Though as a youngster in Venezuela he
played first base enough to gain coordination around the bag (he
began then to work his hands with a Super Ball, which he caromed off the interior walls of his family's house—a practice he
continues to this day), he did not begin playing first regularly as

a professional until late in his minor league career. Cardinals manager Whitey Herzog compares the big first baseman's agility to that of Gil Hodges, whose number, 14, Galarraga wears. But Galarraga himself, when thinking about a model at the position and of all he feels he still has to learn, says it is Hernandez he has in mind.

The first batter in the first inning was a switch-hitting swifty named Otis Nixon, playing in his first season in the National League. This was a batter Hernandez relied on paper charts for, but the information had been quickly reformulated: Nixon generally made contact, sprayed the ball around, had little or no power, was a constant threat to steal if he got on, was someone who could bunt.

For almost any first baseman, the reading of the hitter and the situation were obvious. Anyone playing the corners—whether at first or third—had to be alert for the bunt. Hernandez, however, took alertness one step further.

Rather than position himself on the edge of the grass, Hernandez set himself about ten feet back and then, with the first pitch of the game—a ball—from right-hander David Cone, back-pedaled another twenty feet. The move surely drew Nixon's attention. On the next pitch, Hernandez repeated this rather unorthodox move. The pitch was taken for a strike, only this time, Nixon's hands slid up on the bat. He then committed himself to bunting on the next pitch, which he fouled off. He struck out on the succeeding pitch, possibly never realizing that Hernandez had diddled two strikes out of him by so provocatively inviting the bunt—in effect, limiting Nixon's at-bat to one legitimate strike.

What separates Hernandez from other top performers at the position is just how active he can be. Whether it is an opposing batsman or one of his own teammates—like Gregg Jefferies—Hernandez *engages* those he plays with. He seems to enter into various sorts of dialogue as he moves through a game. Here, with the very first batter, the dialogue was challenge and response. The

situation presented Hernandez with the challenge of a hitter who could turn one base into two or three merely by his reaching first safely. The response was to engage the hitter, distract him if possible. This, in turn, was a challenge to the hitter, answered in his attempt to bunt, which was, after all, a desired answer, because its result was to give the pitcher two strikes to work with, effectively placing the batter in a defensive role at the plate.

Hernandez's sense of "dialogue" is dictated entirely by the moment. He is like a great actor who understands that moment-to-moment life on the stage is determined by a series of active intentions strung together. The intention here was to distract. In another bunting situation, where the sacrifice is called for and where the pitcher is hitting, the intention would be to intimidate. With his own pitcher in trouble, Hernandez, like most first basemen, will come to the mound, but his intention will vary: He will encourage, cajole, pacify, provoke, wheedle, needle, stroke, poke, solicit, conspire, or inquire, depending on who is pitching and what precisely is unfolding.

Hernandez is a believer in putting his glove down prior to a pitch. Many infielders, particularly players at the corners, are taught to do this. The thinking is that with the glove already in proximity to the ground it is that much easier to snare a hot smash. There are no jumpy movements to be made down or up. With a great infielder, something more may be involved. Brooks Robinson, along with other Orioles infielders of his time, was instructed literally to drop his glove to the ground with each pitch. "At first," Robinson says, "I felt very awkward doing that, but once I got comfortable, it was like I started layin' the glove on the ground, the ball was hit—'plop,' it was in my glove." For Hernandez, there is this same talismanic effect.

"From the time I was seven, when my father taught me, I always have had the glove down," Hernandez says. "Earlier this year, I had a bullet hit at me by Vince Coleman that I literally had no time to react to. The ball was there in my glove; my glove was like a magnet for the ball. A lot of times, especially on turf,

when I'm holding a guy on, the ball has gone right to my glove; my glove has just been there." Hernandez adds that he can not count the times balls that he has snagged would otherwise have been base hits but for this placing of the mitt.

(The majority of first basemen now do not drop their gloves. Don Mattingly, free of back pain, does, Pete O'Brien does, Mark McGwire does intermittently. Kent Hrbek, who grew up in northern Minnesota, where the lakes freeze over early for hockey, was a childhood goalie and brought some of that thinking—"nothing gets past me"—to first base. He holds his hands, ready for ball, or puck, at knee level. In the Mets-Expos game that night, Andres Galarraga, as he always has, held his hands up near his waist.)

The top of the first ended routinely with a grounder to short, covered at first by Hernandez, again with a special touch. On a ball hit to an infielder, most first basemen will go directly to the bag to receive the throw. Hernandez's refinement is to move in an arc toward the foul line and approach the bag on a straight line so that the play will be in front of him at all times. Keeping plays out front is crucial to a first baseman in any number of ways: On a pickoff play involving the catcher, for example, correct positioning is to straddle the bag facing second base rather than home in receiving the throw, thereby keeping any play involving the runner out front; on fielding a bunt, the first baseman arcs toward the ball so that his momentum will be toward a force play at second or third. This loop toward the base on a grounder allows Hernandez a good, safe method of planting the foot at the bag, offers a simultaneous view of runner approaching and fielder throwing, and keeps his momentum going forward, enabling him to be better prepared to handle any off-target throws.

Galarraga's first opportunity to handle a routine infield out came in the bottom of the second, when a Mets hitter bounced to short. Galarraga, shifted left about as far as Hernandez had been for him on the play that ended the top of the first, took off directly for the bag, losing radio contact with the play until he turned and planted at the base.

Galarraga's movements, though, were quick and smooth. His footwork at the base was assured. His plant was always with his right foot. As it had been for Mickey Vernon and countless others, simpler was better. Also, the right-handed Galarraga points out, his right leg is his strong leg, necessary as an anchor whenever quick shifting to receive a throw is required.

The Expos took a 1–0 lead on a homer in the second inning, but the Mets' David Cone didn't allow a base runner until the fourth inning, when Tim Raines, leading off, drew a walk. The pairing of Raines, an elite base stealer, with Hernandez, defending at first, provided another glimpse of superior interior play at the position.

The job of a first baseman with a runner on first and an open base ahead is, generally, to hold the runner so that he will be unable to steal or easily advance. One of the advantages a left-handed first baseman has over a righty is that in taking his holding position against a runner, his gloved hand is the one closer to the runner, permitting a shorter turn in and quicker drop in applying the tag on a pickoff throw. Right-handed first basemen take a position at the base with their bodies open toward second base or, in the case of someone like Kent Hrbek, with an even more extreme twist in the direction of right field, so that the gloved hand, extended toward the pitcher, can be dropped more quickly.

Righties and lefties both refine what they do according to the situation. Late in the game with a large lead, the runner will not be held at all. With a slow runner who is unwilling to stray far, the first baseman usually drops back—not all the way but enough to permit him greater fielding room while still allowing coverage at the base. When a runner is speedier, when a hit-and-run play or a bunt may be in order, the task changes again. The first baseman has to hold as long as he can and then break from the base. For many first basemen, this involves a surrendering of too much territory, an opening to be exploited by the team at bat. A really skilled first baseman finds ways to hold his man and cover ground at the same time. First basemen like Mattingly or Hernandez choose their moments to "cheat up" with a runner, com-

ing out with him as he takes his lead, worrying him because they are in such proximity while gaining greater fielding ground at the same time.

In the situation at hand—Hernandez guarding Raines—there was an additional element: talk. Another of Keith's "dialogues" is actual conversation with base runners. While many first basemen yak with runners and umpires (Mattingly, for example, does it to keep himself relaxed), for Hernandez, something else is involved.

He spies—quite literally. Hernandez looks for those who seconds before had been facing ninety-mile-an-hour fastballs and now were willing to relieve themselves with small talk about pitchers and hitting—problems shared by the game's fraternity of batsmen. "Sometimes they'll be dumb enough to tell me they're having trouble with this or that pitcher of ours and I'll just try to draw 'em out, then go tell our pitchers between innings what I've picked up," Hernandez says.

In this particular situation, he knew the man standing next to him very well. "Not all of 'em give away secrets, but Raines, well, he told me once that Ronnie [Darling] gave him a lot of trouble. I never knew that. When I asked him why, he gave me a whole series of reasons," Hernandez said. "I gave Ronnie a complete rundown."

Hernandez and Raines exchanged pleasantries but Hernandez had more fundamental work to do: keep Raines as close to the base as possible. Any runner on first with less than two out means a potential double play, and any first baseman will do what he can to make sure the double play remains in order. To accomplish this with any runner is a plus; to be able to do anything to keep runners like Raines contained goes well beyond ordinary competence.

Hernandez held Raines close. He did not cheat up the base path with him as he took his lead. The strategy, routine enough, was to have the pitcher throw over, keeping the runner as close to the base as possible. Nearly always it is the pitcher who determines when the throw will be made. If he has a good pickoff

move, so much the better, but even an ordinary move, if done persistently enough, can keep runners a step closer.

But Hernandez will sometimes direct this little game within the game. When he takes his stance—left foot on the foul line, right foot by the front inside corner of the bag, Hernandez stretches forward toward the pitcher in such a way that the runner and coach behind him cannot see his *left*—or ungloved—hand hidden near his hip. With the view of the third-base coach also screened by the pitcher, Keith crooks a finger when he wants a throw over. Depending on who is pitching, he initiates throws with less or more frequency. Some of his pitchers—Sid Fernandez, for example—tend to ignore or miss the sign; others—like Ron Darling or David Cone—are more than willing partners in yet another of Hernandez's dialogues.

In this situation, Hernandez was on the receiving end of six throws to the base but when the batter, Andres Galarraga, struck out, Raines was still standing on first.

Also on display here was Hernandez's "release" from the bag. The release is a standard maneuver that a first baseman makes from a holding position to a fielding position lateral to the bag. A left-handed first baseman, facing home plate, will normally move out into a fielding stance with a little preliminary step with his right foot followed by a couple of quick, skipping crossover steps. His movement is sideways rather than straight ahead. A right-handed first baseman, facing more toward second, normally takes a step out with his already extended left foot then swings around into position, using his left leg as a fulcrum as his right leg comes around. A quick left-hander like Mattingly may be able to move eight to ten feet from the bag with his release, more if he has cheated up the base path prior to the pitch. Righties get out considerably less—another reason left-handers are better suited to the position—Eddie Murray, Kent Hrbek, Mark McGwire, and Andres Galarraga get out no more than three to five feet.

With Galarraga batting and Cone throwing hard stuff to help

check Raines on the base paths, Hernandez came out about ten feet. What makes him unlike anyone else is that when he wants to, he can come off fifteen to twenty feet, almost double the area covered by others. This is not because he is long-legged or spring-loaded but because he has changed the mechanics of the release. Having entirely eliminated the little preliminary step out with the right foot, just prior to the release of the pitch, and still holding the runner, he twists his body in the direction of second base. He is lined up toward second almost like a sprinter. With the pitch, Hernandez goes straight forward instead of to the side before swinging around into fielding position, so he is able to cover that much more ground. Simple. Like using a fiberglass pole while the rest of the vaulting class remains in the dark ages with rigid wood.

The Mets trailed 2–0 in this game until the bottom of the fifth, when they tied it. The key to that rally was a poorly handled sacrifice bunt.

The play developed in classic fashion, with the seventh- and eighth-place hitters getting on ahead of the pitcher. For a first baseman defending in this situation, the strategy is even more obvious than the certain bunt that is coming: Charge hard, try to get the lead runner if possible, one sure out at a minimum. Andres Galarraga was able to do neither. The Mets' pitcher, with everyone in the house knowing what he was up to, bunted for a hit—or, rather, laid down a ball that trickled into a midzone of confusion between the Expos' pitcher and first baseman.

It was not clear who was most to blame for botching the play. While sacrifice coverage is simple, it also demands precision and communication. The catcher usually calls which base a throw should go to; primary fielding assignments among first baseman, third baseman, and pitcher, with sliding coverage from second and short, are generally predetermined. This ball was one that the first baseman should have handled because the angle of his approach to the ball gave him a better chance of making a force throw.

· The bunt was good but might have been handled. Galarraga's charge, however, standard for most first basemen, left a sliver of opportunity on the right side. Prior to the pitch, the big first baseman had begun his plateward charge but then pulled up short. When the bunt was put down he was standing poised, about even with the mound—adequate positioning for most sacrifices but not this one. The play was followed by a mishandled fielder's choice that scored one run and then a 4-6-3 double play that scored another.

Because everyone in the game has seen Hernandez's cavalry charge to the plate, it is curious why other good first basemen don't imitate it. Galarraga, reiterating what most other first basemen say, acknowledges that in these situations he does not want to risk having a ball pushed past him or, less likely, having it smashed at him by a batter who decides to swing away. He and generations of first basemen have been taught to play for the sure out no matter what.

Hernandez is able to do more for several reasons. For one thing, he knows exactly when—and when not—to charge. He will regularly charge pitchers, selectively charge other hitters. His central intelligence system has accurately filed who the league's bunters are. He knows that most players, pitchers included, have lost the ability to bunt well, and he also knows that his charge is another "dialogue."

"In that situation, you put the pressure on," Hernandez says, "so that a guy who has to bunt will *have* to go down the third-base line. More times than not, he won't be able to put it down."

There is another motive for the charge that makes Hernandez different, more a throwback than an innovator. Here is George Sisler, that earlier kamikaze flier, on defensing the sacrifice bunt:

> Too many first basemen think they go in to field the bunt merely to get it to the second baseman, who rightfully covers first base in this situation and therefore allows the runner to get to second base. It is to the advantage of the defensive club to have the runner in a

double-play position at all times. This means keeping a runner on first base, in force position. It can be done by playing, always, to force the runner from first base at second. Get the front runner!

Now, if there are runners on first and second, no one out, a close score indicating that a sacrifice is in order . . . as the pitcher pitches the ball, the first baseman starts in with one idea in mind: force the runner at third base!

While the words are Sisler's, the practice is Hernandez's. In sacrifice situations, his focus is on the lead man. All thought, all preparation, goes into this: It is the rally Hernandez is after, the jugular. He knows what most old-time first basemen always understood: that the bunt, particularly the sacrifice bunt, is a powerful offensive weapon and that the ability to take it away, like the ability to defend against the lob in tennis, can instantly reverse the momentum of a game. In defending the bunt, Hernandez's "intention" is simple: to intimidate. "That's the whole idea," he says.

The reasons more first basemen don't revise their conservative bunt strategies are easy to understand. The bunt is going the way of the real grass that would slow it down. As the bunt goes so goes the need to field it. While in the National League the tendency to play for bigger innings is largely responsible, the decline of the bunt in the American League exactly parallels the rise of the DH. (There are, on average, two to three hundred fewer sacrifice bunts in the American League, a league with two additional teams, than in the National.) Anyone looking for a good, solid, practical argument against the DH should focus on what it has done not only to strategy but also to position play at first base. It has literally stripped first basemen of the chance to intimidate (a peculiarly ironic fact for Hernandez—given his move into the American League at the end of 1989). Consider what the DH can mean over the length of a career to a first baseman like Don Mattingly, whose first steps when a ball is hit are quick, whose hands are soft, whose arm is strong. In his time, Mattingly has made fewer errors than any other first baseman in either league,

makes the double play (easier always for a lefty than a righty) as well as anyone, and goes back on flies over his head better than anyone in memory.

The play Mattingly does not make much and that gives him more trouble than any other, he says, is the bunt. It isn't that he hasn't worked on it. He charges a bunt intelligently, coming down the line and then across, allowing himself better throwing position to catch lead runners, and he knows who the bunters are in his league. All that is missing is the play. "They just don't bunt that much over here," he says. Skill and good intentions aside, Mattingly cannot attack the play when it happens the way Hernandez can. "Your back's usually to the base you have to throw to and you have to rely on someone else to make a decision for you when you field a ball. That's never any good for you," the American League's best fielding first baseman admits.

Another play that gives many first basemen fits but Hernandez attacks as aggressively as the bunt is the slow chopper in the hole. This common and seemingly easy play often freezes first basemen because they don't know whether to field it or let the second baseman take it. "But it is," according to Mickey Vernon, "one of the plays that tells you what kind of first baseman you've got."

In that one Mets-Expos game, there were several instances—none decisive—where the play came up. When his chance came, Galarraga, who says that the play is particularly troublesome for him, automatically went to the bag, letting the second baseman field the ball. He has developed a rule of thumb on those plays: "If the ball is hit slowly, I go to the bag; if it is hit hard, I will try to get it. I have to improve there—it's a matter of experience. I need to see as many of those plays as I can."

On a slow chopper in the fifth, Hernandez ranged at least thirty feet wide of the bag and made a soft overhand lead throw to the pitcher covering for the out (the called-for technique; closer to the bag, the throw would have been underhand, also timed to the pitcher's approach rather than simply thrown to the bag itself). In the sixth, though, Hernandez ran to the base on a

slow chopper to second. Both instances were determined by the situation. The fifth-inning play was the third out, there was no one on, and the pitcher was hitting; the play in the sixth started the inning and was off the bat of speedster Otis Nixon.

Hernandez's goal—gained through experience—is to cover ground, the more the better. It is a goal, however, that requires interplay with other defenders. Pitchers have to be able to get to the base; second basemen must be in sync. Unlike Charles Comiskey, Hernandez wants to keep his pitchers out of it as much as possible, but he never shrinks from letting them know what he wants.

Hernandez works with his second baseman as surely as he does with his pitchers. That is yet another of his dialogues and it is one that is almost continual through the course of a game. He moves left or right with a pitch depending on whether or not his second baseman calls out his name. That is a prearranged signal that an off-speed or breaking pitch—easier to pull—is on the way to the plate; Hernandez's gift in return is that by taking more ground to cover, he gives more freedom of movement to his second baseman. A second baseman can cover the middle of the diamond, a tremendous defensive advantage, when a first baseman covers as much ground to his right as Hernandez can. (Conversely, it is a source of frustration when second basemen don't —or won't—move over. Hernandez was never able to budge Tim Teufel, one of the Mets' two second basemen, during Keith's last years in New York.

The game that evening remained tied through nine innings and was decided in the twelfth on a key play—typical for the position, atypically handled by Hernandez and the Mets' middle infield.

The first two batters in the inning, Raines and Galarraga, walked. With the right-handed Hubie Brooks up, Tim Raines the lead runner, and Randy Myers, the hard-throwing, hard-to-bunt-on lefty reliever on the mound, the hope was to keep Brooks from sacrificing, taking the chance that he'd swing away and hit

into a double play. With Hernandez jockeying at his position and Myers throwing high, Brooks fouled off a couple of bunt attempts and then hoisted a twisting foul far beyond first base, down the right-field line.

Hernandez, like any good first baseman, reacted with a quick pivot and pursuit of a ball in full flight. He was able to go for the spot where he thought the ball would come down (poorer fielders are forced to track the flight of the ball all the way). At the same time, he quickly triangulated a relationship between himself, the ball, and the stands, and, like any good first baseman in that situation, he turned inward and to the side when he caught the ball so he would immediately be in position to throw. What he did next, however, was what only a great first baseman would do —and it cost the Mets the game.

Instead of immediately throwing to third base to try to double up Tim Raines, Hernandez had already anticipated that Galarraga, a slow runner, might be trying to advance behind Raines. Even as he caught the ball and saw Galarraga moving out of the corner of his eye, his arm was cocked as he whirled to throw. But then, too late, he saw something else, something Galarraga probably saw as well: *No one was covering second base!* Tim Teufel had also come over to the right-field line, leaving Kevin Elster, the young shortstop, to cover the bag. Elster, watching the play, had either forgotten to cover or had assumed Hernandez's throw would go to third. Seeing the base unguarded at second caused Hernandez to double-pump and then send his throw on to third, far too late to catch Raines. What might have been a brilliant, rally-killing double play instead turned out like the sacrifice Hernandez and the Mets wanted to avoid. The Expos then went on to score and won the game.

The really intriguing part of this play—aside from the Mets' botching it—was that it depended on Hernandez's superior arm. Throwing ability is usually overlooked in first basemen but when it is present it adds another powerful dimension to the position.

The usual throws first basemen make are short: There is the

throw from the back of the bag to the pitcher covering, one that, whether under- or overhand, requires both delicacy and timing but not strength; a lob or somewhat faster-paced throw is called for from the infield grass back to the base in a sacrifice situation; a hard but short throw is necessary to catch an advancing lead runner or to start a double play. The double-play throw is especially important because the release has to be so quick, the timing so perfect, and then the footwork so exact. A left-handed first baseman, stepping forward, has the momentum of his body behind the throw, but a right-hander, dropping a step back like a second baseman, or even spinning counterclockwise so he can open up as he throws, has to battle his body to make the throw. He will always be a split second slower going to second than a lefty. Additionally, for any first baseman the throw is further pressured by the need to place the ball properly for the shortstop —chest- to face-high on the glove-hand side—and then to get back to the bag in time to take the return throw. Most first basemen, Hernandez in particular, do not want their second baseman or especially their pitchers handling the relay for fear of error or injury. In any case, on all these throws, accuracy counts even more than steam.

It is on cutoffs and relays where a first baseman's arm can become a special asset. Normally, first basemen are not asked to make relay throws from the outfield. The job is nearly always left to the other infielders, with the first baseman, a cutoff man, stationed in a direct line between the right-side-throwing outfielder, the relay man, and the base being thrown to. In that situation, the first baseman determines whether to let a throw go through to the base or to head it off and redirect a short throw to another base where there is a more likely play. With the Mets, Hernandez was employed according to convention, with his throwing almost exclusively a product of his role as a cutoff man. When he was with the Cardinals, however, he took position play at first to limits probably not imagined even by men like Hal Chase and George Sisler. Because of his arm and because from childhood he

has been "programmed" so thoroughly about where to throw and when, under Whitey Herzog he became a kind of roving ambassador to the Cardinals' outfield.

On hits to the alleys or corners in right with men on base, Hernandez went farther out—thirty to forty feet—than the average second baseman to receive an outfielder's incoming throw. From there, entirely depending on the moment in the game— who was running, what inning and score it was—his throw went to the necessary base. As a consequence, opponents *had* to react more cautiously on the base paths. Their game changed with Hernandez handling relays the same way it did when he was handling bunts!

Perhaps because of that, or because Whitey Herzog himself is so creatively committed to defense, the most revolutionary way Hernandez was used on relays was in handling throws from left center and even left field. On hits to the alleys, the usual relay man on the left side is the shortstop, with the first baseman acting as a backup or trailer to the play; on a hit down the line or deep to straightaway left when there is a possibility of a play at the plate, the usual relay man is the third baseman, though, again, the shortstop can be used if it is felt he possesses the stronger arm. For a first baseman to be used is simply unheard of.

"From the start with the Cardinals, I was the guy who went out on doubles down the line in right; the second baseman was the trailer," Hernandez says. "When Whitey came in, he also wanted me to be the arm in left." The task was sometimes impossible. Playing on a turf field, where balls travel faster, there was just no time to move from one side of the field to the other on certain plays. When he was holding a runner at the bag, he had a chance, he said, but when he was positioned deep behind first base there was too much ground to cover. "We tried it and tried it and tried it," he says. "It got to a point where the third baseman, Ken Oberkfell, would just look at me and see that I couldn't get there and he'd take it—I could get over if it was in the gap, but not beyond."

Watching any first baseman through any single game tells you only so much. As it is with hitters, perhaps even more so, you have to see a defender over a span of games to get a full sense of what he does. But this one game—and it could have been almost any other—showed just how much play was involved at first base, just why, in other games (like the one in Chicago a year later) a player like Hernandez is able to do so much more.

After one accepts a standard of physical skill shared by many major league players, what separates the great from the good player is his sense of command at the position. Hernandez comes to his work like a general, not a private. The secret of his game is that from the first to the last pitch, without break or pause, he is looking always for that extra advantage. Ordinary players, good ones, are content to cover their base well. Hernandez, as did earlier great first basemen, senses the largest possibilities of the position.

Like a chess master, Hernandez thinks of the different moves on the board not so much in terms of where different things go —those were the lessons of childhood—but of what the situation is. The rook is worth more than the bishop, but not always; sometimes victory or defeat hangs on a pawn. The name of the game is controlling the board, and it is a never-ceasing process until the game is won. You control the board to make sure you win. There is no other purpose in chess or baseball.

The advantages Hernandez works so hard for have a statistical corollary. Among career leaders in fielding percentage and double plays, he is the all-time leader in assists, a statistic that, even more than total chances, suggests how much range a first baseman has. (Right behind him in career assists are George Sisler and Mickey Vernon; the top fifteen include Jake Beckley, Joe Judge, Stuffy McInnis, Gil Hodges, and Jimmie Foxx. Another leader is Bill Buckner, whose one error in the 1986 World Series will probably forever obscure the fact that he was actually an excellent defensive first baseman.)

Hernandez's eleven consecutive Gold Gloves almost guaran-

tee that we will not soon see his like again. But as great as he is, it is well to keep in mind that the position he occupies is far older than he is and that what he has accomplished at it, shows his has been an office of trust, faithfully executed, not one of exclusive or even peculiar ownership. Hernandez has distinguished himself and his position because he has been able to enter into the flow of a game so much more than other first basemen. But here is Alfred Spink in *The National Game,* on turn-of-the-century first basemen Jiggs Donahue and Fred Tenney. Tenney, in particular, caught his eye:

> The wizardry which Tenney and Donahue worked in the art of first base play was something almost uncanny. Both of them could make dazzling pickups of wide-flung balls, hitting the ground in any old spot. They were enough to drive the fans hysterical. Both could leap high, reach up the gloved hand and pull down the frantic throws. Both were marvels at chasing foul flies, or snapping up grounders cutting across the line. Tenney, in particular, was the king of all first basemen when it came to mixing into plays around the bases. Old-time first sackers contented themselves with working in a sort of sturdy, mechanical fashion, doing just what came straight into their hands to do and never dreaming of interfering in the complicated plays that were coming off in other sections of the field. Tenney changed all that and forced himself into every play that was happening around the circuit. He taught the other first basemen things they didn't imagine possible.

Fred Tenney died in 1952, one year before Keith Hernandez was born.

SECOND BASE

We travel on to second base
And Brainard there is found;
He beats the world in catching "flies,"
And covering the ground.
And as the pitcher of our nine,
Whene'er 'tis best to change
The man will find that plays behind
That "Asa" has the range.

① **WILLIE RANDOLPH** *takes a double-play throw. Notice the base between his feet. He makes his pivot almost flat-footed, refusing to give an inch to the oncoming runner.*

THE CALIFORNIA ANGELS

② **NAPOLEON LAJOIE,** *the Hall of Fame second baseman, had a team named after him—the Cleveland Naps. A lifetime .339 hitter, his play at second base was noted by contemporaries as unusually smooth.*

NATIONAL BASEBALL LIBRARY

③ **BILL MAZEROSKI** *of the Pirates was called "No Touch" or "No Hands" because of the speed with which he turned double plays. No sooner did a double-play throw touch his glove than it seemed to be on its way to first.*

THE PITTSBURGH PIRATES

④ *Acrobatics for* **FRANK WHITE** *are just part of the repertoire. Doing things gracefully has been his hallmark—but it is also the secret of his extraordinary consistency.*

UPI/BETTMANN NEWSPHOTOS

⑤ **JOE MORGAN** *taking a catcher's throw as Davey Lopes of the Dodgers attempts to steal second. "The two prerequisites for playing second," Morgan says, "are quick feet and intestinal fortitude."*

THE CINCINNATI REDS

DURING THE BASEBALL STRIKE of 1981, I began watching minor league games in Connecticut. The team I traveled to see was a Red Sox affiliate playing out of Bristol, an old industrial town that had seen its share of hard times but, surrounded by mountains older than hard times, looked particularly beautiful sillouetted against the sky on soft summer evenings. The team played out of Muzzy Field, an old WPA park situated in the middle of town, a Norman Rockwell setting for a team whose skills seemed to belong more to that era than to one of megabuck player salaries and nationally televised Games of the Week.

The affiliate Red Sox didn't seem like much. They were a last-place team when I began watching them in late June and early July. But by the end of the season they improbably had risen to first in their division. They traveled Bull Durham country in their worn bus with the sort of storybook luck that seemed to go far beyond their talents. Not one of these players ever had more than a proverbial cup of coffee in the majors, while the teams between them and a championship were well stocked.

In the first round of the playoffs, they eliminated a team from Reading whose best player was Julio Franco, the highly prized second baseman, then a highly prized shortstop. In a five-game final series, they took out a White Sox affiliate whose big guns were Greg Walker and Ron Kittle.

The key to Bristol's success was some reasonably effective pitching and the play of the team's second baseman, Erwin Bryant. Bryant never really had a chance to go further in his career, but for this brief time he was a perfect second baseman, a

sort of Everyman at the position. In fact, he was known to his teammates as "E-Man," "E. Bryant," or just plain "E."

E. Bryant killed Reading and then Glens Falls the way Everyman Brian Doyle took out the Royals and then the Dodgers for the Yankees in the 1978 playoffs and World Series. Bryant, an indifferent minor league hitter, hit. He sent beebees into corners and alleys, frozen ropes into no-man's-land. He set up rallies, extended them, capped them. And E. Bryant fielded. How he fielded!

In the first of the playoff games, Everyman preserved a scoreless tie by making three different plays in one inning. He took a ball to his left, going headlong toward the right-field line, spun, and threw his man out. He went to his right, took a sure hit backhanded across his body, straightened up, and had enough on his throw to nail his runner at first. Then he went up the middle again on a ball rocketed off the pitcher's glove—a certain hit. E. Bryant seemed to switch gears in midflight as he dove for the ball and then again as he snared it, and somehow managed to get to his feet in time to cut down his man.

The team's manager, Tony Torchia, told the local press afterward that that one play alone lifted his team. "I'm not in the habit of giving out game balls, but this time I would," he said.

Bryant continued his heroics through the games that followed, into and including the championship round.

My memory of all these games is that this player, who never spent a day in the majors, was everywhere. He made catches over his shoulder and speared line drives in places he shouldn't have been, sometimes turning hits into unassisted double plays; he took balls slowly bounced off the grass and devoured them going left and right when they were struck hard along the ground; he fed balls to his shortstop, starting double plays, snapping them sideways or shoveling them underhand when he was closer to the base. He was the middleman on double plays, standing in blind, getting his certain peg off in time, going up in the air, coming down again as though, through twenty-odd years of life, he had

learned an old secret of the gods—that dancing feet were more effective than prayer in warding off ruin.

In a few short weeks, though I had followed the game all my life and seen a number of great second basemen, it was Erwin Bryant who made me forever aware of the position. The harshness of professional judgment being what it is, it is likely that E. Bryant, like B. Doyle, was, after all, only a Roman candle, but he was a real light nevertheless.

Because he did so much in so short a space of time, it was like watching a hurry-up film of a growing plant, the flowering of second base.

What any second baseman is asked to do first is cover ground. He must be able to move left and right, to go back for balls over his head and in for balls slowly chopped, and his hands must be soft enough to handle hot shots, quick enough to separate ball from glove in time to make double plays and relay throws. His feet need to be even quicker, so he can, in moving left or right, in or out, upright or scrambling, get that one extra step that makes the difference between the play made or not made. Above all, his feet better work on double plays, precisely, quickly, perfectly, because there the margin for error concerns not only the play but the integrity of one's body.

So many of the second baseman's moves and plays count. If he handles a relay throw, an extra base or a run is always on the line. If he is the trailer on a relay from the other side of the field, he may have to align things for the shortstop and make sure he gets him to throw to the right base, or, if he sees that he has a chance to get back to second in time for a play on an advancing runner, he has to decide that in a flash, and get back to cover; the double play he makes—or fails to make—is sometimes the difference between winning and losing.

Strong- or weak-armed, he must be able to throw skillfully. On the double-play throw, for example, the second baseman may come sidearm to force an incoming runner down, the peg just clearing the runner's head on a line to first; if he has time, he will

also try to grab the ball across the seams as he transfers it from glove to hand in attempts to keep his throw from dipping or sailing. On relay throws he will set up facing the outfielder, giving him as wide a target as possible, and then, as the outfielder unloads, he will align his own body so that when the ball hits his glove he will already be in position to throw. He must master throws that are no more than little underhand flips, and equally throws where he is spinning counterclockwise, losing sight of the target he must find. On seemingly routine balls, because his throw is short, he has to cut down the motion of his arm to reduce velocity while at the same time using a peculiar snap of the wrist to guarantee there will be enough on the ball when he gets rid of it. (The inability to do this may have been behind the peculiar rash of simple throwing errors that plagued Steve Sax several seasons ago—at least so Davey Lopes, a teammate of Sax's, surmised.)

Second basemen, alternately, turn into first basemen when they cover on bunts, into third basemen when they are playing in to cut off a run; they are outfielders when they go back, shortstops when they play deep, catchers when they are on the receiving end of throws where tag plays are to be made at the base. Physically, they must be able to be everywhere at the same time —or at least appear to be. They must be simultaneously quick, smooth, and tough as nails. Base stealers, in profusion, come from their ranks: Eddie Collins, Napoleon Lajoie, Frankie Frisch, Snuffy Stirnweiss, Jackie Robinson, Joe Morgan, Willie Randolph, Harold Reynolds, Billy Doran, Ryne Sandberg, Juan Samuel, and Steve Sax are just a few. The very same list suggests still another dimension: second basemen are expected to provide some offense.

BEFORE HE VANISHED into the world beyond the last outfield fence, E. Bryant, neither a base stealer or a hitter, refused to make much of what he did. Second base was his job, and a second baseman's job, he said with the simplicity of Aristotle, was to "cover the position."

For me, there is a peculiar correspondence between Bryant and one of the game's first great second basemen, a pre–twentieth century player named Bid McPhee. McPhee, like E., has also suffered the injustice of being overlooked—not then but now. He is one of a number of players who, though clearly deserving, have never been voted into the Hall of Fame. Unknown to most of us today, McPhee played over two thousand games through eighteen years and to this day remains a career leader in most fielding categories for second basemen. He was one of the first who understood what it meant to "cover the position."

Bob Carroll, in his essay "For the Hall of Fame: Twelve Good Men," noted that McPhee "led his league's second basemen in putouts eight times,"

> assists six times, double plays eleven times, total chances per game six times, and fielding average nine times. In every one of those years, he led in at least one category and usually in several—but he never led in errors.
>
> And remember . . . only in his final three years, long after the glove became standard equipment, did he begin to cover his hand with leather. . . . Bid accepted 14,241 chances, and that comes to a greedy 6.7 per game. To put it another way, in the average Cincinnati game, he accounted for about one-fourth of their opponents' outs. The only one involved in more outs was the scorekeeper.

To be sure, it is not McPhee's numbers that make me think of E., nor even the fact that both men, in very different ways, suffered the injustice of being overlooked. McPhee's defensive achievements, accomplished between 1882 and 1899, suggest a way of thinking about his position that was revolutionary then but was part of a trust, an inheritance that E. Bryant and every real second baseman since has carried with him into the field. McPhee thought about second base probably the way the Wright brothers thought about flying.

McPhee's thoughts are gone with his career, so in his case the numbers have to do the talking. And what they suggest is that he

got around. McPhee piled up those records because he roamed farther and did more than other second basemen dreamed possible.

Just a decade or so before McPhee began playing professionally, *Beadle's Dime Base Ball Player* reiterated in words what pictures of the time told us about position play at second: Second basemen played close to the bag.

> This position [second base] is considered by many to be the key of the field, and therefore requires an excellent player to occupy it. He should be an accurate and swift thrower, a sure catcher, and a thorough fielder; he should play a little back of his base, and to the right or left of it, according to the habitual play of the striker, but generally to the left, as most balls pass in that direction.

But by the time McPhee and other pioneers of the time like Fred "Sure Shot" Dunlap, Fred Pfeffer, and Cupid Childs left the game, second basemen had swung far to the right, transforming the nature of the position.

From the early part of the century right through the present, second basemen have almost had to have a manager's sense in the field. Napoleon Lajoie, the Hall of Fame second baseman for the Cleveland Naps (so named for him), was known for his elegance and smoothness afield. He was "a natural." But his mind was nailed to everything he did. He was one in a long line of managers including Bucky Harris, Frankie Frisch, Earl Weaver, Billy Martin, and Davey Johnson who were originally second basemen. Lajoie, in the wake of Bid McPhee, described what he did in the field for *The National Game*. He might have been writing a coach's manual for the position today:

> I play a deep field and change my distance from the base according to the style of pitching. You must size up the man at bat and know the style of ball the pitcher is to feed him. It is always best to go in and meet the ball . . . I never make up my mind how to take

the ball until it is very close, for it may take a jump if you set yourself for the regulation bound.

On working in tandem:

I always have a perfect understanding with the shortstop and catcher, as to who will cover the base, and play a bit closer when out for a double play.

On taking fly balls:

A second baseman should go for short flies, and depend on the outfielders for the coaching, as they are in a better position to judge the ball.

On turning double plays:

If there is no chance for a double play, you should hold the ball. . . . In turning to throw, step in front of the base and throw regardless of the man coming down, as he will generally look out for himself and is not anxious to get hit with the ball. . . . I instinctively start for the base as soon as I see the ball is hit to the right of me. It pays to be at the bag in time to help the throw from short or third, for a fraction of a second will lose a double play.

Then and now, play at second base begins with positioning. It is hard to see from the stands because sometimes only a step or two may be involved, but being in the right place to make a play is, more often than not, the only hope that the play will be made. It is not as simple as it sounds. As always, the prerequisite is an understanding of situation, i.e., who is pitching, what pitch is being thrown, who is hitting, what the count is (players alert to positioning will adjust with each pitch of a particular at-bat).

Slower second basemen depend that much more on positioning. Marty Barrett, second baseman for the Red Sox, told Roger

Angell that from one batter to the next he sometimes moved twenty to thirty feet. The Royals' seven-time Gold Glover Frank White, Barrett said, could in the same circumstances hold his ground and still cover the same territory.

White, in turn, said that he moved as much in the beginning of his career as Barrett but cut down when he was more familiar with the hitters. As a result, he jokingly told Angell, "I'm playing better but getting noticed less."

The play that ended the 1962 World Series between the Yankees and the San Francisco Giants was a bullet off the bat of Willie McCovey, the huge left-handed slugger, right into the waiting mitt of second baseman Bobby Richardson. The play has been talked about ever since as the epitome of correct positioning. Had Richardson been a foot or two to either side, so goes the consensus, there would have been no play. And in the context of the situation—two out, runners on second and third in the last of the ninth inning of a 1–0 game, Series tied at three games apiece, the narrow difference of feet meant a World Championship.

But Richardson himself never saw the play that way. "Actually," he remembered recently, "I had some room. I thought I could have gone a couple of yards more to get the ball if I had to. But that was because I was not only in position, I was ready for it."

The ball McCovey hit was *smoked*. But not directly at Richardson. Another look at the film shows the second baseman actually moving left and toward the ball, almost as if the ball itself pulled him into the play. The play was *not* shot-catch, but Richardson moving to meet the ball and take it with him as he headed for the dugout, the locker room, the plane he had to catch—as though McCovey's ball was somehow an afterthought on his way to the airport.

Of course, Richardson couldn't have made the play unless he had been correctly positioned. Even though the Yanks and Giants did not regularly play each other and hence were not that familiar

with each other's personnel, it was no secret that McCovey was a dead pull hitter and that the Yankees' pitcher Ralph Terry, in his ninth inning of work, was mainly throwing the kinds of pitches —sinkers and sliders—that would likely induce a pull hitter to pull. Swing to the right, way to the right, for McCovey.

But through six games Richardson also had been able to "read" McCovey. For example, he knew from earlier games and from an earlier at-bat in this game just how McCovey pulled and, more important, how the ball came off his bat; McCovey hit balls hard and with tremendous overspin on them. Actually, Richardson first thought McCovey's ninth-inning shot was going over his head. But then, in a split second, reading the tremendous overspin, he knew the ball was going to sink. But why do this for Bobby Richardson? Here is his account of the play. Call it positioning plus:

"Matty Alou had opened the inning getting on with a bunt, right? Then we got a couple of outs, I think, and there was Mays's double. The thing I remember about that was the great cutoff Maris made on the ball. Because Roger had a really strong arm, I knew I could position myself for the relay closer to the infield. I did. All the while I could see in the back of my head that Alou was going to score, I'm thinking, 'Home, home, home.' Roger hit me perfectly and then the throw I got to the plate took too big a bounce. But I was in a good position to throw and that may have had something to do with holding the runner. Alou didn't try to score.

"With McCovey coming up, Houk came out to talk to the pitcher, to see if he wanted to pitch to McCovey or put him on —Orlando Cepeda was on deck. I was standing at second with Mays and Kubek. Kubek said to me—you may have heard this— 'I sure hope they don't hit the ball to you.'

"Now we'd roomed with each other for eleven years so I said, 'Why?'

"He said, 'Well I'd hate to see you blow it at this time.'

"I went back to my position but I was thinking, 'I want the

ball; hit the ball to me.' I also remember, just before the pitch, as Terry was going into his windup, the second-base umpire said to me, 'Hey, Rich, I'd like your cap after the game for my little cousin'—I was even thinking about that.

"I was moving before the pitch—which I think was a breaking ball—if you're an infielder, you want to be moving, up on the balls of your feet—I was moving right towards the ball. I know it's been said that I was smoothing dirt and I just happened to stay way over towards first but that's not the case. I knew how McCovey pulled; I played him in the hole earlier in the game on a ground ball he hit there. I had an extra yard or two on the ball he hit because I was moving towards it. There would have been nothing if I hadn't been. I thought for a second it would be a hit because of its height off the bat—but I picked up that topspin right away; it had such tremendous topspin on it—same as Mantle's—but I was ready. I was on my way off the field."

There were several things going on simultaneously, all direct results of positioning. Begin with anticipation.

Jim Lefebvre, the Mariners' manager and a former second baseman for the Dodgers, says that the very first thing he looks for in middle infielders is great anticipation. "The better middle infielders are the ones who best know what they're going to do with the ball when it's hit to them," he says. From Mays's double to the last out of the game, what Richardson did sprang from his sense of where he was on the field, what was going on, and what he had to be alert for. His description is technical and psychological. He talks about having to get on the balls of his feet, to be moving forward toward the play, rather than waiting for it to happen. This is standard, to be sure, what fans can see just before a pitch: the idiosyncratic dance routines that bring defenders forward into motion. But from the stands we are seeing very little.

How a player is "in" the game is largely not visible to the naked eye. And while being in the game is also fundamental, instruction manuals can never lead a player step by step to the informal and spontaneous moments with other teammates—and even with

neighboring umpires—that punctuate the tensest situations on the field and that, in the most practical ways, allow for grace under pressure.

Positioning is dynamic and explosive. Watch an Olympic sprinter, poised in the blocks with all that is going on inside him before the starter sounds his gun. Now watch an infielder just before a pitch. An infielder waits for more than the sound of a gun and a surge of energy. How much range he has, how well he reads situations, where he goes, what he does when a ball is in play—everything that makes the difference between three feet and five, between three fifths of a second and one whole second, all is there poised in that initial moment.

Joe Morgan, the two-time MVP and five-time Gold Glover, says there are really only two essentials to playing second—quick feet and courage. For Morgan, these standards are as formidable as they are simple. "By that I mean you have to be tough enough to stand in there and make the double play first and worry about your body second," he says. "Very few guys are able to do that. There are many people who play second, very few who are real second basemen."

Morgan was a real second baseman. His quick feet and knowledge of the game enabled him to be in almost full flight on balls hit to either side of him. Going to his right, usually the more difficult side for second basemen, he was a sheer terror. A film clip I have of him during a Dodgers-Reds game in 1977 shows him moving deep behind the base, making a scrambling, backhand stop a good *twenty feet toward shortstop*, leaping and throwing—completely against the momentum of his body—in time to get his man. He also went to his left sufficiently to protect his slow-moving first baseman, Tony Perez, and enough to place him among the game's career leaders in assists, total chances, and double plays at the position.

IT WAS THE double play that challenged Morgan the most. As with everything else, he attacked the play with ferocity. He got

to the base quickly, got his body under control, hit the bag with his left foot as his hands (left hand covered with only the smallest of gloves, the better to draw the ball from) extended for the throw; then, catch, right-foot plant, throw, in one seemingly shutter-speed blink; then, sometimes a collision, more times a leap, a pirouette over the hurtling body of the incoming runner. Twenty-three years of this left Morgan's legs looking like highway maps of scars.

Morgan says that his role model among second basemen was Bill Mazeroski, in the latter stages of his career as Morgan was starting his. Mazeroski, like Morgan and so many other second basemen, was a converted shortstop, converted because his arm was not particularly strong. But just because he lacked a strong arm, he had to find ways to compensate. He reduced each move he made to its essence. His throw—he was called "No touch" and "No Hands" because of his relay—took no time between the touch of ball to glove and its flight to first. Mazeroski took no extra steps to get out of the way of oncoming runners. His pivot, the very one Morgan adopted for himself, was one of the most daring and effective ever. He never cheated. He couldn't afford to. He didn't want to. Making the play was everything.

"There are a lot of guys today who people say are good second basemen," Morgan says, "but only a few have been willing to stand in and take a shot. There are a lot of guys who are getting rid of the ball and getting out of the way at the same time, and they don't make the double play—they just miss it. In the ninth inning with the game on the line, they just miss it—it never even looks like a mistake, but it's the difference between a true second baseman and a guy who just plays the position."

The double play has always been the key to playing second and to the interior of the man playing there. Remember Napoleon Lajoie on the double play? "Step *in front of the base* and throw regardless of the man coming down." In 1989, Mets manager Davey Johnson used bullfighting imagery in teaching his rookie second baseman, Gregg Jefferies, how to turn double

plays. "Think of yourself as a matador. Your left leg, planted on the bag, is the red cape, the runner is the bull," he counseled.

Eddie Collins, at the top of the career lists in almost every fielding category, was small, light, fast, and had large hands. A great deal is known about how he hit and ran, less about how he turned the double play. He surely knew about double plays, though. One of the unbought White Sox in 1919, Collins later measured the World Series scandal in terms of how his shortstop did *not* stand in on double plays. "In almost every account," Collins said years later, "it has been stated the sellout was clumsily arranged. I don't agree. . . . Players contrived to look good while not giving their best . . . like [Swede] Risberg taking my throw on a double-play pivot, reaching back with his foot to tag second . . ." Like Joe Morgan, Collins knew all about making or just missing the play.

According to George Sisler, second baseman Rogers Hornsby, nasty, cantankerous, and absolutely fearless, usually turned double plays by stepping across the bag and throwing sidearm. Unlike Morgan and Mazeroski, Hornsby hit the front corner of the bag with his right foot, came over with his left, then threw across his body from the side—not the optimum way to throw—forcing the runner to hit the dirt.

Frankie Frisch, the old Fordham Flash, faced the shortstop or third baseman with his left foot forward, right foot planted, to receive double-play throws. He then touched the bag with his left foot and dropped it back to the outfield side to make his throw. It was usually sidearm to get the runner down, but because he was driving off his pivot foot, he had the option of an overhand throw as well.

Nellie Fox was a good second baseman for the White Sox. He became a great second baseman at about the time he taught himself to make his double-play throw from the middle of the second-base bag.

Joe Gordon, a great and underrated second baseman for the Yankees and Indians, popularized a more histrionic move. He

frequently hit the base with his right foot, planted it there, then simply went airborne as he got his throw off to first base.

The way all second basemen say they avoid injury is by getting into the air. If you are hit in the air, they say, you may get cut, you may come down hard, you may make the back-page photo of the tabloids, but you won't be seriously injured.

The way earlier second basemen turned the double play obviously required quick feet and an abundance of courage. Until 1977, when the rules were changed to limit the approaching runner to a direct slide into the bag, second basemen were fair game for anything thrown at them. According to Sisler, the style signatures of Hornsby, Frisch, and Gordon were the most heavily copied by major league second basemen. For three quarters of a century, courage was a fundamental, its absence a noticeable liability. Standing in and taking it, was, well, just standard. Second basemen were protected only by their agility— and their refusal to be intimidated.

Red Schoendienst, a post–Gashouse Gang successor to Frankie Frisch, had his own way of standing in. A quiet, modest man who never looked for—or ducked—fights, Schoendienst says the goal always was to stay in the game, "to make the play." To do it consistently, he had to do it right—no backing off, no peculiar steps. Catch, plant, throw. He expected to be hit.

"Every once in a while, someone'd try to hurt you," he says. "So I could step on 'em if I had to."

Step on 'em?

"Yeah. I had one guy once—I won't mention his name—he came into me on a force-out. He was out by fifteen feet. And all I did was catch the ball from the shortstop for the third out—the inning was over. He wasn't anywhere near me, so what does he do, he comes crashing right into me. I turned around and said, 'What the hell are you trying to do? You're out by ten, fifteen feet and I'm off the side of the bag.' He says, 'You play your game, I'll play mine.' I says, 'Okay.' Well that same ball game I was hoping he'd get on first, then come into me again. He got on.

He came into me. I waited for him a little bit, and I got him. I stepped on his neck."

The late Billy Martin was a real second baseman long before he was employed by George Steinbrenner. Second-base play today has changed, according to Martin.

"They don't knock guys down the way they used to," he said in one of his last interviews. "You see double plays not being made that should be made because you see second basemen coming across the bag instead of staying in there and getting knocked down. Years ago, you went across the bag, they'd still come out and get you. Second base, to me, was really toughest in making the double play. It was tough on your knees, tough on your legs —I only got scar tissue left there now—everything was body to body. When you get hit by a guy who weighs two hundred and forty pounds and you're one sixty—in football they call it a clip and give you fifteen yards. In baseball, you just get up, dust yourself off, and hope you're not missing a wheel."

This is the way Billy the Breakable Kid taught himself how to take control of second base:

"I did it by never letting anyone know I was hurt even when I was. Pitcher hit you with a pitched ball, you never yelled or threw a bat, you just took it in the ribs and walked down to first. You take one extra step, you don't make the double play. Guy's a fast runner, you have to stay on the base and get creamed. A lot of times you throw the ball and never see the DP. Sometime later, someone figured out you could tape a piece of plastic to your shins—we were never smart enough for that. I learned to relax after I got hit, that's all. Instead of standing firm, give—they knock you on your ass but they wind up hurting themselves more than they hurt you.

"I'd get guys down, too. If they come in high, I'd drill 'em. Once they really know you're going to do that, they'll either go wide or slide early. I threw at Walt Dropo one day halfway between first and second. Did I nail 'em? Right between the eyes. I tell you this, too. If a guy didn't come after me, I didn't have no

respect for him. That's why I never had no respect for Ted Williams. He always ran wide."

IN OUR TIME, one in which, ironically, there is far more violence on the field, the frontiers are settled and the rules more exact. But second basemen, particularly the older ones, who learned their trade in the time of cross-body blocks and sharpened spikes, are no more timorous than their forebears. And some of them may be even quicker afoot.

Frank White, the Royals' thirty-nine-year-old second baseman, reminds many old-timers of Charlie Gehringer in his smoothness. Gehringer, said J. G. Taylor Spink, in *The Sporting News,* "was to the infield what Joe DiMaggio later became to the outfield. He had the same loping grace that Joe has, the same flawless timing. He covered more ground than any rival."

Fluidity, ease of motion, and grace all describe Frank White. But just as these terms were more than points of style in Gehringer, who, though quiet, was tough to the point of daring (Gehringer took no steps at all on the double play—he simply straddled the bag and threw!), White's elegance and toughness also go far deeper than style.

White, who grew up in Kansas City, and used to watch A's games, was athletic without ever being "an athlete" or having dreams of one day being a ballplayer. He joined a group of friends who had heard that there were going to be tryouts for the now extinct Royals Baseball Academy. White knew nothing at all about the Academy but was selected as a student during an intra-squad game in which he played third base. He played there for the next six months, then a bit in the outfield, then much more at shortstop. He became a second baseman only as a major leaguer. His quick feet, quick mind, and very soft hands were useful anywhere he played. But when he reached the majors—having spent just half a season in the minors—it was as a backup second baseman to Cookie Rojas, aging but still superb at his position. Rojas, White says, taught him something essential about style:

"I learned that there were certain shortcuts to getting things done. You do things fluidly and easily because that is the easiest way to do them. I like to be known for that, yes, but there is something more—being fluid, to me, means being consistent. If you are consistent, there are no surprises. If you do things the same way all the time, you make the plays more often, your teammates know what you're doing and, most important, the umpires give you the calls. They pick up your rhythm. If it is the one they recognize, they don't have to think about anything; if somehow your rhythm goes off, they'll unconsciously say to themselves, 'I haven't seen that before, something must be wrong.' "

White learned from Rojas. "You learn from people who have really been successful," White says. Rojas taught him how to go to his left. Most second basemen till then simply stretched out or dove, then straightened their bodies as best they could to make the short throw to first. The difficulty in making the play is having to gain control and then come back across the momentum of your body to make the throw.

Rojas was one of the first second basemen to go with the force of the hit, to turn his body around and into the throw—to spin rather than fight back against the grain. Particularly on artificial surfaces, this move not only was more elegant but opened up far more coverable territory. White—and every other second baseman who followed him—could then angle back into the outfield on balls that would otherwise have gone through for hits, and with the spin, gain rather than lose momentum on the throw to first. "Doing it that way, you can even throw overhand to first—you cut down the chance of having the ball sink or just plain get away from you," White says.

Rojas taught White another useful shortcut. When a second baseman went up in the air following his double-play throw, he could do more than simply avoid injury. He could come down on the runner.

Learning to stand in and make the double play was the most difficult thing White had to learn. Though he is too modest to

talk about his own courage (in his vocabulary the operant word is "consistency") for Frank White, turning the double play has been a private trial.

"You make double plays any way you can, obviously," he says, "but I think you have to find one way, one ideal way, that is most comfortable—and stay with it."

White went through seven or eight ways before he found the one that best suited him. At first he made a lot of errors; in 1976, his first year of full-time play, he committed eighteen. The problem, he says, came mainly from being distracted by oncoming base runners.

"At shortstop, everything was always in front of me—I could always see the runner. At second base, You don't see the runner till you're actually making your throw to first. You never know where the guy is. I know when I first started playing in '76, the majority of my errors were dropped balls right on top of the base —because I always had that impulse to look before I received the throw, and the ball would always hit and fall by my feet or whatever."

There really was no shortcut to help overcome this. In fact, the important thing, the secret that went to the heart of the play, was learning to slow down—getting slow in order to become quick.

"I practiced and practiced," White says. "I had to learn to become more deliberate. You know, catch the ball, throw the ball, catch the ball, throw the ball, until after a while it was just there."

"After a while" for White turned out to be a year. In 1977, he committed only seven errors at his position and won the first of his record eight Gold Gloves (Mazeroski won eight in the National League), and since then has been simply the best at his position in both leagues, among the very best ever.

But the way he chose to turn the double play perhaps says about him what he would not say himself. Like Charlie Gehringer, White cut his throwing time to the minimum by straddling

rather than crossing the base. The trick he picked up from Cookie Rojas here was to *use* the base—the runner would have to hit the base before hitting him—and then jump.

"Basically, the base is between your feet—you have almost a side view of the runner—and you're accepting the throw," says White. "As the throw's coming, you're shifting your weight to the right side, so you're pulling up across the base with your left foot as you're making your throw. Then you make a little jump turn out of the way, it's a little half-moon turn, which suddenly gives you an advantage over the runner. It's another one of those things Cookie taught me."

White, learning to be smooth, long ago found his own cutting edge. But at thirty-nine, he is still finding ways to add to his game. In the past few seasons in Kansas City, where there has been a rapid turnover at shortstop, White has learned to deliver his double-play throw to second more quickly. He has taught himself to deliver the sidearm flip—usually done from just a few feet away—from deep in the first-base hole. Cal Ripken, Jr., swears that at a clinic he saw White make one of these flips from a distance of ninety feet! White says he is uncertain he can make the throw at that distance but, in any case, as with so much of his game, young second basemen—including Billy Ripken—have begun to copy it.

Lou Whitaker is an old-timer by now as well. It seems only a day ago that he was a baby-faced recruit in the Tigers' system, brought along to play middle infield for the parent team with a shortstop named Trammell.

Though Whitaker had arrived in the American League only shortly after White, the interregnum was significant because in the meantime, the so-called McRae rule, forbidding football-style takeouts at second base, was adopted. (The new rule, which mandated sliding and staying within the base paths, was named for the Royals' Hal McRae, who regularly demolished second basemen with rolling cross-body blocks as he attempted to break up double plays. On one such effort in the 1977 playoffs, McRae

nearly dismembered the Yankees' Willie Randolph. The rule change, it was said, was hastened into effect for the '78 season largely as a result of that single play.) Regardless, Whitaker had already learned his trade, and was prepared for midfield mayhem. His aggressive style was a throwback—and a model for future second basemen—even after the old regime was thrown out.

His way of taking the bag was initially difficult anyway, because he was a latecomer to playing second. A third baseman when he signed his first professional contract, he did not begin playing second until 1977 in Double A. Learning where his feet went was much more than figuring out dance steps.

"What it took was learning the bag," Whitaker says, "because you're making the double play. To make the play precisely, so many other things go into it. At the same time, you have to be prepared for so many different things: You have to be ready for the ball in the hole, to protect your first baseman when he's there holding a runner; you then have to be alert to the middle also. The runner may steal, there may be a hit-and-run, there may also be a double-play ball—you have to be prepared for everything. There's just a lot of movement and a lot of thinking on *every pitch!*"

Whitaker learned what all pivotmen have to learn: that there are a number of steps to take, seemingly all at once, in turning the double play. You get to the base under control, you set your feet for the throw (body slightly turned if the throw is coming from third or from the mound, foot in contact with the bag if the throw is wide), then make the catch specific (on the throwing-hand side if possible, and down in the palm of the mitt so the ball can easily be withdrawn), and then you make the throw.

Whitaker was at first confounded by the bag. He got too close to it when he fed balls to the shortstop, and tended to waste time crossing it when he had to throw. What he eventually learned to do, he says, was move back of the bag when he was the lead thrower, getting out of the shortstop's way, and, when receiving a lead throw, staying in. "I learned to take the bag, take my right

foot back so I could throw through the runner," Whitaker explains. He is not talking about cheating or setting aside laws of physics any more than Billy Martin was.

Among second basemen, Whitaker is a powerful thrower—a third baseman. Once he had his feet under him and understood that he had the ability to leap, staying in was not difficult for him. He worked on his throw, adapting it to second base. Technically, what he did was learn to drop down, to throw from the side and underneath, but what he really learned was a second baseman's climate of mind: With his throw, he learned to intimidate rather than be intimidated.

"I was very fortunate to have a really strong arm," Whitaker said, recalling how he used to use it. "At first my tendency was to throw around people and to throw over the top—the way I had at third. It took a couple of years to learn to throw through people. I remember one play that changed my thinking. I got a double-play ball with Bruce Bochte running. He just stood up, so I threw over his head—right into the first-base stands. Maybe it took that—or just playing against Kansas City with runners who were fast and could hit you—to learn something different. I learned how to come down low. I always throw with something behind it, always, and I try now—I've done it for years—to go right through the runner. I have no sympathy for him. It's not just about having an arm. In my career," Lou, who is called Sweet, says, "I've tried to use some smarts."

Smarts. With second basemen it is interchangeable with *courage*—and sometimes even with *quick feet*.

Sweet Lou is slow for a second baseman. Long before he acquired the first of his three Gold Gloves, he learned that his feet took him only so far. He sought out Frank White. "No one I've ever seen plays the position better than he does," Whitaker says. "I can't imagine that anyone ever played it better."

What he learned, technically, was lateral movement, particularly to his left. Whitaker had watched White's spinning move for years, never quite understanding it. "What I picked up from him

was not the spin so much as the angle he took going after the ball —towards the outfield rather than the ball itself." Because White could go left that way, Whitaker realized, he could guard the middle better, he could position himself better to dominate the middle of the field—no cheating, just taking ground and control. Quick to the left meant more room to intimidate.

After Frank White, the dean among contemporary second basemen is Willie Randolph. Randolph began as a shortstop in the Pirates' organization, and still takes ground balls at short during warm-ups, teasing midfield mates that he's after their job, but for years he has been synonymous with textbook play at second. For most of that time, spent in the Bronx, he had to be doubly courageous, guarding his position and also his sanity. More recently, Brooklyn-born Randolph has found his way to the prodigal Dodgers.

A measure of Randolph's mettle has always been the way he stands in on double plays. Among second basemen, no one has refined the move quite the way he has. His usual move is no movement; he sets his feet and throws almost from a standstill. Unheard of—the very thought of it conjures the many injuries he has sustained over the years. Randolph's knees have been savaged, the flesh all scar tissue. Years ago, before the advent of arthroscopic surgery, he tore cartilage in one knee and had to have the entire cartilaginous pad removed rather than repaired in order to continue playing—though with chronic and incremental pain. Then he tore cartilage, surgically repaired, in the other knee. (In addition, he has regularly been afflicted by hamstring pulls— a curse of the trade that may be related to those tiny balls-of-the-feet preparatory moves before a pitch. The consequent overdevelopment of quadriceps muscles in the front of the leg, Randolph believes, makes the hamstrings particularly vulnerable.) His body has always had to pay the price of his courage.

Nevertheless, Randolph has been a five-time All-Star. He has been co-captain of storm-tossed teams great and almost great, a steadying influence where steadiness seemed more certain in every

other port of call in organized sport. He played with thirty-three different shortstops during his tenure with the Yankees. Yet throughout he has remained completely reliable: a consistent hitter, always better under pressure, among league leaders each year in almost all defensive categories. And despite the terrible battering to his legs, he has remained a swift runner—not the explosive base stealer he once was, but fast enough to create problems whenever he gets on.

For all that, Randolph might have had a more durable, more lucrative, and hardly less celebrated career had he been willing to take an extra step across the base, to let his arm try to gain back the additional inches yielded by more cautious feet. No one would have known—except Randolph, of course.

But Randolph has never presented himself in a hair shirt or had to boast about anything. He has so obviously, so thoroughly and gracefully, done his job, no one in their right mind would ever have thought to wonder, watching him in that standstill pivot of his, if his single-mindedness in getting things done was not slightly crazy. Why would anyone be willing to take the punishment Randolph has; what are the limits to courage at second base?

On the wall of his locker through most of his years at Yankee Stadium, Willie Randolph kept a picture of Joe Louis. One of his heroes, Louis also represents a lifelong interest Randolph has had in boxing. As a youngster, he was part of an organized neighborhood boxing program in Brownsville. To this day, he regularly works out on a speed bag and acknowledges that he is "pretty good" at it. But it has also helped his hand-eye coordination in the middle of the field, he says. Quickness, not love of punishment, is what he counts on at second; his hands are lightning fast, his arm unusually strong. Is there any better, faster way to turn a double play?

Quickness. Speed. It is a matter of mind, a rhythm in the body, it allows you to *think* a certain way, it even gets into patterns of speech:

"I can pivot almost from a standstill because I have quick hands and quick feet and the arm for it. People may not see that because I have this quick little pivot, you know—*boom, boom,* it's here, it's gone," Randolph says. "I can do that."

Like all of the good ones, he relies on becoming airborne to protect himself after he gets his throw off. The move—he calls it a pirouette—comes from his schoolboy football days and allows him both to fall properly and to deal properly with contact. Contact, for Randolph, is an extraordinary challenge, which he responds to in a simply extraordinary way:

"I learned early that if you're going to be intimidated by contact you're not going to be a good second baseman. You almost have to have blinders on. I try to get a picture in my mind of where everything is without having to look at it. I visualize the speed of the runner, the velocity of the ball when it's hit, the likely velocity of the throw from short or third or from the pitcher —all that's going through my head as I'm approaching second base. I know where the runner is; I know exactly where he is without looking. When I get the ball, I don't worry about being knocked down or upended because I already know I have that split second to throw; I've seen it before it's happened and that's all I need."

Randolph does not seem to go out of his way to intimidate anyone—just to keep from being intimidated. His combativeness comes out in his commitment to the play. Like any second baseman, he has been the victim of cheap shots—including the one he took from Hal McRae. He throws to keep runners down but seems not all that concerned about protecting himself. For a reason.

"A lot of guys get off on upending you," he says. "It's like they're saying to themselves, 'Look at that, I knocked him upside down—did I take him out.' Bullshit. The play's been made. If you get me, get me in the act of throwing—but if you haven't gotten me there, you haven't done your job—I have."

His quick-handedness combined with Steinbrenner's heavy-

handedness have cost Randolph. He has been pushed to play through injury. And what does it mean to reorganize a middle-infield combination not once but thirty-three times? Joe Morgan argues forcefully that second basemen and shortstops need to have nearly identical rhythms of movement in order to work most effectively and that when combinations are constantly juggled, middle infielders become conservative, working within very mechanical limits.

Randolph, while never criticizing a single shortstop he has played with, praises one—Bucky Dent—above all. Having been impeded in ways the Principal Owner and, possibly most fans, never imagined, Randolph speaks of the advantage playing with Bucky Dent afforded him:

"When you turn a double play, you don't always get a routine one. . . . Each of you has to know what the other is going to do —if you're unsure of each other, you just don't make the play. It means having a sixth sense about each other. A ball's hit slowly in the hole, someone's barreling down on you—a shortstop, if he's looking out for you, he's gonna give [you] the ball on the back of the bag. Another shortstop who doesn't know [you] will just give [you] the ball on the base . . . Bucky knew what to do . . . that's why we didn't miss too many and why, even on plays where we seemed to have no chance, we'd still do it, because we'd know exactly what to do if a guy was on top of me, if it was a routine play, if he was gonna flip it to me where I had to come across and *boom, boom,* just go. . . . It was really knowing each other to the point where if there was a crucial play, there was no room for indecision or hesitation to where you miss the play by just half a step—and that half step turns out to be the ball game, run scores or next guy hits one out—the big thing that makes you not see the little thing that didn't happen."

Randolph has played with other infielders who have made his game easier. Working with Graig Nettles for so many years helped him considerably with the more distant, more difficult throw from third, for instance. "Graig's ball was always absolutely

straight and accurate. A lot of times, a third baseman's double-play throw sails," Randolph says. "Graig would put the ball right there for me ten times out of ten. That made my positioning easier." So did playing with first basemen like Chris Chambliss and Don Mattingly.

Nevertheless, Willie Randolph has had to celebrate his skills largely by husbanding them. He has not been able to be as fine as he might when taking and feeding double-play throws. He asks new shortstops simply to get him the ball "over the bag"; he will do the rest. "It is easier for them, takes some of the pressure off them," he says.

Randolph seems to add a dash of style to everything he does —but it is for the play and the people he plays with. Like Maze-roski, Joe Morgan, and many other second basemen before him, he carries an unusually small mitt. "It's my muffin," he says, per-sonalizing this work of the hands that must be done. He takes a grounder the way infielders are taught to, drawing in his hands up toward his body as he receives the ball. But then he adds something: He takes the ball and seems to tap it once in the mitt before he throws. There is a faint aroma of hotdogging in this but the purpose is to make sure his fielder on the other end *sees* the ball before it is thrown.

Anyone who has watched Randolph play recognizes just how he has incorporated natural quickness into a mature style. He dives going right and seems to bounce into throwing position almost immediately. *Boom, boom.* The double play he initiates at a distance—the body is down, feet apart, left foot behind the right —is converted out of a crouch by a quick twist of the upper body and a dartlike throw that is *overhand* rather than from the side. It is a flashy move that gets the ball to his shortstop—whoever he is—with something on it and with a minimum of movement. Ten times out of ten.

Because his left flank has been so well covered—he now plays with Eddie Murray—and because he has played most of his games on a slower natural surface, Randolph has never had to be as inventive going that way as Frank White has. It is too bad.

Once, in a minor league game, Randolph went left, extended as far as he could, had no time to spin and catch the runner streaking to first, so instead passed the ball from glove to hand *behind his back* and made the throw for the putout! Randolph says that he has wanted to try that in the majors but that if he ever got it wrong, "I'd be called a hot dog forever." Not by anyone who really understood where he was coming from.

It is a good time for second basemen. Masters are still playing, and the lessons of masters before them have long been incorporated into the routines of the position. Billiard-ball playing surfaces and rules changes have created a demand for even more quickness without sparing any of the consequences of that one extra step that is the difference between plays made and those missed.

Players in the middle or even at the beginning of their careers seem able to challenge gravity itself. Ryne Sandberg, the Cubs second baseman who set a major league mark for consecutive errorless games at second in 1989 and who has captured a record seven straight Gold Gloves at the position (Mazeroski and Frank White have won more but not consecutively), has what some call the best feet in the game. This has nothing to do with fashion, and everything to do with balance. In simplest terms, it means that he is able to keep his feet always in position to make a play, even when laws of gravity make this unlikely.

I saw Sandberg, who is taller than the average second baseman, make a leaping catch of a line drive in which the force of the ball might have knocked him over backward. But somehow he had managed to turn sideways as he went airborne, coming down with the ball in the tip of his glove and his feet firmly in place beneath him—or at a forty-five-degree angle to the play!

Charlie Fox, then a Cubs advance scout, said that Sandberg had the balance and quickness that would allow him to play anywhere. "Watch him when he makes a throw, any kind of throw," Fox instructed. "His feet are always perfectly set to make that throw. You can't really teach that."

But Sandberg credits this ease with the fact that he broke in

at his position playing alongside Larry Bowa. The season he began playing second (he had been a minor league shortstop and third baseman) he turned up at spring-training camp several weeks early to work with Bowa, the Cubs' shortstop.

"We just did things over and over, the only way to do it," Sandberg said. "He kept after me all the time. He helped me a lot on positioning, on hit-and-run plays, on coverage—you have to be aware of not leaving your position too early. He taught me to keep an eye on the hitter when a guy's stealing—just in case he does swing the bat. I used to think along with Bowa for a long while, till I reached a point where I could think for myself—and actually tell him some things."

Sandberg is sure of the plays he makes. When he goes left to take a ground ball, he has done it enough so that he can go into his spin with his target already in mind. If his throw goes back to second base from this spin, his movement off his back foot up into the air is done with the necessary sense of balance to make what would otherwise be an awkward or impossible throw.

"I do things enough so they become instinctive," Sandberg says, "but I never just let myself spin—as I do it, my mind is already on what I have to do next so that I can make the play."

Because he is tall, Sandberg pays special attention to his feet, which allow him to make up for what the length of his body might interfere with. He is on the balls of his feet, always moving before any play. "I'm ready for a ball to be hit to me on any pitch in any situation," he says.

On double plays, this allows him more movement at the bag than other second basemen enjoy. He is freer to move behind, in front of, or in back of the bag to take a throw. He is freer to quickly go airborne with a runner coming into him.

"As long as your spikes aren't dug in, you're going to be all right when they hit you. When you go up in the air, it looks like you've really been creamed—but you haven't been if your feet have given."

Roberto Alomar, the Padres' twenty-one-year-old second

baseman, seems like he has played the position all his life—and perhaps he has. His father, Sandy, played second for five teams, and Roberto was around the clubhouses as soon as he could walk. He was once batboy for the Yankees. The partners he induced to hit him paper balls bound with tape included Catfish Hunter and Chris Chambliss. His father says the key to Roberto's game is incredible quickness coupled with a professional's sense of confidence, which even at the age of nine seemed to border on cocksureness. For his part, Roberto says his father is the only hero he's ever had, and that his youth does not in the least add pressure or get in the way of his game. Nothing gets in the way of his game. Watch him.

He takes a minimum of forty double-play balls in practice every day—takes them from every angle, rapid-fire, machine-gun style, so his hands and feet will never be surprised. He hasn't, like Frank White, decided on one optimal way to pivot, but so what? No one will *ever* move him out of the way, and he will get his man—both of them.

He wants the whole field if he can get it. Outfielders *must* call him off any short fly to the outfield he can reach; on foul flies, he sets the spot he will go for, farther than second basemen have any right even to think about, then, as he arrives there, 250, 260 feet from the plate, he slides another 10 feet to make his catch.

When you watch his rightward move on ground balls—possibly the best in the game—he is even more spectacular. Once again, a slide is involved. He goes as far right as he can and as he extends for the backhand stop, he slides on his left thigh like a base runner—while other second basemen would dive. By doing this, Alomar is able to recover more quickly, to come up instantly with his right foot planted, in position to make a strong throw. He has somehow managed—it seems almost an optical illusion—to reverse the momentum involved in the play that ordinarily would preclude the likelihood of any throw at all.

And if all that were not enough, Alomar goes left just as well. In one game last season, playing on a natural surface, he stopped

a hard-hit ground ball in right field and turned it into a 4-3-5 double play!

SECOND BASEMEN have this audacity that is absolutely wedded to agility. There is no such thing as just looking good, any more than courage at the position means anything without magical hands and feet. And second basemen are keenly appreciative of what it is they do. Rogers Hornsby, the greatest right-handed hitter in the history of the game, might be expected to have picked any of dozens of batting feats as his outstanding achievement in the game. Instead, in his autobiography, *My War with Baseball,* he recalled one comparatively easy defensive play he made, a tag at second on an attempted steal. Second basemen make this play all the time, nearly always by taking a straddling position to the side of the bag, catching the ball, then dropping the glove to the ground without going for the runner, in effect allowing the runner to put himself out by sliding into the tag. Here is what Hornsby said:

> My biggest thrill in all baseball was making a simple tag on a runner trying to steal second base. The play was the biggest surprise of my career, and I'd have to say the biggest break any of my teams ever got. It also goes to prove that the World Series is not won—it's lost. The guy I tagged out—and by a mile, too—was Babe Ruth. Babe just decided to take off and he merely slid into my glove and tagged himself for the out that gave my St. Louis Cardinals the 1926 World Series championship over the New York Yankees. The Yankees were 15-1 favorites to beat us in the Series.

Ready. Ready for anything and able to do almost anything at the same time. Shibe Park, Philadelphia, 1951. It was the last day of the season, and the Dodgers and the Phils were tied 8–8 in the bottom of the twelfth inning. The Dodgers had to win to tie for the pennant and earn the right to face the Giants in a three-game playoff. The Phils loaded the bases against righty Don

Newcombe, who was in his fifth inning of work and had pitched a complete game just two days earlier. Eddie Waitkus, dangerous and left-handed, was coming up. Waitkus, of course, would make contact in this, his 610th at-bat of a season in which he had struck out only twenty-two times. Jackie Robinson, jockeying up on pigeon toes to be ready for anything, was thinking, "Right—he will hit the ball right." But Waitkus, with Robinson shifted over toward first, didn't pull. He hit a low, hard line shot straight up the middle. Somewhere, somehow, out of the shadows and flood-lights of late afternoon, Robinson literally flew into the picture. He took an impossible headlong dive and, in a great cloud of dust, made the catch that saved the Dodgers for another, bloodier day, soon to come. Never mind how he got there or whether he caught or only trapped the ball (some still wonder), he was, beyond reason or expectation, there. He was ready.

In all of baseball history, there have been eight unassisted triple plays. In the 1920 World Series, a second baseman, Bill Wambsganss of the Cleveland Indians, made one. But for the fact of his making the play he might have passed into oblivion as just another Everyman at the position. Wambsganss chafed at the notion, but almost a half century after he made the play, he remembered exactly what was involved. This is how he explained it to Lawrence Ritter:

> It happened this way. It was the fifth game of the Series, and we were tied with the Dodgers at two games apiece. The date was Sunday, October 10, 1920. We jumped out to an early lead when Elmer Smith hit the first grand-slam home run ever hit in a World Series, and at the end of the fourth inning we were way ahead, 7–0.
>
> The first man up for Brooklyn in the top of the fifth inning was their second baseman, Pete Kilduff. He singled to left field. Otto Miller, their catcher, singled to center. So there were men on first and second, and none out. Clarence Mitchell, the Brooklyn pitcher, was the next batter. Well, in a situation like that, with them behind by seven runs, we didn't expect them to bunt or hit-and-run or

anything. We figured they'd just hit away. Mitchell was a pretty good hitter. And, being a left-handed batter, he generally pulled the ball to right field.

So with all that in mind I figured to play pretty deep for him, not especially caring whether we got a double play or not, not playing close for that. We didn't need a double play. Just stop the rally, that would be enough. So I played way back on the grass.

Well, Jim Bagby was pitching for us, and he served up a fast ball that Mitchell smacked on a rising line toward center field, a little over to my right—that is, my second-base side. I made an instinctive running leap for the ball, and just barely managed to jump high enough to catch it in my glove hand. *One out.* The impetus of my run and leap carried me towards second base, and as I continued to second I saw Pete Kilduff still running toward third. He thought it was a sure hit, see, and was on his way. There I was with the ball in my glove, and him with his back to me, so I just kept right on going and touched second with my toe *(two out)* and looked to my left. Well, Otto Miller, from first base, was just standing there, with his mouth open, no more than a few feet away from me. I simply took a step or two over and touched him lightly on the right shoulder, and that was it. *Three out.* And I started running to the dugout.

The fans, he said, didn't seem to know what had happened. But he did. He was ready.

THIRD BASE

And lest the boys should thirsty get,
When after balls they've ran,
We take with us, where'er we go,
A jolly "Waterman."
Upon Third Base he stops hot balls,
And sends them in so fine,
That all have said that jolly "Fred"
Is home upon the nine.

① *This picture of* **MIKE SCHMIDT** *fully extended offers just a hint of his extraordinary defensive ability. A ten-time Gold Glove winner, Schmidt was bigger, faster, and had more range than others. "Third base is a skill position, like shortstop or center field," Schmidt says—probably because he played it that way.*
UPI/BETTMANN NEWSPHOTOS

② *Gotcha! The all-time leader in fielding average at third,* **BROOKS ROBINSON** *also handled 9,165 chances at his position—almost 2,000 more than his nearest rival.*
© TADDER/BALTIMORE

③ **PIE TRAYNOR,** *the Pirates' Hall of Fame third baseman in the twenties and thirties. Never particularly fast, Traynor's great edge came from his superior sense of "tactical situation" in a game.*
NATIONAL BASEBALL LIBRARY

ONE EVENING BEFORE a game late in his career, Graig Nettles was sitting in the visitors' dugout at Shea Stadium, looking out across a field wet with rain. There was no infield to take that night, and there was little chance that he would see action in the game, if it was played. He was no longer a regular. His once glorious career was reduced to occasional appearances as a pinch hitter and as a stand-in at third, where, for the decade following Brooks Robinson's retirement, his name had been synonymous with the position.

I was interested in the 1978 World Series, in which he had given one of the bravura performances at third base in baseball history. Nettles was noticeably older now, some ten years later. His balding pattern—just beginning in the seventies—was far more distinct, his curly blond hair turned gray. His body, which had taken a career-load of caroming baseballs and belly flops onto infield surfaces as hard as empty swimming pools, seemed already soft with middle age. His eyes, though, were the same—a clear baby blue that in any aging face is always a surprising reminder of youth.

Of course Nettles recalled the Series, but in the peculiarity of this setting—during one of his last trips to the city where he had done it—it was as though his whole career and not any set of games stretched out before him. He had third base on his mind. He looked at the empty base not twenty feet from him and, almost as an aside, summed up his own career by summing up what he thought was most essential about the position he played.

"I was never very fast," Nettles said, "but you don't need speed for third; you need quickness. I always had more range

than other third basemen because my first two steps were quick —that's all. That's the most important thing playing in close to the hitters. It's really a position of two or three steps to one side or the other—if you make those two or three steps quicker than other guys you're gonna have more range."

This image of a narrow lane of action can be deceiving. The third baseman has fewer tasks than other infielders. In the mirror imagery of the diamond, the left-side cornerman is actually a poor reflection of his counterpart at first—he can go whole games without making a putout and his footwork around the bag is limited. Third basemen, no matter how good their range, cannot begin to cover the ground middle infielders can. They initiate but do not turn double plays; they range backward in pursuit of flies along the foul line and stands but cover less ground going into outfield spaces than shortstops and second basemen.

What a third baseman does, basically, is field ground balls and make throws. He has other plays to make, to be sure: He covers his base for force-out and putout throws; he is the cutoff man on some relay plays coming from left field; he is a principal defender against the bunt and must be able to make one of the more elegant plays of the game—the bare-handed, one-motion pickup and throw. Like other infielders, the better he is at communicating with his partners, the better for all concerned. But what third basemen have been known for—from the time of old Fred Waterman of the 1869 Red Stockings—is stopping smashes hit at them in that narrow lane of two to three feet.

Perhaps because third basemen have so limited a job description they have traditionally been underappreciated. Only eleven of them have been elected to the Hall of Fame (the fewest for any position). Third base is usually reserved for slower players with some offensive potential—or so conventional wisdom has it.

But ask any third baseman and he will tell you that his is a "reflex" position. Because he is stationed so close to the action and because his lane of coverage is really confined not by lack of speed but by the incendiary nature of what he is asked to handle, it is his autonomic nervous system, even before his mind, that

counts. He cannot do his job unless his hands and feet, impossibly, work faster than his brain. It has always been that way.

During a 1988 game in Boston between the Red Sox and the A's, Wade Boggs made a remarkable stop on a bad-hop ground ball. It came at a time when Oakland was rallying to get back into a game that they ultimately lost 7–5, but the play will really be remembered for itself. The A's batter, Dave Henderson, launched a supersonic ground shot directly at Boggs. Coming in at groin level, the ball took a crazy last-second carom upward directly at the right side of Bogg's face. He had no time to throw a deflecting glove in the way. Instead, he put up a bare hand and actually caught the ball. The sheer force of the blow knocked him flat on his back, from which position he somehow managed to scramble to his feet and get off a throw—too late—to first.

Acrobatics aside, what was most startling about the play was what did not happen: Boggs was *not* struck in the face. After the game, he said the play had scared him "nearly to death," but he also said that he had never been particularly afraid of being struck in the face playing third. "I don't know why, but I've never been afraid of that—that one play as it happened, yes, but not before and not afterwards. I've sometimes been afraid of taking one in the cup, but not the face."

This turns out to be an unofficial test for third basemen. It has nothing to do with masochism, but everything to do with reflex, the invisible component that makes it possible to play third at all.

"I have never been afraid—ever—of taking a ground ball in the face," says Terry Pendleton, the Card's Gold Glove third baseman, "because I've always known that I could get my head out of the way in time. The head is actually the first part of the body that moves. People may not know that, but any good third baseman does."

Brooks Robinson knew it.

"I always felt I wasn't going to take one in the mouth. I knew I was quick enough to protect myself that way," he said.

The game's earliest third basemen knew it too. Bob Ferguson,

captain of the Brooklyn Atlantics, was the fielding leader among third basemen in 1873. He had a nickname, "Death to Flying Things," which may have derived from how he handled himself at third—or, more likely, from his sometime work as a catcher. Ferguson was one of the first catchers to move into position behind the batter. He did his work there without glove, chest protector—or mask. In any case, third base was easy on his face.

Will White was another nineteenth-century fielding leader at third. He played the position wearing glasses, decades in advance of high-density polymer plastics. "White wore spectacles," wrote Alfred Spink in *The National Game*, "and players who saw him playing at third, often wondered how he ever escaped with his life." Apparently it was something White never wondered about.

To be sure, players *have* been struck in the face at third—the most recent being Howard Johnson, the Mets' third baseman, known more for his bat than for his glove. Hall of Famer George Kell, notes writer and researcher Jim Kaplan, "had his jaw broken by a Joe DiMaggio smash [in 1948]. Reacting instinctively, Kell picked up the ball, crawled to third for the force out, and then fainted."

The concomitant to reflex at the position is, of course, fearlessness. It is helpful to trust one's reflexes, but that alone is not enough. Overcoming fear at third must also be a matter of experience and skill. Like other fielders, third basemen begin in a set position. But because they are up so close, their set becomes that much more important. When the lane is two or three feet to either side, inches and milliseconds are crucial. The third baseman's concentration must be riveted on the immediate situation, such as who is pitching (life and limb are at stake in knowing that the left-hander out there is a breaking-ball pitcher, or that his right-hander tends to work inside). What about that hitter? If he's left-handed, does he have a good "inside-out" swing that can send a ball whistling to third? If he's a righty, does he have a slow bat or a quick one? What inning is it? What is the score? What about a bunt or a squeeze? Or a throw from the catcher? Getting

to the balls of his feet and having some forward motion toward the play is a third baseman's way of readying his reflexes for a hair-trigger response to a *variety* of possibilities within his limited lane.

Getting the glove down and the body positioned so that it is facing the ball squarely is just as essential. Nearly all sound coaching in fielding fundamentals teaches that keeping the glove down is preferable because coming up for a ball is always easier than going down. The glove in the down position promotes "soft" hands—this and keeping a wide base in the body, eyes on the ball, toes parallel, bent elbow and wrist, bringing the ball into the body, are especially important for third basemen because everything happens so quickly at the position. Forewarned is forearmed at third. It cannot be otherwise.

Turn-of-the-century player Jimmy Collins, the first Hall of Fame third baseman, knew what the third baseman had to do as well as anyone. "He must be ever alert and fearless," he said in an interview in *The National Game* a few years after he retired in 1908, "for no man has the hot shot to handle as the third baseman."

The plays, Collins noted, all seemed to come out of this heightened sense of alertness. "A player should have his mind made up before the ball is pitched as to which base he will throw to. In fact, a player should never take his mind off the game."

The bunt and the swinging bunt, always exceedingly difficult for third basemen because of the tremendous disruption in timing, were even more difficult in Collins's time, when the bunt was more prevalent.

"A clever batsman that can bunt and also hit away will keep you guessing at third. I play quite deep on all and come with the pitch," Collins said.

In fact, Collins depended heavily on anticipation:

"I want to know the kind of ball the pitcher is about to deliver," he said, "that is, whether a curve or straight ball, as it improves one's ground covering at least twenty-five percent."

Twenty-five percent? Remember the lane. Collins knew all about the different kinds of ground balls: It was a "science," he said. On balls chopped slowly toward short, "I always cross in front of the shortstop for the slow grounders as I can get to them first."

And it was important, if extension was required, to do it one-handed, because the time to throw would be limited and the one-handed catch "gives a better chance to get into position to throw."

Balls to his right, even slowly hit ones, were also to be taken one-handed for the sake of the throw.

"Trapping the ball is the most scientific department of baseball," Collins said. Play the short rather than the long hop, he stressed, watch out for in-betweeners, and take the ball right at you so that it will have "no chance to come up"—but if it does, the correct positioning of body and glove are essential. "The best way to play all kinds of ground balls is to be on the move and trap them just as the ball is about to come up from the ground, being well over the ball, with the side of the hands close together in such a position that the ball . . . can be scooped when not held the first time."

There were other dangers to consider, like throwing. How, precisely, does a third baseman throw? This is one of the least understood and most easily confounded of the third baseman's skills. Because players like Brooks Robinson had a stronger throwing release than arm, it has sometimes been assumed that having "an arm" at third is not really that important. Nothing could be farther from the truth. Terry Pendleton came into the 1988 season with a sore arm, and began piling up throwing error after throwing error. Orioles shortstop Cal Ripken, Jr., who began his career as a third baseman, recalled that in his first years in the minors he regularly tried to gun the ball to first but found that he had no control, so he had to learn to throw sidearm, and more easily, to correct himself. "But at clinics," he said, "I always point out that that's exactly *not* the way to learn how to throw. A

young player must learn to throw over the top, not just for accuracy's sake, but because overhand throwing is the way you build arm strength, and that is absolutely essential."

Jimmy Collins put it a little differently. Before anything else, he said, "a third baseman must be a good thrower." Collins believed—a half century before Terry Pendleton was born—that "third basemen should be about as careful as the pitchers in starting out in the spring, for a lame arm is a hard thing to get rid of and without the arm in the pink of condition, a third baseman will carry a big handicap."

The handicap derives not just from loss of arm strength but from loss of *throwing ability*. Gunning the ball is just one throw a third baseman makes. He must, like a pitcher, be able to throw accurately at different speeds. He sometimes will have to throw from deep behind the bag with everything on it, sometimes from in close and underhanded. He throws to second differently than he does to first.

"With a chance for a force-out at second," Collins said, "the ball should be thrown for the bag at a medium pace, trusting the second baseman to get there. When trying for a double play with a fast man at bat . . . put extra steam on the throw to second." Be a pitcher not a thrower.

It is a permanent loss to us that we don't know more about old artists like Collins. Would that we had the video equivalent of daguerreotypes to catch the style of old Death to Flying Things Ferguson and Will White. It would have served far more than nostalgia to see Hick Carpenter, who played 1,059 games at third between 1879 and 1892. To this day, he remains among career leaders in putouts and total chances per game. But the thing about Carpenter, who played at a time when bunts and contact hitting were common, was that he was left-handed. Conventional baseball wisdom long ago rejected the idea of anyone left-handed playing third (Don Mattingly did for a few games several years ago), but Carpenter did it with distinction for a career.

By all accounts, the best third baseman prior to the modern

era was Pie Traynor, whose entire seventeen-year Hall of Fame career was spent with the Pittsburgh Pirates. Traynor, of course, was a hitter; he had a lifetime average of .320 and seven times drove in over a hundred runs. But his fielding is what he will be most remembered for.

Tall and rangy, Pie was able to go right better than anyone. He did not really dive the way third basemen do today, a motion, perfected by Brooks Robinson, that allowed third basemen to hit the ground, then come up throwing. Traynor did it somewhat differently—so well, *Sporting News* correspondent Bob Broeg noted, that telegraph accounts of games would sometimes jokingly include descriptions like "Smith (or Jones or Hornsby or Hafey) doubled down the left-field line but Traynor threw him out."

The way he did it seems almost incredible. "I've seen him make that play bare-handed," Charlie Grimm, the late manager and first baseman, told Broeg. "Pie had the quickest hands, the quickest arm of any third baseman. And from any angle he threw strikes. Playing first base with him was a pleasure—if you didn't stop too long to admire the plays he made."

Sometimes Traynor outdid even his best. According to Broeg, "They even talk about . . . Traynor lunging backhanded to his right, gloving a smash and, losing balance, flipping the ball to his bare hand and firing a side-armed strike to first base before taking a header in the dirt."

Pie Traynor wore a small glove. After he'd retired, he reflected on how the equipment—and the position—had changed.

"The glove, not the hands, does the work now," Pie said in 1959. "I wonder how the players can even handle the weight and be dextrous at the same time. . . . In my time, the idea was to skin down the glove, to make it as light as possible. Jimmy Caveney [the Pirates shortstop] would rip almost all the stuffing out of his glove. It looked like a sick pancake.

"I liked to take the padding out of the thumb of my glove so I could get a better feel of the ball, a more secure grip. In my

time, this was the style, a light loose glove with plenty of room for finger action."

Traynor, like Jimmy Collins, played his position so long and so well that he simply knew it better than others. Whatever his natural gifts, they were transformed into mastery through experience.

Experience taught Pie many things: work as far left as possible on grounders; make double plays with runners on first and second by going to second, unless the act of fielding itself brings the third baseman close to the bag; taking bunts, Pie said, means being able to direct the throw of the pitcher when he fields the bunt as well. It is also mandatory to cover the base against runners: straddle the back corner of the bag for incoming throws, and leave the bag when the throw is not going to be close. "Never let the runner on third take a long lead," Traynor warned, having lived for years on the edge of squeeze plays and attempts to steal home; "always feint the runner back [to the base]."

This particular skill—the ability to hold runners at third—has eroded along with the frequency of the bunt and the steal of home, and it is too bad, because some artistry has gone with it as well. Judy Johnson, the Negro League third baseman elected to the Hall of Fame in 1975, once described a play that in a game between his team, the Pittsburgh Crawfords, and a team of touring major league All-Stars. According to his teammate Ted Page, Johnson worked out a routine with his catcher, Josh Gibson, when runners reached third base. "He and Josh Gibson," Page told John B. Holway, "boy, they trapped more men off third base! Judy'd put a little whistle on to Josh . . . and I'd say, 'Oh, oh, they got something cooking.' "

In this particular game, Leo Durocher, one of the All-Stars, had reached third and had begun his move off the base to distract the pitcher. Johnson began whistling.

"Durocher moved in towards home," Johnson said, "and I moved with him. Then I just backed up, put my foot about two feet in front of the base. Josh had the best snap, wouldn't move

to throw, just snapped the ball. I caught it. Here comes Durocher sliding in and the umpire says, 'You're out.' " Twenty years later, according to Holway, Durocher was still talking about the play.

WE ARE NOW in the twilight years of a golden age at third base. In the last quarter of a century there have been more outstanding players at the position than the game had seen in almost the entire century preceding—Brooks Robinson, Mike Schmidt, Graig Nettles, George Brett, Buddy Bell, Ken and Clete Boyer, Sal Bando, Ron Santo, Doug Rader. Why this is so is perhaps another of the game's mysteries. But there also may be explanations closer to home—or third.

Begin with Brooks Robinson. No player in his time has so completely dominated a position in the field. Whatever third-base play was before him, it has been redefined since. Even the most casual look at the record book suggests why. Robinson is a career leader in almost every fielding category. He has played more games, made more putouts and assists, handled more chances, started more double plays than anyone at his position. In addition, he just happens to be the career leader in fielding average.

Robinson, now a broadcaster in Baltimore, where he spent his entire playing career (twenty-two one-year contracts, another of his amazing stats), says that it was only an aging body that took him from the field. "I love the game just as much now as then," he confesses.

Actually, though, he was physically limited from the start. He signed with the Orioles as a second baseman but soon learned he was not fast enough nor able to cover enough ground there and was moved to third, where it was felt a narrower range of coverage would better suit his good, soft hands. As well as being slow afoot, Robinson initially was not much of a hitter. In his first full season with a team that finished sixth among eight teams, he hit .238 and had just three home runs and 32 RBIs. (His left-side partner was not yet Mark Belanger but Willie Miranda, an adequate but not great defender and an even lighter hitter than Robinson.)

But if Robinson—or his team—harbored any early doubts about his own future, he knew two things clearly—that the position he had been moved to was a "reflex" position, and that his own reflexes were special.

"There are a lot of things you can do to improve yourself anywhere you play," Robinson says, "but the real key . . . is God-given talent, an instinct for what you're doing. Ever since I can remember, I had that little sense of timing where I could just tell. Like rebounding in basketball."

As a high school basketball player Robinson was a formidable rebounder—not because of his height (he was under six feet), nor because he was unduly fierce, but because he had an "instinct" for the ball as it was coming off the rim. He was able, he said, "to jump neither too soon or too late."

He had always been fascinated by this gift of his, he said, especially when it came to baseball. There was never anything else he wanted to be in life except a ballplayer.

"Fielding was always my pride and joy," he said. "I played all the positions as a kid, I was a pitcher, catcher, everything—but there was always that little sense of timing, anticipation, getting that little extra jump."

And when he played those solitary games off a stoop with a rubber ball, it was as though third base was in his blood ten years before the Orioles thought of moving him there from second base:

"I played games, you know—go to your left, go to your right," Robinson said, "and it wasn't like I played way back—it was from here to there—hit the top step, it bounced down here, skip it it would come off on a fly . . ." When he finally did get to third base as a professional, he said he felt like he was coming home.

Though he had been playing brilliantly for the better part of a decade, Robinson didn't really come to everyone's attention until the 1970 World Series. The Orioles took the Reds in five games that year, and Robinson was simply in orbit the whole time.

In the first game of the Series, after throwing away the first ball that came his way—something that Robinson said unnerved him and reminded him of a poor Series he had had the previous year—he made several outstanding plays, including an impossible stop of a smash off the bat of Lee May far behind the bag at third, which he converted to an out at first. The play came leading off the sixth inning with the score tied at 3–3 and was immediately followed by a walk and single, which would have broken the tie. Instead, the Orioles won on Robinson's homer in the next inning.

In the second game, also at Cincinnati, Robinson turned a certain first-inning double down the line into a force-out, limiting a big opening rally by the Reds. Then in the third, he converted another down-the-line smash into a 5-4-3 double play. The Orioles, with a late rally of their own, won 6–5.

He made several more spectacular plays in the third game, each one demonstrating what reflexes at third mean: With runners on first and second and no one out in the first, he made a leaping stop of a ball chopped over third, stepped on the bag for one out, then threw to first to catch the slow-moving Tony Perez for the double play, rather than going to second in pursuit of the swifter Bobby Tolan. An inning later, he charged a topped roller down the third-base line and made a one-motion pickup and throw to get the out at first. Later, he made a sprawling, diving catch of a line drive in the shortstop hole off the bat of Johnny Bench.

Robinson, who went four for four including a home run in the fourth game, had only one play in the field, taking a sliced, spinning ground ball off the bat of Bernie Carbo and turning it into an unassisted, inning-ending force play. In the fifth game, though, he made the play that has since been on almost every World Series highlight film. It was a diving catch going to his right—into foul ground—of a line drive off the bat of Johnny Bench.

When the dust cleared from this Series, everyone in America

was aware of what Brooks Robinson had done. But they might have missed nuances that teammates and rivals had been aware of for a long time. He did everything *correctly*. When he had to make his one-motion throw, he came in on the ball, almost over it, left foot forward, having slowed his body to gain control, so when he took the ball with his bare hand, his momentum was already into the throw.

When he fielded hard ground balls, his glove was down, open to the plate; his body, perfectly balanced, was pitched forward, in motion even before the batter had swung. He shifted left with one batter, right with another—even between pitches. Look at the film again and you can almost pick up the slight rightward lean of his body when Mike Cuellar is out there delivering junk to the inside corner, or the slight leftward lean when Jim Palmer is throwing hard for the outside corner. Watch Robinson on bunt plays. In an obvious sacrifice situation, he is fifteen to twenty feet in on the grass, almost charging with the pitch—as he was in the first game, second inning, with pitcher Gary Nolan up. But in other situations Robinson is just at the edge of the grass: first game, seventh inning, two men on, none out, the right-handed, slap-hitting Tommy Helms up with left-hander Dave McNally pitching. The position of his body is slightly different, facing a few degrees in toward the pitcher rather than directly toward the plate. With the pitch, Robinson looks toward second to see what the lead runner is up to, then begins moving in, but not so far that he can't get back to third to anchor for the force-out if there is one. All of this is simply correct—the way third basemen are supposed to but don't always do it.

And then there was the way he dove. Third basemen in the past tumbled into the dirt going left and right, but no one had made a habit of this headlong dive through the air—more like an Olympic swimmer beginning a race than a third baseman going for a ball.

Whether or not Robinson actually was the first to dive that way is beside the point; he was the first to make it a standard part

of the repertoire. All third basemen do it now. But when he started it, even in Robinson's mind, it was something that seemed to belong more to the realm of mystery than to that of mastery.

"I don't know why I started diving—it was just something I did," he says. "It was funny—balls would be twenty feet to my left or right, I knew I had no chance, but I'd dive anyway. There'd be a rocket, you knew you couldn't reach the ball if you ran, so you dove—and you'd say, 'What the heck did I do that for?' "

He credits a lot of what he did to knowledge of his pitching staff and help from shortstop Mark Belanger. Belanger would usually signal breaking or off-speed pitches by calling out to Robinson, "Be alive," and he was always there to extend positioning yet another foot. But Robinson, with whatever assistance, was supremely creative at the position, and he simply changed the way third basemen play.

The most recent stars at the position know all about what Brooks Robinson had done. Mike Schmidt says that Robinson was the only player he really ever paid attention to when he was growing up, the closest any major league player ever was to being his hero. He saw Robinson in that Series in 1970, the year before he signed his first professional contract as a shortstop, and has thought about him ever since. Asked what it was he had seen in Robinson, Schmidt, perhaps the best all-around third baseman ever, says without a second's hesitation, "consistency, consistency, consistency. He was consistently part of everything. He played on a grass field and his concentration level was just awesome. Awesome."

SCHMIDT AND every other third baseman who has followed Robinson have played a significant percentage of games on Astroturf. For Schmidt, whose home field through his entire eighteen-year major league career was the carpet of Veterans Stadium, turf meant a game that was faster, requiring even more mental and physical quickness.

Schmidt was big and fast—faster, perhaps, than any third

baseman. He was a base stealer earlier in his career and still relied on speed afoot to complement his quickness around the bag at the end. If anyone played a wide lane at third in the time of artificial turf, it was Schmidt, who won an unprecedented ten Gold Gloves at the position. He moved more like a shortstop than a third baseman. Third, for Schmidt, as he saw Brooks Robinson first play it and as the demands of the game brought it out of him, was "a skill position—like shortstop, second base, catcher, or center field. If you don't have the position filled by a skill player today," he says, "you can't win. It's as simple as that."

The speed of the game made him ready for anything. Runners on first and second and no one out? Schmidt anticipated every-thing from a sacrifice to triple play, as though the old teaching—anchoring, playing for the bunt, readjusting to go for the force at second—had, like the lane at third itself, been widened to include greater possibilities.

"If there's a man on first and second, there's a lot of things that can happen and a third baseman is involved in them," Schmidt said. "If they hit it to your left, you go to second; if it's to your right and it's the right ball, you can step on third, go to second, throw to first—it's an around-the-horn triple play. And I was ready for that all the time—just needed the right play. You might get a bunt dropped on you, a line drive hit down your throat, a ball caromed off the pitcher. If the right ball's hit, *lots* of things can happen."

Schmidt, like Judy Johnson, like any good infielder, used feints and fakes.

"There's always a runner to be had rounding the bags by faking a throw to first base," he said. "You can catch someone at second or coming too far off the bag at third . . . by faking a throw to first on a grounder or a cutoff. There's just a lot of opportunities for outs that generally players don't see or take advantage of."

In terms of physical and mental quickness, Robinson showed what was possible, and turf fields have made it almost mandatory

that those possibilities be incorporated into play. Under these circumstances consistency, the professional's goal, was possible only with the sort of "awesome concentration" that Schmidt admired in Robinson.

Any third baseman today, no matter his size or shape, no matter the surface upon which he plays the majority of his games, seems to understand the need to incorporate this dimension of additional quickness into his game. Many of these third basemen were not born fielders and have made themselves known far more by what they have done offensively than by what they've done defensively. But they have had to be equally assiduous in developing skills at their position that might give them that hair's-width advantage in making plays.

Wade Boggs, gradually accepted by observers as a solid third baseman, has, every January, returned to his old high school in California to polish his fielding skills. As with his hitting, he practices every day at the same time, 3 P.M.: ground balls, ground balls, ground balls. He says that with experience, learning hitters, situations, he has picked up an extra step, the difference, he underscores, "between having range and no range at all."

Carney Lansford, the A's third baseman, a batting champion and base stealer, has been less valued for his fielding. The numbers show that he winds up with fewer total chances each season than many other third basemen—an indication that though he is fast he may not be quick. But leaving aside the fact that Lansford has regularly played on teams that feature strong right-handed, fly-ball pitchers (Nolan Ryan in California, Dennis Eckersley and Mike Torrez in Boston, *all* of the current starters on the A's), the numbers tend to obscure rather than illuminate what he has done.

If you watch Lansford closely during a game, you will notice that prior to each pitch, he doubles over, nearly to the ground, his feet spread wide apart. This set of his is like no other current third baseman's. But it is like Clete Boyer's. After an error-plagued season in 1984, Lansford spent the 1985 spring training working exclusively with Boyer, then the A's third-base coach, on

just this. "Clete believed that playing down close to the ground like that would enable me to see the ball better, to pick up all those funny little hops that seem to give a ball a life of its own." The spread before a pitch also enabled Lansford to stretch out his leg muscles, the better to get a quick start toward the ball. Since 1985, the most errors Lansford has had in a season is seven. He had regularly racked them up in double digits before then.

The best of the recent "turf" third basemen even more pointedly show how quickness can be developed. Gary Gaetti, third baseman for the Twins, had not played many games at third when he broke in as a professional in 1979, two years before joining the Twins. Till then, in high school and junior college, he had been predominantly a shortstop.

As a third baseman, he has focused on training his already soft hands to get there just a bit more quickly. On one level, that has been simple: take ground balls by the bucketful. Yet, because it is easy to do this by rote but qualitatively different to do it with gusto, part of Gaetti's approach has been to find ways to keep his mind as active as his hands and feet. So he plays a game with one of the coaches. The coach moves closer and closer, trying to fungo the ball past him; the idea is to get one ball through the wickets—line drives don't count—and the winner, determined by either a preset number of balls or a miscue, is treated to dinner.

"You absolutely have to be feeling good to do this," Gaetti says. "You have to feel yourself get into a groove and then stay there—and then remember it."

Gaetti, like any good fielder, has learned to read situations. Knowledge of hitters, pitchers, specific moments in a game all help him to be one step left, two steps right, three in, four back —that much closer to a ball he might otherwise have no chance for. That is the whole objective of quickness: to be there more often; to be able to do more once there.

Gaetti constantly seeks to sharpen what he calls an "edge" he maintains at third. He says that he remembers hitters better than he does pitchers, that remembering itself is an especially impor-

tant part of a third baseman's game. "My memory is better defensively than offensively," he says, "because I really remember every mistake I make." He recalls an incident in a game where a batter dropped a bunt on him and he was not prepared for it.

"The peculiar thing in that situation was that I had this hunch before the play that there was going to be a bunt—and I didn't follow my instinct. I was standing there at third and I remember thinking that in this same situation in a spring-training game, this guy had bunted. I remembered the game, the inning, everything —and then, for some reason, I stayed back—told myself, 'Nah, there's two out,' and then got burned." Gaetti shakes his head. "I still can't understand how I let that happen."

Gaetti has learned, literally, to see how plays develop. Through his first seasons, he experimented in different ways with trying to "see" the baseball as it left the pitcher's hand on its way to the plate.

"I tried a lot of different things to get that right," he explains. "They teach you to follow the ball into the plate but I found that wasn't right for me. Eventually I found that you can get a sort of picture in your head, right in front of you: It's like you see the hitting zone and then you can look in that general vicinity for the ball, you can actually see the ball out of the corner of your eye. It's not about knowing the pitch—you may or may not know that—it's about getting a better jump."

Because there is a danger of this sounding more like magic than fielding, Gaetti takes pains to point out that this laserlike ability to focus depends on several other factors, all of which contribute to getting "a better jump" on a ball.

"You read so many things in a moment," Gaetti says. "You're looking at a batter's face, maybe you're playing games with him. I remember when Gorman Thomas was playing in the league. He was such a dead pull hitter and I'd see him peek down at me. Then I'd take my glove off and just lay it there as he came walking up to the plate. I'd be laughing at him—and sure enough, he'd hit one my way. He couldn't help it.

"Because you know what a hitter's likely to do, because you tell yourself *everything* is going to be hit to you, you get to a point where you just feel yourself in the flow of the game. You get into a rhythm where you can see the pitch coming and you can see the hitter's timing and the ball coming your way out of that zone."

Perhaps the quickest third baseman currently playing is the Cards' Terry Pendleton. Like many others at the position, Pendleton played elsewhere first. An outfielder when he finished his college career in 1982, Pendleton acknowledges that he had always been more interested in hitting than in fielding. But in the Cardinals organization there was little room to be so one-sided. There was also very little time to prepare for what was ahead.

Out for almost the entire 1983 minor league season with an injury, Pendleton found himself in Triple A in 1984 and then, when Willie McGee was placed on the disabled list in July of that year, in the majors.

"Frankly, I was scared to death," Pendleton remembered. "I thought I was gonna be there for seven games and then go back down—unless I was so brilliant they couldn't send me back." Pendleton explained that his manager, Whitey Herzog, considerably lightened his load by assuring him that whatever happened he was "just to go out and play and forget about everything else, that even if I was sent down, I would soon be back." Pendleton never returned to the minors.

In the beginning, though, he did not handle his position well. He hit, which kept him in the majors, but he had a hard time in the field. "I always told myself the majors were different than Little League, college, or the minors—that wasn't what got me. I was an offensive player; I always thought of myself that way," he said. "My defense was all right but I found after the '84 season when I hit so well, I came back wanting to work on my defense. I knew I had played poor defense at the major league level."

Pendleton's relatively high error totals in his early years (seventy-eight in his first three and a half seasons) seem to confirm his self-criticism. But from the start he had the sort of range other

third basemen did not. When Mike Schmidt talked about third base as a "skill" position, he singled out Terry Pendleton for his ability to cover unusual amounts of ground.

But Pendleton had to find his way. He joined a team loaded with defensive stars and traditions. "The Cardinals," Pendleton said, "played defense on the field and talked about it off the field." In addition, Pendleton's teammate to his immediate left was Ozzie Smith, who never let him forget for a moment that there were always ways to improve.

Through '85 and '86, Pendleton said, he was at the ballpark every day by midafternoon to take ground balls—twenty, fifty, one hundred, or more. He tried diving. "I mean you don't want to go divin' for balls in practice, but I was doing that, too." It was all for quickness rather than range, the sure play rather than the tentative one.

"You watch Ozzie and you know you can't practice the way he does—no one is that quick. But you learn," Pendleton said. "He taught me that you could work with your hands—have a coach hit the ball hard to you, keep your legs still, and just move your hands this way and that way at the ball, almost like you're slapping at it except your hands are loose. Your hands can get faster."

In the beginning, the high chopper to third was the most difficult ball for Pendleton. His first reaction on any ball, he said, was aggressiveness. "But as anyone will tell you, if you let the ball play you, you'll be in trouble. My way of letting the ball play me," he said, "was to go straight for it. I'd try to get it on the quick hop and fire to first—but if I didn't get the hop, I'd blow the play."

As his hands became more practiced, Pendleton learned that he could backhand a ball, take it higher off the ground, more to the side, if necessary. He could move with the ball without letting it play him.

On bullets hit at him, he learned that he did *not* have to play the ball immediately. "I used to throw the ball, fast, right away,"

he said. "Well I've learned that here I have time. I've learned that on a smash hit at me, I can let it turn me around; I have time to get myself under me, and then go. You make the ball your dance partner," he said.

Pendleton is one of a very few players who practices with a small training glove (about the size of one of those old turn-of-the-century mitts), the better to work those minute movements in the hand that create "softness" and quickness.

In almost everything Pendleton says about covering his position, there is this emphasis on things happening at higher than understandable speed. There are his teammates on the left side of the field, for example. Because Vince Coleman and Ozzie Smith are that fast, a high fly to short left or down the left-field line—a ball that might be out of the reach of players with only average speed—is catchable.

"It's funny," Pendleton says. "Oz has this thing where he ribs us, tells us that Whitey says he's got to get to everything he can because those other guys—Vince and I—can't play. Well, it's a thing with us. When a ball's hit, we *all* react. I'll go down into the bullpen in left, as far as I can go; I'll go until someone calls me off. Sometimes I can get to balls the other guys can't, and vice versa. One time I got to a ball in left Vinnie couldn't reach. I told him, 'Hey don't be afraid to holler, "You've got this much room! You've got this much." ' We actually are looking for ways to help each other all the time."

Pendleton has by now acquired the savvy—and the hands—to play his position at that Cardinal tempo. He makes plays that sometimes are even a surprise to himself:

"I made a play at the end of the '87 season against Montreal. They had a runner at third and two out in a one-to-nothing game with Joe Magrane pitching. Galarraga hit this thing down the line, and to this day I don't know how the ball ended up in my glove. But it did and I turned around and acted like I knew what I was doing and threw the ball to first base. And then I saw the replay—and I still don't know why or how I ever made the play."

Sometimes, largely because of Ozzie Smith, the way other players make plays can be just as surprising: "I'm not like Ozzie Smith going out to play shortstop," Pendleton says. "He knows his position like the back of his hand. But just because of that, I better know mine. It's like bases loaded, ball hit to the second baseman: He flips to Oz and then suddenly Oz throws to me instead of going to first! You've got to be so into that moment!"

More than anything, Pendleton has learned to relax: that is, as a third baseman. There is, to be sure, a lightning bolt's worth of difference between ordinary relaxation and this almost mystical state of heightened awareness that enables a player to feel at ease at third base. Some of this requires preparation—taking extra time to walk out on a field hours before a game and study the way a ball rolls along a baseline or in the grass. "Know the field," George Kissell, a minor league instructor in the Cards' organization once told Pendleton. He has learned the fields.

Being more relaxed also means easily handling the consequences of the inevitable errors. "I can make an error now and say to hell with it," Pendleton says. "Before I couldn't."

Above all, this relaxation flows from knowing his position. It is brought about as much by the number of games played as by the condition of one's nervous system. Here is Pendleton at his position, readying himself for two of the batters in the league toughest for him to defense:

"Juan Samuel and Ryne Sandberg are murder for me to defense. Samuel may be the toughest guy in baseball. He'll walk up and bunt a ball, he has the greatest speed in the game going from home to second, he can knock you down if he turns on a ball—so you don't know whether to come in and take the bunt away or stand there and be killed on the next pitch. All you have to go on is the situation and trusting that you'll be loose enough. You got a runner on first and nobody out, I won't give in to him but I'll take a little more of the hitting game than the bunting game away from him. You know, if I back up a little, maybe I'll *make* him think about bunting, distract him from his game a little.

Good bunter and slasher like him, or Sandberg—I'll walk up when he steps in the batter's box. They always take a look down there—Sandberg's so good at that; he'll peek down there while he's fixing something on his uniform—oh, it's a game, it's a game."

For this third baseman, it has also become a dance.

ONE DAY LAST summer Buddy Bell played his last major league game. Bell was never underrated as a third baseman—he won six consecutive Gold Gloves in the American League and, arguably, should have won another in his first year in the National League, 1987, when he made seven errors in 142 games, best in both leagues. At some juncture long ago, possibly even in childhood, he tiptoed, without realizing it, through the masonic trials of third. Even though he did not begin playing there seriously until his second season in the majors (he, like Brooks Robinson, is a converted second baseman), Bell came to his job with his psyche fully prepared for what he had to do; he brought a standard with him that he well might have taken with him when he left.

Though his father is Gus Bell, the home-run-hitting outfielder who played primarily for the Pirates and Reds during the fifties, Buddy says his father had little to with his early training. "The last thing my father wanted to do when he came home was play more baseball," Buddy remembers with a laugh.

He laughed because baseball—and his father's influence—really turned out to be important. Buddy learned on his own, and that, he said, was everything. "The biggest thing my father gave me was the chance to make my own adjustments," he said, adding that too many young players are tampered with by coaches and instructors in a rush to change things. The process of trial and error worked out for oneself is the securest one, Bell suggested, because what is gained in addition to technique is the sense that a player has it within himself to overcome his own deficiencies. "I think I got a lot of this subconsciously from my father," Bell said. "I do know that I learned early that there was a right way to

do things and that if I was having trouble with something I always seemed to be able to deal with it through hard work."

But Buddy Bell's idea of hard work was a child's, not a taskmaster's. He was baseball drunk from the start. The work was never grim or monotonous. He never worked on specific "problems"—a habit he carried with him to his last day. "I never really sat down and weeded my bad habits out; you sort of knew they were there and you worked on them."

Instead, he played.

"I threw balls off walls all the time," he says. "I was always looking for someone to throw with. A lot of the kids, you know, were playing with trucks, doing other things. There just weren't kids to play with so you played with walls. A lot of that was making great plays—that was the whole idea—later on when you became a professional you had to be more precise, you had to make the team play. But when you were a kid . . . the fun of it was: 'This is the seventh game of the World Series, score's tied, two on, one out'—oh yeah, I would do that for hours."

Bell loved playing defense. To him it remained child's play, from which he made himself fundamentally sound. "It was repetition—I had no alternative but to become good," he said. But he meant something more than becoming proficient.

"What makes a good third baseman great is his aggressiveness," Bell says. "You can't just *be* like that. There are a lot of guys who are good, who can make the outstanding play—but they don't really want the ball all the time. Obviously, there are plays where, if you make them you're great, if you don't you're fucked. But the key to watching a third baseman is how he makes the routine play. That goes with all infielders, but third basemen in particular—you want to get to every single ball you can and you think every single hitter is going to come your way."

Moving laterally left and right, diving, charging and throwing, getting down for a smash hit directly at you, making recoveries and quick throws, every play a third baseman makes, Bell says, flows from knowledge of the game—situation—and, from that, how to anticipate.

Bell anticipated somewhat differently than others who play the position. Many third basemen want to know exactly what a pitcher is throwing. As Brooks Robinson had with Mark Belanger, as Graig Nettles had with neighbors to the left, third basemen usually learn what is about to be thrown from the shortstop. Knowing the pitch helps them anticipate. Bell skipped the help.

"I didn't like to get any signal because I found myself leaning one way or the other," he said. Even a pulse beat of movement one way with the ball going another meant a play lost rather than made. Nor did Bell "watch" a pitch into the hitting zone. Instead, he says he tried "to get a picture" in his mind of the hitting area and then watch for the ball out of that. "You can kind of see it out of the corner of your eye," he says.

To Bell, any attempt to watch the hitting zone was a hindrance more than a help because he could not count on the accuracy of what he was seeing—the plane of vision was distorted. The slightest skewing of vision, like the barest misdirection of the body, means a ball past you that might have been played. Early in his career Bell learned to impose upon his nervous system the severest and most challenging of restraints: no cheating. Purity all the way, not for heaven's sake but for the sake of those few hellish millimeters and fractions of seconds.

Up close, Buddy Bell looks different than he did from the stands or in pictures, which invariably make him seem cherubic and eternally young. His longish hair seems more colorless than blond. His face is worn, with pouches under his eyes, and his complexion pale. Over the years, the pounding of more than two thousand games and ten thousand ground balls took a final toll on his career. Multiple knee operations, as much as reduced playing time, hastened his decision to retire.

But as his body slowed, his sense of the position he played only deepened. With his eighteenth and final big-league season, he played more games than any other third baseman in history save four. He is a career leader across the board: the eleventh-ranking third baseman in fielding average, third in assists, second in assists per game, third in total chances, a close fourth in starting

double plays. Younger, faster players will be hard-pressed to match him.

GRAIG NETTLES, at forty-five, was the oldest man ever to play third base in the majors. He took a record book full of achievements with him into retirement (second in games played, assists, total chances, and double plays—Rubinstein to Brooks Robinson's Horowitz), but he has also had the great fortune to play more postseason games at third than anyone, including one game in the 1978 World Series that brought his skills to the attention of everyone. Remember?

Through the first two games of the Series, the Yankees played as though they were suffering from adrenal exhaustion after a long and miraculous season highlighted by the Fenway playoff with the Red Sox and the ALCS joust with the Royals.

In the Series opener in Los Angeles, the Dodgers, with Tommy John pitching, hammered the Yanks 11–5. The next day they beat them 4–3, with the Yankees leaving runners on in almost every inning and looking very much like a team already on its way to winter vacation.

The third game, however—and ultimately the Series itself—turned on Nettles's play at third base. Back in Yankee Stadium, the New York pitcher that night was Ron Guidry, normally a sure bet for a team down and trying to get back. But Guidry was pitching on only three days' rest, coming off starts in the Fenway playoff, where he had only two days' rest, and the ALCS start against the Royals three days after that. He was not in form for the Dodgers.

Sitting in the Dodgers' dugout that night, players from one end of the bench to the other could see this.

"Every shot we were hitting from the opening inning on was hard," remembers Bill Russell, the team's shortstop, now a Dodgers coach.

"We felt we were going to take that game," says Joe Ferguson, the team's reserve catcher. "They were going with their best and it was clear he didn't have his best stuff."

The Yanks, though, got off on top, scoring single runs in the first two innings. Then the Dodgers stirred. Guidry walked lead-off batter Billy North, who promptly stole second and moved to third on an infield out. Moments later, North scored on another infield out. It was 2–1, the switch-hitting slugger Reggie Smith was coming up, and the Dodgers were gearing up for more. Enter Graig Nettles.

Nettles made a spectacular diving stab of a ball hit over the third-base bag, scrambled to his feet, and threw Smith, a speedy runner, out at first. Instead of a game-tying double, it was an inning-ending out.

In the fifth, the Dodgers mounted an even more serious threat. With the score still 2–1, Dodgers catcher Steve Yeager drew a one-out walk, Guidry's fifth of the evening. Davey Lopes followed with a single to left, and one out later Reggie Smith came up again. And once again, he lit into a Guidry slider and destroyed it—with nearly the same result. If anything, the ball was hit even harder than the first, but Nettles somehow managed to knock it down and keep it in the infield—a single loading the bases rather than a one- or two-run double. Still 2–1 Yankees. There's more.

The very next man up was the power-hitting Steve Garvey, the Dodgers' leading batsman and clutch hitter extraordinaire. Garvey hit a ball (he later called it one of the hardest he had ever hit in his life) down the line, just inside the third-base bag. Nettles made another of those man-out-of-a-cannon dives to his right, then got his feet set under him just in time to make a force throw to second, ending the inning. Instead of three runs scoring, zippo. Still 2–1 Yanks.

Wait, there's more.

Next inning the Dodgers again loaded the bases. A throw to the wrong base on an outfield fly had put runners on first and third with two out and Manny Mota, the Dodgers' premier pinch hitter, drew Guidry's sixth walk, bringing up Davey Lopes and another chance for the Dodgers to break open the game—and the Series.

Of course Nettles made another impossible diving play behind third: force-out at second, three more runs wiped out.
Could it have been otherwise on this particular night? When the
Yankees finally won the game 5–1, it was as though fate itself
had touched Graig Nettles and everyone else associated with him
on both sides of the field. It was the greatest single-game performance by a third baseman that anyone could remember.

"He personally took ten or eleven runs from us," Dodgers
manager Tommy Lasorda said (immediately after the game, Lasorda had correctly counted *six* runs, but these legendary games
have a way of growing in memory like the length of Pinocchio's
nose). The actual number of runs aside, Lasorda had it just right:
"Nettles single-handledly beat us and did it in such a way that he
revived their whole ball club. It's hard to describe unless you were
actually there but I've never seen anything like it. He single-
handedly turned the Series around; he was the reason the Yankees
won it."

Ten years later, sitting in the dugout shadows against a twilight softened by rain, Nettles reflected on his performance and
what it meant to his team.

"We were down two games to none—and it helped us win
that one game and turn the momentum our way, and we went
on to sweep four games," Nettles said, adding, with what I first
assumed was requisite modesty, "but I was lucky."

He explained that Guidry's being a lefty provided a built-in
advantage. And on top of that, lacking his good fastball, Guidry
relied heavily on his slider, which bit down and in to right-
handed batters, making it more likely that balls would be pulled
to third.

"I was lucky in that they hit so many balls to me. I might not
have been able to show anybody what I could do if they were
hitting the ball to right field," Nettles said.

As we talked, it gradually dawned on me that Nettles was
really more grateful for than modest about his performance. It
was a career, not a game, a standard, not a one-night stand that

had given him the real opportunity to show what he could do before a national audience. If luck was really involved, it had more to do with how things had worked for him over the long haul. He first signed with Minnesota when Harmon Killebrew was the third baseman, but a few years later was traded to Cleveland, where Alvin Dark, the manager, gave him the chance to play third regularly. He was subsequently moved to the Yankees, where he had the chance to be a star among stars.

Talking about his game that night, it was clear just how much his prior years of experience leading up to that moment counted. Knowing how Guidry pitched, what shape his arm was in, what pitches he was throwing were all part of Nettles's everyday approach to playing. He was one of the third basemen who liked the shortstop to signal him from pitch to pitch. This was as calculated for him as getting no signal was for Buddy Bell—or as a good hitter "looking" in a specific zone before swinging. "The key thing is not getting the signal but the pitcher having control," Nettles said. "If the pitcher's all over the place, I don't lean. I get the signal—and ignore it."

When Nettles described the diving plays he made that night, he talked about the range he had: those first two steps that made him quicker than other third basemen. He had a view of diving that went beyond the runs he saved in any one game. There were two keys to it, he said. The first was being able to bounce up quickly to make a throw. "If your dive isn't too long," he said, "then your own momentum will get you up; you try not to get stretched out or to have to reach up when you're in the air."

The other key, according to Nettles, was adrenaline. The ordinary adrenaline flow of a game, so necessary for the position, was protective when it came to diving. As a grown man, he never practiced diving because he would injure himself. But in a game, when adrenaline was flowing, there were no injuries. "When I dive in a game—and I catch the ball—I don't even remember hitting or feeling the ground. If I miss it, I suppose I do," he added with a mirthless laugh. Amazingly, Nettles said that he

could not remember a single game in twenty-two years when he was without his flow of adrenaline. "When you get out there in front of a large crowd, especially like the ones we had in New York," he said, "it's just there."

Nettles's real achievement at third became crystal clear to me when I talked to some of his old New York teammates about that World Series game. They acknowledged his performance but were uncomfortable being asked to make so much of one game.

"I made him look good by being lousy," Ron Guidry joked. "Truthfully," he said, "I *expected* him to make those plays because he always made them. Yeah, they lifted us, but you don't see him right when you pick out one game full of great plays."

Chris Chambliss, the Yankees' first baseman in those years, remembered Nettles when they were teammates on the Indians. "Graig was that good when we were in Cleveland," Chambliss said, "and no one would have ever noticed if he had stayed there instead of coming to New York—and they still might have missed it if it weren't for the opportunity he had to show it before a national audience in that one Series game."

That was Nettles's own view:

"Normally players don't ever get the credit they should for defense. I did. I was able to really do something to help us win, which is all the gratification I could want. But it doesn't change the fact that people still don't see much of what we do in the field —unless it is spectacular and in a very bright spotlight."

Nettles's legacy, like those of Brooks Robinson, Buddy Bell, and Mike Schmidt, was consistency. It was only because he routinely defended his position so well for so long that he could, when the moment came, defend it so memorably.

SHORTSTOP

Our shortstop is a man of worth
We hope he'll never die;
He stops all balls that come to him;
He's grim death on the "fly."
The many deeds he has performed,
We will not here relate,
But tell you now that "Johnny How"
As a player is first-rate.

① *What Willie Mays was to one generation,* **HONUS WAGNER** *was to another. As a shortstop, noted one contemporary, "he just ate the ball up with his big hands, like a scoop shovel, and when he threw it to first base you'd see pebbles and dirt and everything else flying over there along with the ball. It was quite a sight. The greatest shortstop ever. The greatest* everything *ever."*

THE NATIONAL BASEBALL LIBRARY

② **DAVE CONCEPCIÓN,** *Joe Morgan's double-play partner with Cincinnati's Big Red Machine of the seventies, was a role model for succeeding generations of Latin shortstops. He was the game's first outstanding "turf" shortstop.*

THE CINCINNATI REDS

③ *If* **OZZIE SMITH** *seems able to walk on his toes it is because he probably can. As he defines it, artistry has something to do with defeating not only opponents but laws of gravity as well. The standard he has set for play at short may well be applicable for another century or two.*

④ **TONY FERNANDEZ,** *a veteran at twenty-seven, is the game's outstanding young shortstop. He goes to his left better than anyone and no one can make the throw going deep into the third-base hole as well as he does.*

THE TORONTO BLUEJAYS

A RECENT EDITION of the *Elias Baseball Analyst,* that rich-as-chocolate-cake annual of baseball numbers, tried to measure the worth of Ozzie Smith, the best shortstop and arguably the greatest defensive player in the history of the game. The question the editors set for themselves, the only one they felt was either answerable or worth the effort of number gathering, was how many wins Smith's presence in the lineup meant. By calculating the number of runs allowed per nine innings when he played compared to the number allowed when his backups played, the *Analyst* came to the conclusion that over the course of a season, Smith was worth slightly less than 3 wins to his team—a not especially impressive total compared to the number of wins star hitters and pitchers represented (the average for top hitters was 4.6 wins, for pitchers 5.2).

For numbers players, the *Analyst* is an elegant companion— smart, provocative, cheeky, and keenly on guard against the use of mirrors and phantom figures to support dubious conclusions. But the editors ran into some trouble here.

The *Analyst*'s numbers showed that Smith saved the Cards 27 runs a year. This, it was calculated, added up to fewer than three wins a year because "For a low-scoring team like St. Louis, every 9.5-run swing makes a difference of one win."

Never mind that St. Louis's average margin of runs scored to runs allowed (less than 1 per game) was a far better barometer of what 27 runs in a season might mean, or that Smith's substitutes played too few games for a meaningful comparison, or that one of the subs, José Oquendo, has been a pretty fair fielder in his own right. Clearly, the method used to compare Smith in the

field with other players at bat or on the mound was impossible. Defensive numbers—always tricky—and offensive numbers just do not mix.

Yet the question posed by the *Analyst* could not be more to the point: Just how valuable to his team is this shortstop who is probably the only player on the planet to have been paid more than $2 million a year for his glove? The answer to the question may, curiously, have less to do with Ozzie Smith than with the position he plays. Shortstop is the lynchpin position on the field. As incomparable as Smith's gifts are, it is hard to imagine that they would have commanded quite the same amount of attention —or cash—at another position. The man who plays short, like the thirty-seventh Hohenzollern or the forty-seventh Hapsburg, has a realm waiting for him.

Shortstops, like second basemen, are expected to cover lots of ground. They can range thirty feet to their left and thirty to their right to handle grounders: I have a film clip of slow, slow Cal Ripken making an over-the-shoulder catch of a fly ball in the medium right-center-field alley beyond any conceivable reach of the infield-fly rule; I have another of Walt Weiss, the Athletics shortstop, snaring a ball in the left-field corner at Fenway Park.

The shortstop must also be a man for the smash; on the edge of the infield to cut off a run, at double-play depth, even in normal position, his hands *must* be quick and soft. Unlike any other infielder, he cannot misplay a grounder and still get his man. He must be equally sure-handed in getting to slow bouncers —he must be able to get to these quickly enough and with his body under enough control to execute the requisite dance steps and skewer his man at first, force him at second, or cut him down at the plate. While he doesn't have the tough pivot of the second baseman, he is just as much a main man on the double play. Feet, hands, courage, improvisational ability are all mandatory as he sweeps across the bag—or behind it or in front of it or above it —as he turns one out into two.

He is a general, a quarterback, a strategist. He may be the one

to call coverage on steals, hit-and-run plays, pickoffs; he signals pitches to his third baseman, sometimes to his outfielders. He has to be ready to cover not one but two different bases on tag plays. On bunts, he may be the spoke on the "wheel" that protects third while the third baseman charges. Like other infielders, the better he "dekes" and fakes, the tougher he makes it on base runners. If his sense of the game is sharp enough, he can steal hits. Lou Boudreau of the Indians made a play once where he took a ball out of position in the shortstop hole and flipped it to Ken Keltner, his third baseman, who threw to first for an out. Incredible —except that Boudreau and Keltner worked on the play that year in spring training. Boudreau also devised the famous "Williams Shift," an overbalanced arrangement of fielders on the right side of the diamond designed to distract Ted Williams as much as thwart him.

And then the shortstop is a thrower, different from his mirror at second in that so many of his throws are long. This throw to first simply changes things, making almost everything he does qualitatively different from the responsibilities of other infielders. The longest throw to first made by a second baseman is a little more than 90 feet; for a third baseman the longest throw is a bit more; the *average* throw to first for shortstops is about 110 feet, and the tough throws from the third-base hole or from short distances in the outfield are 30 feet longer than that. There can be simply no overestimating the demands that places on the position. Shortstops need not be guns but they must be maestros.

Like all good defensive players, good shortstops rehearse what they do; they want to know what's coming. But when so many difficult plays are to be learned, the task of what Mark Belanger calls remembering is prodigious. Davey Concepción, the great Reds shortstop, who has been the inspiration for a generation of Latin middle infielders, said shortly before he retired in 1989 that he still took eighty ground balls daily. He had the balls hit to every part of the infield he was responsible for, from near the third-base bag to the right of second, in close, back on

the grass, at double-play depth, "anyplace on the field where a play might conceivably come up for me." Over the years, just because he had seen so many plays, taken so many ground balls, he had a deeper appreciation of just how much happened in the middle of the field. "You get to a point where you think you've seen everything and then something happens," he said. "Just a year ago, in winter ball, a guy hit a sharp ground ball to me. Hit it so hard the cover actually came off the ball. The cover went one way, the ball went the other, and I didn't know what to do," he said with a laugh. "I hadn't seen that before."

More than any other on the field, the shortstop position seems to have been created for improvisation. When the number of position players was finally fixed at nine in the early years of the game, shortstop was almost an afterthought. Anchored to no base, he was something of a roamer, stationed between the mound and second base, sometimes moving to the outfield, working the field left to right—a short fielder (the actual name of the position then) more than a shortstop.

The player who changed that, according to several baseball historians, was a five-foot-three-inch short fielder named Dickey Pearce. "Pearce's height probably limited his range," surmises Tom Heitz, the chief librarian at the Baseball Hall of Fame. "He was too short to cover ground in the outfield, so he probably looked for ways to do as much as he could in the infield." Bob Carroll's list of twelve overlooked Hall of Fame–caliber players includes Pearce:

> He was, as a matter of fact, the first to play what we would consider the shortstop position. Until Pearce came along in 1856, the "shortstop" was a fourth outfielder whose job was to catch flares . . . and to take short throws from the deep outfielders and relay them to the infield. (The early ball was so light no one could throw it more than 200 feet or so.) Dickey noticed that many more base hits were bouncing safely between second and third than were pop flies coming into his grasp in the outfield. Accordingly, he moved himself into the breach.

Maybe. There's another story, which, if more apocryphal, suggests even more sharply the way surprise seems to have been biologically encoded in the position. Pearce, so this supposition goes, may have invented the infield double play in a classic game between the Brooklyn Atlantics and the Cincinnati Red Stockings on June 14, 1870. It was a classic because this was the game that ended the Red Stockings 139-game, year-and-a-half-long winning streak and because a key play in the Atlantics' 8–7 win was a deliberately mishandled fly by the quick-thinking Pearce that he then turned into a 6-4-3 double play.

Almost certainly, the routine three-sided double play developed earlier (though probably out of the same scramble of surprise and opportunity), but when Pearce changed things and set himself up in the breach, even though he was a step slower than other short fielders, he was able to do things defensively that his fleeter counterparts couldn't. He actually wound up giving himself more—not less—ground to cover because the ground he took in close was out of the reach of other fielders, completely his own.

Beadle's Dime Base Ball Player of 1865 said nothing about shortstops or second basemen turning double plays, but it was clear by then that changes in the position wrought by Dickey Pearce opened wide the doors of possibility. Henry Chadwick, the editor of the annual, had a sense even then of just how much could happen at short:

> On the activity and judgment of the Short Stop depends the greater part of the in-fielding. His duties are to stop all balls that come within his reach, and pass them to whatever base the striker may be running to—generally, however, the first base. In each case, his arm must be sure, and the ball sent in swiftly, and rather low than high. He must back up the pitcher, and, when occasion requires, cover third base when the catcher throws to it; also back up second and third bases when a ball is thrown in from the field. He should be a fearless fielder, and one ready and able to stop a swift ground ball; and if he can throw swiftly and accurately, it would be

well to be a little deliberate in sending the ball to first base, as it is better to be sure and just in time, than to risk a wild throw by being in too great a hurry. His position is generally in the center of the triangle formed by the second and third bases and the pitcher's position, but he should change it according to the striker's style of batting.

It is remarkable that a position so newly formed should so quickly have developed its set routines. Chadwick's introduction to the work of hands and feet seems altogether modern. And our observer is positively sophisticated when he gets into the demands of positioning and throwing.

Baseball historians are rightfully fascinated and frustrated by these early years of the game. They know that great bare-handed shortstops played then, but they cannot really re-create their game for us. The Red Stockings shortstop George Wright was celebrated in song and story in his time. As much as Dickey Pearce, he was a pioneer at the position. Harry Ellard's 1907 book *Base Ball in Cincinnati* described Wright as

> the model ballplayer in the United States. He could play second and third base in superb style, and he was a fine catcher and change pitcher, but he shone most brilliantly at shortstop, and in this position was unapproachable. He was an old player before he came to Cincinnati . . . He covered more ground in his position than any other man in the country, and he and [second baseman] Sweasy made a pair that could not be surpassed. He was as active as a cat, and the way he pounced on a hot daisy-cutter and picked it up, or made a running fly catch, was wonderful.

But we have only hints about his obvious charisma. A century in advance of Ozzie Smith, he was, says Ellard, "much given to indulging in a little by-play, that amused the crowd greatly; yet, though, apparently careless, he was always on the lookout, and was sure to cling to any kind of ball that was near enough for him to reach.

"Wright was a very swift thrower, and the quickness and dispatch with which he picked up and fielded the ball, often enabled him to make double plays."

The roster of fielders compiled in William Akin's essay "Bare Hands and Kid Gloves: The Best Fielders, 1880–1899" includes a number of shortstops. Jack Glassock, who played for several National League teams between 1879 and 1895, Akin says, had range, arm, and speed. He led all shortstops in fielding average and in assists six different times; "he dominated his position more than any National Leaguer of the period." The American Association, while having no similarly dominant shortstop, featured Bid McPhee's teammate Frank Fennelly and then Germany Smith and Bill Gleason of the old Browns. Again, only hints.

Herman Long of the Boston Beaneaters was a dominant player through the nineties into the turn of the century and was something of a hitter as well as a fielder. In 1900, he led the National League with twelve homers, finished with a lifetime batting average of .279, and stole 534 bases to go along with fielding marks among career leaders in putouts, putouts per game, assists, and assists per game (he remains first on the career list in total chances per game).

Long also left behind some clues about how he played the position. Emphasizing the primary need for a shortstop to be a skilled thrower from "long and short distances," Long said in *The National Game,* "I play the position very deep, well to the right for a left-handed batter, figuring that the third baseman will come across for the slow grounders."

In addition, Long said, he set up according to what his pitcher was throwing. He always took signs from his catcher—before each pitch, on pickoff plays, even on coverage in steal and hit-and-run situations. Different as that was from the modern approach, where middle infielders call coverage, Long's principal worry was not leaving his position too soon, "in this way preventing the batsman from knowing who will leave a place open for a grounded ball."

Long had words of practiced advice that any shortstop playing now would clearly understand. Going left, at or on the other
side of the bag, the shortstop, even on slow-hit balls, he said,
should always make his catch one-handed for the sake of being
able to keep his throw under control. Making tag plays correctly
was a matter of both avoiding injury and, even more important,
getting calls from umpires. *Style* was involved, not in order to
look good but to control what it was an umpire saw when he
made his call: "Never go after a man [on his slide into the base]
the second time, for the umpire is usually in sympathy with the
fielder who handles the ball in good style."

The proper way to pursue fly balls (go after everything till
your outfielders call you off), to make relays (go as far out to
meet the ball as you have to and throw low rather than high), to
make short throws (practice underhand tosses and all throwing,
"as no other position is called on for the variety of throwing as is
the shortstop")—these, for him, were by then the ABC's of the
position.

Among early shortstops, the most illustrious was Honus
Wagner. "The Flying Dutchman" was simply the player of his
time—as Willie Mays was in his era. The record books tell the
story in numbers: Wagner had a lifetime .329 batting average,
3,430 career hits (sixth on the all-time list), 651 doubles (fifth),
252 triples (third), and 722 stolen bases (fifth) to go along with
101 career homers (a robust number in the dead-ball era). In
addition, Wagner was, despite making a large number of errors,
a superb fielder. He led the league in fielding percentage only
twice in twenty-one years, but that says almost nothing. He remains among career leaders in total chances and chances per game
and even the numbers can only suggest who he was and what he
did.

To see this first superstar of the game as a fielder, it is mandatory to skip the stats and go to descriptions—like the one of a
double play he started in a 1908 game against the Giants, reported in the *New York Press* on July 25, 1908:

Honus Wagner has turned many a clever trick when opposed to the Giants, but never before anything quite so smooth as he sprang yesterday, in the third inning, when Willis issued his only pass of the day to Wiltse. Tenney tried to sacrifice and the little pop fly looked good when [third baseman] Leach sat down as he started for it. But Wagner raced in like a streak of lightning over half the distance to the plate and scooping it up with his bare hand an inch from the carpet fired to Swacina for the grandest double play ever seen in New York.

Even better are the stories about Wagner, like the one Paul Waner told Lawrence Ritter:

I did see Honus Wagner play, I really did. Honus came back as a coach with the Pirates during the thirties. He must have been sixty years old easy, but goldarned if that old boy didn't get out there at shortstop every once in a while during fielding practice and play that position. When he did that, a hush would come over the whole ball park, and every player on both teams would just stand there, like a bunch of little kids, and watch every move he made. I'll never forget it.

Or a story about Wagner at the beginning of his career: Tommy Leach, just starting out himself, was looking for a team that had an opening at third base. He was advised to stay away from Washington because they had a third baseman named Wagner. Instead, he signed on with Louisville in the National League:

I hardly had time to get settled before it hit me that this guy the Louisville club had at third base was practically doing the impossible. I'm sitting on the bench the first day I reported, and along about the third inning an opposing batter smacks a line drive down the third-base line that looked like at least a sure double. Well, this big Louisville third baseman jumped over after it like he was on steel springs, slapped it down with his bare hand, scrambled after it at least ten

feet, and fired a bullet over to first base. The runner was out by two or three steps.

I'm sitting on the bench and my eyes are popping out. So I poked the guy sitting next to me, and asked him who the devil that big fellow was on third base.

"Why that's Wagner," he says. "He's the best third baseman in the league." . . . Do you know what happened? There was a Wagner with Washington, all right. But it was *Al* Wagner, Honus' brother. Honus was right there in Louisville.

Tommy Leach, of course, got around to playing third base for the Pittsburgh Pirates. He remained a teammate of Honus Wagner's for fourteen full seasons and perhaps saw better than anyone just what was so special about him. Wagner was a great third baseman, a great left fielder, center fielder, right fielder, second baseman, as well as shortstop, Leach said. (Wagner also pitched eight scoreless innings with six strikeouts. The only position on the field he never played was catcher.) Tommy Leach was there when Wagner finally settled in at short:

> That year, 1903, was also the year Honus became a full-time shortstop. Up until 1903 he played almost every position on the team, one day at short, the next day in the outfield, the day after at first base. He didn't look like a shortstop, you know. He had those huge shoulders and those bowed legs, and he didn't seem to field balls the way we did. He just ate the ball up with his big hands, like a scoop shovel, and when he threw it to first base you'd see pebbles and dirt and everything else flying over there along with the ball. It was quite a sight. The greatest shortstop ever. The greatest *everything* ever.

The fact that Honus Wagner might have been as great at other positions as at shortstop curiously underscores the relative value of his principal position. Wagner *could* have played anywhere, but he mainly spent his career at short. Whatever his greatness, Wagner was really the first modern shortstop more than half a century

before his time. The multiskilled ability he brought to the position, eye-opening then, has become the sought-after standard today.

Because so much is required from the shortstop defensively, teams over the years have been reluctant to compromise their standards for the position. If shortstops could hit—like Mark Koenig or Joe Cronin or Lou Boudreau or Marty Marion or Vern Stephens or Pee Wee Reese or Ernie Banks—so much the better. If they could hit and were also strong fielders—like Reese, Marion, and Boudreau—pennants and world championships usually followed. But teams sometimes worried more about run prevention than run production. Mark Koenig, shortstop for the 1927 Yankees, generally considered the strongest baseball team ever, was traded shortly thereafter to make room for a lighter-hitting, surer-handed shortstop; Ernie Banks, "Mr. Cub," spent the second half of his Hall of Fame career as a first baseman. Has there ever been a "good-hit, no field" shortstop?

For all that, shortstop, true to its beginnings, is the most changeable of the positions. A century and a half after its birth, it is still evolving like a new star.

At first glance, Luis Aparicio, the Hall of Famer who played for three teams between the fifties and seventies, seems like a typical shortstop. A light hitter, barely five feet seven and 150 pounds, he made his way to the majors from Venezuela on the strength of his fielding and his speed. Aparicio not only could make the plays, he made more of them and from parts of the field where shortstops, even very good ones, usually did not go. He regularly made plays from the right-field side of second base; he made plays in the hole completely against his momentum that other shortstops did not even dream of. And among his innovations was a simply unheard-of one-handed style of fielding grounders that succeeding generations of shortstops have made routine.

What allowed Aparicio to do things differently was speed. There were shortstops before him who were fast, but he was

special. A dazzling base stealer—he regularly stole twice the number of bases than anyone else—he was in full flight from the start, whether going for a ground ball or going for an extra base. Combined with sure hands and an unusually strong arm, he was simply unlike others—quicker, stronger, more fluid. When Al Lopez, Aparicio's first major league manager, explained what was so special about him, he might have been Paul Waner talking about Honus Wagner:

"At shortstop," Lopez said, "you must pick up the ball clean or you don't throw the man out. It is the most important position. First, second, third, you can knock the ball down. At third, you don't need good hands. At second you don't need good hands or a good arm. At first all you need to do is to be able to catch the ball. Shortstop requires the most ability: catching, arm, hands, experience. Luis has great hands, great arm, great speed. He covers ground from all the angles, positions. I've seen some great shortstops, but he does everything as well. I think he could play the outfield. He could play any position except catch."

Though Aparicio made thirty-five errors in his first season (out of a league-leading 759 total chances), there was nothing untutored about him. It was as though he had come to the position full-blown and fully taught—which he was. Aparicio was tutored by his father, Luis Aparicio, Sr., the top shortstop and most celebrated player in Venezuela until Chico Carrasquel went north to play short for the White Sox just before Luis Junior.

The story of Luis Senior passing the torch to his son is still told in the barrios of Maracaibo, Caracas, and all across Latin America. Having haunted ballparks his father played in, having spent months and years learning his secrets, Aparicio was nineteen and playing for an amateur team in Barquisimeto. Luis Senior, nearing forty, shortstop and co-owner of the professional Maracaibo Gavilanes, was thinking of retiring as an active player. He mentioned his plans to the team's manager, Red Kress. Kress asked about Luis Junior as a possible replacement and, after some hesitation on the part of the father, who feared his son was too

young for the hard life of a professional ballplayer, an uncle was dispatched to bring the boy to Maracaibo. At a Gavilanes night game on November 18, 1953, Luis Senior took his usual position at short. After the father made his initial play in the field, the game was stopped and the son left the dugout and trotted out to his father's position. Luis Senior took off his mitt and handed it to Luis Junior. The two men embraced and, along with everyone else in the stadium, wept openly.

But this ceremonial act was far more than a family affair. While Luis Junior's predecessor on the White Sox Chico Carrasquel was a hero in Venezuela, Luis, with far greater skills, became a national and even an international hero. Young baseball players not only followed Aparicio's career, they also tried to follow in his footsteps. "I think the big reason there are so many shortstops from Latin America," says Eppy Guerrero, super scout for the Blue Jays, "is because so many players heard about Aparicio and tried to imitate him."

One player who tried to imitate him was Davey Concepción, another Venezuelan, who became an even more inspirational role model and, in terms of playing short, a more revolutionary influence.

Concepción, like Aparicio, grew up with a ball in his hand and a father who owned a baseball team. Concepción's father ran an amateur team out of Aragua, a small inland town near Venezuela's east coast. But, Concepción said, his father was not his tutor—or his hero. An old pro named Luis Rodriguez was. Concepción had role models, but they were neither Carrasquel nor Aparicio, who played in the States. Concepción followed his father's team, of course, and the pro team in Valencia, whose double-play combination of Obregón and Hill had a national reputation. Above all, Concepción wanted to be a ballplayer, a better one than anyone else.

From childhood on, he played a wall game still popular in Venezuela. (Concepción says he plays the game today with his own children: no gloves, a hand-drawn line to two bases; miss a

ball spiked off the wall, watch it become a home run.) Fielding the ball counted; fielding it cleanly—with everything in so close —counted even more.

Concepción played baseball beginning in the morning before school, finishing at dark, each day, every day. In more organized fashion, he played soccer. He was an accomplished center, and the skilled footwork of the game, he believes, helped him as a middle infielder. Above all, he says, he had this feeling about catching ground balls. "Catching a ball is like juggling. I can't juggle but I can catch baseballs. I always could. It's a great feeling —I don't know how to describe it—it's the same feeling you get when you hit the ball on the sweet part of the bat or when you make love."

Whatever this affinity was, Concepción had it when he came north. He spent a year in the lower minors, split a season between Double A and Triple A, and then took over at short in 1970 for a Reds team many baseball people believe was as strong as any team in this century.

Concepción says the Reds' middle defense of the seventies— Johnny Bench, Joe Morgan, himself, César Gerónimo in center —made things easier for him. "I don't think there was ever a team as solid up the middle as we were," he says. But there were two additional and highly unlikely components to Concepción's impact on the game: Astroturf and television. Playing with a powerhouse team that regularly got to the World Series, Concepción had a chance to showcase his abilities before millions of fans in both North and South America. His career, unlike Aparicio's and Carrasquel's, was visible on the nearest television screen.

Turf, of course, changes and warps the whole game, but at short the challenges it presents are more arduous than anywhere else on the field. Turf giveth and turf taketh away. Concepción wound up blessing the name of the stuff.

He positioned himself more deeply, as shortstops on plastic now do as a matter of course. He fielded balls in the short parts of the outfield—in left when he took a ball in the hole, in center

when he went deep behind the bag—converting hits to outs. No one had done that before.

When Concepción went toward third base he also looked to follow rather than break his momentum. Because his arm was strong enough, he could fire across the diamond even as he moved toward the left-field foul line. And when he suffered an elbow injury in 1980 that limited his throwing ability, he invented a one-bounce throw from the hole that many shortstops have since copied. It was Concepción himself who realized, when his arm grew strong again, that his one-bouncer actually seemed to add speed to the ball coming off the turf.

Concepción makes no special claims for himself as a "turf" shortstop. He was just a good fielder, he says, someone "who had sweet hands and could glide." Though he never stops insisting on the importance of defense, and his own love for that side of the game, he makes no mention of the fact that he won five Gold Gloves and was among career leaders in a number of fielding categories.

In his mind, where he may have changed things at short was in his offensive ability. What distinguished him from most good fielding shortstops was that he could hit. Surrounded by Murderers Row Midwest, he was no odd man out. He laid wood to the ball, hard and often. He was from time to time one of the murderers. From 1972 (following a season in which he played with a broken wrist) to 1982, he frequently hit above .280, twice hitting over .300. Though he wasn't really a power hitter, he had sixteen homers one season, fourteen another. Twice he drove in over eighty runs. And he was a base stealer—not like Aparicio, but good enough to be a threat whenever he got on. His eight All-Star appearances were based, certainly, as much on his accomplishments at bat as on those in the field.

And since Concepción began playing, shortstops have increasingly become part of the offensive picture. With the evolution of the twenty-four-man roster, it has become almost mandatory. Cal Ripken, Tony Fernandez, Alfredo Griffin, Ozzie Guillen, Garry

Templeton, Barry Larkin, Shawon Dunston, Jody Reed, are all sure-handed shortstops who from the start have been hitters. Alan Trammell and Ozzie Smith, defensive specialists at the outset of their careers, have since made themselves over into formidable offensive players.

But, in addition, almost all of these shortstops underscore that what was unique and unheard-of only a decade or so ago has become a matter of near routine now. They can play deep, can bounce throws on the carpet, have the sort of acrobatic control of their bodies that permit them to use their momentum going away from the direction in which throws have to be made. Things are just different out there today than they used to be, and the nature of the position has changed accordingly.

Another key figure, a bridge between generations, a sort of Saint Paul of the shortstops, is Mark Belanger. When Belanger first joined the Orioles in 1965, the team's regular shortstop—and the man in the way of a steady job—was Luis Aparicio. Aparicio, Belanger says, had been his idol. But when he actually saw him make plays up close, he was awed.

"When I signed, they took me to Baltimore to watch a game," Belanger says, "and I saw him take an impossible ball backhanded—and they said to me, 'Someday you'll be making those plays.' No way I could believe that."

Instead, Belanger, who remains convinced that he never had the physical abilities of Aparicio or of a number of other shortstops, studied what he had to do and then tried to apply it. He was probably as well schooled in the fundamentals of shortstop play coming into the big leagues as most shortstops are exiting them. Like Alan Trammell and Cal Ripken, players without outstanding speed and acrobatic ability, Belanger had to do things "right" in order to compete. No one-handed pickups, nothing fancy, everything by the book. Belanger was able to define the revolution that was under way by his own limitations—as Trammell and Ripken have since defined it.

When Belanger saw Aparicio at work the first spring they were together, he sought him out.

"He wouldn't talk to me at all," Belanger remembers. "I'd never knock Luis—he had to know why I was in camp—but I'd ask him questions and he'd say, 'Get away from me, kid, get away from me.' So, instead . . . I watched him all the time. I watched every move he made."

For Belanger—and for the legions of shortstops who have gone by the book—there was a right and a wrong way to do everything. Taking a grounder, for example, meant, first getting in front of the ball, taking it with both hands, "receiving" it rather than stiff-handing it. Belanger believed that it was especially important to move low to the ground in fielding a ball, to keep one fluid, unbroken motion fielding and coming up to throw. Above all, he wanted to take a ground ball off the left rather than the right foot. The instruction manuals all correctly pointed out that taking the ball off the left foot allowed the fielder to immediately set his right foot for the throw. But Belanger also knew that this allowed a more natural and relaxed positioning of the hands, with the glove completely open rather than at an angle to the incoming ground ball. It was imperative to be clean.

But when he saw Aparicio go for a ball, he saw something different. Rather than doing everything he could to "slide" right to get in front of the ball, Aparicio stepped directly toward the third-base line, went down, and took the ball—off his left foot—backhanded, his glove open, his hand soft and relaxed.

"It took me four or five years to learn that it was actually easier to take a ball and quickly get into throwing position that way," Belanger says. What might have seemed flashy in the stands turned out to be fundamentally sound on the field. The slower Belanger learned then (and later passed on to Cal Ripken) a way of conquering some of the extra territory faster shortstops like Aparicio seemed to take automatically. As for a third baseman, the first step the shortstop takes toward a ball is crucial. The impulse is to step out with the foot nearest the path of the ball. But Belanger found that if he pivoted on that near foot he could step directly forward—toward the third-base line one way, toward the second-base bag the other—allowing him quicker and

greater lateral movement. He was able, literally by the turn of an ankle, to make fundamental what otherwise would have been "impossible."

Belanger went for balls differently all over the field. On flies to the short outfield, he went to a spot and then took two additional steps so that he would be behind the ball with his momentum coming into it when he made his catch. Whenever he could, he approached grounders at an angle rather than going directly for them.

By watching Aparicio, Belanger learned the most fundamental law of shortstopping: Always look for the easiest way to do things.

Eventually, apostle and master did talk:

"I picked up how he positioned his body. . . . we were entirely different people, on balls in the hole he'd much rather backhand it than get in front, but what he was doing was always making things easier for himself, looking for the easiest way to get things done. You looked at his body position and how he threw, how he could throw from such a position, and I tried to figure that out too—till I did. He threw every day; he threw hard every day. I asked him, 'Why do you do that—doesn't it hurt you to do that?' He said you could throw through pain and be stronger, and he was right. I threw the ball hard and I threw the ball long . . . I started out with my arm weak but I got muscle and elasticity back . . . I did that all through my career till the very end."

Till the end, Belanger was an overhand thrower, devoutly believing that however hard on the arm, this was the soundest way to get a true throw—easier for the first baseman to handle—across the diamond.

Belanger worked with his second basemen on throwing, footwork, and coverage with equal meticulousness. He learned exactly where his second basemen wanted to receive balls on double-play throws—high, low, front, or back—to the point where he could divide the bag into six-inch slices of its inside and

outside portions. The type of throw—underhand, overhand, high, low, inside, outside—varied, depending on how the ball was hit, where it was hit—close or far from the bag—what the situation was, who the player was at second. One second baseman —Davey Johnson, say—had to be thrown to differently than, say, Bobby Grich, who Belanger believed was better at turning the double play. The first time he threw without looking to Rich Dauer, another second baseman, he had to explain what he was up to:

"He couldn't believe that after I knew where he wanted the ball that I could throw to him without looking. He wanted to know why I did it and what I got from it. So I had to explain to him that it comes from a feel you have—that you really develop a feel for these things by doing them enough times. He never really understood what I was saying. He'd keep saying, 'How do you *do* that?'"

Belanger also developed a special feel for the second-base bag itself. He regarded it as both his home and a place of danger. It was home in the sense that he was constantly aware of it, gauged his position on the field in relation to it. It was a place of danger because almost anytime he approached it, if he did not do things correctly, injury could result. He moved across the bag as he moved elsewhere, trying to keep a flow of continuous motion— fluid, easy, smooth. In completing double plays, it was possible to cheat, come wide of the bag, but only if the shortstop's motion was unbroken. "You have to touch the bag; you can't get away without touching it," he says, "but if your motion is unbroken, you touch the bag, keep your motion going to the side, make your throw, get up in the air, the umpire will give you the call— because he sees the tag and he's caught with the ease of your rhythm—you've given him something that looks routine and al- lows him to make a routine call."

Belanger used every trick of hand and eye to gain for himself those additional inches and feet his body did not naturally give him. No one was ever smarter about exploiting the specific mo-

ment on the field; no one ever used his teammates more. With Brooks Robinson playing third alongside him, Belanger nearly always took advantage of *his* range by moving a step or two toward second; with the control pitchers like Mike Cuellar and Jim Palmer had, he could move a step one way then another during the same at-bat.

By the end of his career, Belanger had run an eighteen-year clinic on how shortstops who were not blessed with great speed and great natural ability could survive and thrive in the age of fast grass and faster legs.

Alan Trammell and Cal Ripken both acknowledge the limitations of their gifts and the way they have compensated through excessive attention to doing things correctly. "I can't be an Ozzie Smith or Tony Fernandez and play everyone in the middle of the diamond and catch everything to my left and everything to my right," Ripken says. "I have to cut down my area, and concentrate on fundamentals."

"Tony Fernandez is unbelievable," Trammell says. "I can't do a lot of the things he does but I'm a stickler for detail. I don't really make great plays—they're a bonus—but you can be successful making the routine plays. The bottom line is getting the job done."

Both these players acknowledge the influence of Mark Belanger. Ripken was actually taught by him, beginning at about age seventeen. "He would tell me things," Ripken says. "I'd find myself unable to do what he was talking about—but it was, like, planted in my mind and later on I'd understand and be able to do it." Trammell, who was tutored by another stickler for detail, Eddie Brinkman (who held the major league record for consecutive errorless games at short—seventy-two—until it was broken by Kevin Elster of the Mets in 1989), also acknowledges Belanger. "I respected Brinks a lot coming up—and Belanger. Belanger was still playing when I started out. No one was ever smarter at the position. I watched him all the time."

Like Belanger, Ripken and Trammell have made a virtue—

almost an art—out of limitation. Take the matter of throwing. Neither of them has a great arm but both have used methods of release that make them better, smarter throwers than other short-stops. Ripken, who has the stronger arm, actually had to find a way to slow his throw, so he learned how to throw sidearm. By correctly gripping the ball across the seams, he found when he dropped to the side that he could be accurate. And from the side, he could throw more easily. This not only made for improved accuracy but could be better timed to the movement of the first baseman as well. "The throw was like a timed pass in football," Ripken says.

Trammell also has learned to slow his throw, though he stays over the top. He throws with just enough on it to get the runner. That is the objective always. That, and staying in his rhythm of motion. Trammell does not time his throw to the movement of the first baseman. He takes into account who he is, but he throws to the bag. Sometimes he "rainbows" his throws, sometimes he puts more on it; rarely, and only if necessary, does he unload.

Each of these "traditional" shortstops has the same respect for fundamentals. "You try to make everything routine," Ripken says. "Smoothness" is the word Trammell uses. He wants to look smooth in what he does, not because he's vain but because he is impeccable. "When it looks smooth, it *is* smooth," he says.

Ripken and Trammell both emphasize the importance of po-sitioning, knowing the hitters, the pitchers, the situation, and of the correct alignment of hands, feet, and body.

The little preliminary movement just before a pitch is crucial to both men because it puts them in motion, gives them an extra step, before a play develops. That first step toward a ball is almost a kind of prayer bead for Ripken: "If your first step is quick, then your second one will be; if your first step is slow, your second will follow."

From the first day of spring training to the last day of the season Trammell works on everything in slow motion. Prior to each game, each practice session, he has a coach hit ground balls

directly at him, to his left, to his right. The balls are hit slowly and Trammell moves after them so slowly he looks as though he is performing *tai chi* exercises. On each grounder he seeks to do the technically correct thing: On balls he can get in front of, he makes the catch with two hands off the left foot; on balls that are backhanded, open glove off the left foot; on balls where he must extend, he drops the hip back so the front left shoulder swings around and is pointed in the direction of the throw to be made.

"I want to feel my body making every exact move it has to make," Trammell says. "I want to feel myself taking a ball off my left foot and planting with my right; I want to feel that first step I make towards a ball away from me. I need to feel that so that when the game comes I'll do it instinctively."

Both of these players have made maximum use of their teams and teammates. Ripken, whose father was an Orioles coach in the glory years and a manager in the gory ones, grew up in a system that preached and practiced defense. Trammell has had another kind of support: Through his entire career, save during times of injury, he has played with only one second baseman. Trammell and his middle-infield partner, Lou Whitaker, are the longest-running double-play combination in baseball history. Trammell regards this as something beyond good fortune, a kind of fate. "How many teams ever have their two middle-infield positions open up at the same time? It happened in our case [in 1977]. That's what I mean by fate. You can't ask for anything more," he says.

Working with a double-play partner like Whitaker, Trammell is able to do things by instinct, almost by extrasensory perception, that he would not be able to do with a fledgling or little-known partner. He is able to deliver a ball to Whitaker without looking, perfectly confident that his throw will be the right one; he is able to cross the bag and take a throw, perfectly confident that what he will be receiving will enable him to complete a double play. Most times, when a runner is bearing down on the base, the shortstop must move to the side to complete his play. "Unless

you've got an easy play, you must get out of there," Trammell says. "I try to hit the base with my right foot to the middle to the left side of the bag, slide it, turn my hips so I'm lined up shoulder to shoulder for my throw."

The basic mistake young players make, Trammell says, is stepping on top of the base and then into the base path. The mistake is easily made, he believes, because it is especially hard to keep body control—continuous motion—coming across the bag. In clinics, Trammell teaches students to "feel" the rhythm of what they do at the bag, then move back three feet, five feet, ten feet so they can extend this sense of controlled rhythm as they approach and cross the base. Partnering with Whitaker, however, has involved a kind of symbiosis, developed over years.

The first time Alan Trammell saw artificial turf, he knew he hated it. In the first inning of his first major league game, at Toronto, the Blue Jays' first batter hit a ball to him. It was low, hard one-hopper. Trammell readied his open glove at knee level and the ball stayed down, striking him in the ankle and ricocheting out into right-center field. He has since adapted himself to turf not only by familiarizing himself with how differently the ball comes off it and with what additional spin ("All the more reason to use two hands," he says), but by working harder at understanding ground balls (there are different types of them—balls with pace, with ordinary bounce, slowly chopped) and bad hops (you can read most of them thirty to forty feet away; the body should be held slightly to the side to avoid being handcuffed). But turf never has and never will be his game. That is where other, faster shortstops come in.

When you watch players like Tony Fernandez and Ozzie Guillen (Guillen plays the majority of his games on grass) it is as though they came ready-made for the faster game. If manufacturers of turf could also have provided player-salesmen to demonstrate the advantages of their product, they would have chosen players like Fernandez and Guillen, who simply have the sort of range, reflexes, and hands that might delude some people into

believing that such great human talent was tied first to plastic and only second to ability.

Fernandez and Guillen began playing baseball and dreaming about the majors early, like thousands of other young middle infielders in Latin America. Though they grew up in very different countries with very different cultures and traditions, they shared a common baseball idol: Dave Concepción.

"Everybody in my town, in the street, they want to be Davey Concepción," Guillen says. "I'm the only guy in the barrio who followed him into professional ball, so right now they love me—but they still want to be Davey Concepción. I asked my own kids, 'How do you wanna play shortstop?' They said, 'Like Davey Concepción.' He's the best I've ever seen going left," adds Guillen, who goes left as well as anyone in the game.

"When I was a kid, I saw Davey Concepción on TV," Tony Fernandez said. "I watched everything he did, read everything I could about him. I looked at him and said, 'Someday I want to do that—I want to feel like him. But that's impossible because there's only one Davey Concepción. When you think of Concepción, you think of his range. It was amazing how he could get to balls other shortstops couldn't get to."

Guillen and Fernandez, like scores of others from the poorest, hardest fields of the Americas, began converting their baseball dreams into near-professional skills before they had even reached their teens. Fernandez's large family lived in a house situated behind the right-center-field fence of a ballpark in San Pedro de Macorís, the small town in the Dominican Republic that has a higher per capita representation in the major leagues than any town on earth. As a child, Fernandez began hanging out—and working out—with ballplayers; he made gloves out of cardboard milk cartons, baseballs out of tape, bats out of sawed-off sticks, so he could play. By the age of thirteen, he had been singled out by Eppy Guerrero, who trained as well as scouted local talent for the Blue Jays.

Guillen, before he was a teenager, was spotted by an uncle of

Luis Aparicio's, who, along with Aparicio's father, had a long involvement with professional baseball in Venezuela and who had been responsible for signing Aparicio himself. Guillen moved into the uncle's house and lived there for three years, working daily in a sort of minicamp run for a handful of players. Guillen remembers many of the fundamentals and fine points he learned from the uncle—showing the ball to the second baseman before throwing it, learning how to come across the bag with the right foot forward already *in* throwing position, learning different rhythms in the feet when making plays to different bases—and, of course, Concepción's new, revolutionary one-bounce throw:

"One day, we saw Davey Concepción on TV throw the ball on the carpet—you know, one hop to the first baseman. We went out after that," Guillen says, "and every day Aparicio's uncle worked with me on that. 'Don't throw all the way,' he'd say. 'It takes too much time.' So ever since, I've done that. I get a ball in the hole on turf, I throw right on the carpet. It saves time."

These two young shortstops—Fernandez, the better known and more experienced, is twenty-seven, Guillen is twenty-six—still have their best years ahead of them. But they are already ahead of themselves, more polished in their skills than most veteran shortstops. Their approach to what they do, perhaps because their lives were so sorely tested so soon, is, literally, professional. Fernandez, whose dream is to one day complete his high school degree, works as hard at being a shortstop as he would at being a doctor. "In a way, baseball is like medicine," he says. "You never stop learning and if you ever think you have something down that's when you fall back."

Both these players work for consistency and rhythm, constantly sharpening their basic skills. But their approach even to fundamentals somehow seems innovative as much as traditional. Guillen says he still works on "receiving" grounders, looking the ball into his mitt. He also says he talks to the ball because each one is different, each one requires special attention. In the minors, he went through a couple of error-plagued seasons, an experience

common to young shortstops. To better teach himself to stay down, he began in infield practice to use a training glove, a thin, tiny mitt barely larger than his hand. He *had* to stay down because his glove left no margin for error, but at the same time he was working on making his hands quicker, softer. "You have to catch the ball in the pocket just right or you hurt your hand," he says.

Fernandez also works on things as elementary as staying down. But he does this by having short hoppers hit at him, imagining that the ball will stay down, then reacting to whatever it does, a dangerous way to work on a fundamental but one that allows him to come up into the ball rather than breaking his rhythm with a safer but jerky downward movement.

But both these shortstops have defined what they do—and what shortstops who follow them will be doing—by their amazing quickness. "Tony Fernandez and I both go to our left better than anyone," Guillen says. And they go to their right too. Fernandez takes a ball farther in the hole than anyone in the game and then what he does seems simply impossible, more like an optical illusion than an actual play. Fernandez keeps going after he backhands a ball. He does not plant and throw. On the run, never breaking stride, with even more fluidity than Concepción, he slightly twists his upper body and throws *underhand* back across the diamond to first base!

Guillen, left and right, does things a little differently. He leaves his feet—dives headlong, like a third baseman—but somehow, even from the impossible depth of the shortstop position, is able to recover and throw across the diamond.

It is not just that Fernandez and Guillen have enough range and throwing power to take them where other shortstops cannot go, but that they have learned to work innovatively at exploiting these gifts. Fernandez, like the very best traditional shortstops, works to make all his movements smooth and easy. But the key to his amazing throwing ability is in his feet, not his hands. He works endlessly at speeding his feet so that he can be slow in his upper body, thus gaining the control necessary to make the diffi-

cult throws. Watch him. His feet, whether moving across the bag or deep in the hole, have a completely different rhythm than do his hands and arms. It is as though the upper and lower halves of his body have separate lives of their own, the one high-torqued, piston-driven, the other as slow and smoothly flowing as a violinist drawing his bow.

Guillen is probably the only person in baseball who actually practices diving. Any player will tell you that you cannot *work* on diving, that it must be left to the adrenaline flow of the game. But every two or three weeks, and only when he can do it on grass, Guillen practices leaving his feet. The goal is not to punish himself but to make his catch with hands and elbows up rather than extended along the ground—so the ball will hold in his glove with his hands already in throwing position.

WHEN OZZIE SMITH, who won his tenth consecutive Gold Glove in 1989, talks about diving, he tends, as with every other technical aspect of his game, to be mysterious. The word *technical* itself seems cross-grained to him because, in his mind, it does not really explain what he does in the field. Diving, he says, is really important. But because it is dangerous, he does not practice it. He just does it. But then he grows mysterious:

"When I moved from San Diego to St. Louis," Smith says, "one of the things people said was 'Well, now we have a shortstop that doesn't have to dive for the ball—he can get in front of it and make the play standing up.' . . . But diving allowed me to be quicker because I had the ability to scramble to my feet and make the play. Not too many people can do that, but don't ask me how I do it because I really don't know."

I asked Smith anyway and he grew even more mysterious:

"I do know that I don't dive the way you dive into a swimming pool; I dive with an arch in my back so that my motion is going down and coming up at the same time. Now you've got to do this in relation to where the ball is—as opposed to how you dive, what technical steps you take to dive. It is timing more than

how. The timing part of that is like a 'snap.' You time it so that you're coming up at the same time that you're going down to the ground."

With a player as extraordinary as Smith, there is a strong tendency to lose sight of what he does for the magic involved. And why not? Smith regularly makes plays that require a willing suspension of disbelief—and then once in a while makes them in a dimension beyond that. Consider this one:

In the ninth inning of a 1988 game between the Cards and Phils, tied at 4–4, the Phils got a runner on with one out. Von Hayes, the next batter, spiked a ball to the Cards' first baseman, Bob Horner, as Smith moved quickly from short to take the lead throw. But Horner threw wildly behind Smith as he was crossing the bag. Without even seeming to change gears, Smith, in full flight, dove back the other way and caught the ball, all the while *keeping his foot on the base* for the force-out!

Or this one:

In a 1984 game at Wrigley Field against the Cubs, with two out and a runner on first, Smith fielded a slow bouncer on the right side of second base, twenty or thirty feet in on the infield grass. Seeing that he had no chance to get the fast batter, Henry Cotto, Smith, not even breaking stride, merely flipped the ball behind his back to his second baseman, Tommy Herr, for the force and continued on into the dugout. Credit Herr with having enough presence of mind to have handled the throw, credit Smith with, what, astral projection?

Then there was this most celebrated of all Ozzie Smith's plays.

In a 1978 Braves-Padres game (Smith was still with the Padres then), Jeff Burroughs hit a rocket up the middle. Shaded right for the power-hitting Burroughs, Smith got his usual quick jump on the ball, a one-hopper about to kick into center field. He dove headlong, fully stretched out, but the ball kicked off a pebble and ricocheted back toward the shortstop area that had been vacated. *In midair, with his gloved hand already extended for the catch he could not make, Smith reached backward and snared the ball*

with his bare hand! Then he got to his feet and threw Burroughs out.

Metaphors of magic and wizardry so surround Ozzie Smith's game that it is all too possible to overlook the fact that he is perhaps the most consistent as well as the most innovative short-stop who ever lived. He is, first and last, a shortstop. It is not smoke and mirrors but reliability that got him where he is. The real problem and challenge that he presents for his successors is that he is just too hard to copy.

"Good defense," Smith says, "means taking momentum away from the team at bat and giving it to your team." To that end, he is constantly "on." At his position, he doesn't just set himself into motion before a pitch, but seems to stalk his opponents, never the same way, never predictably. He will pace forward, backward, then forward again, setting himself distractingly close even when power hitters are up, only to do it completely differently when that hitter comes up again. It is his intent to distract as much as to position—anything to gain even the slightest advantage.

He barks midgame instructions and suggestions to those who play alongside him. Terry Pendleton remembers Smith yelling at him "during pitching changes, between plays, from pitch to pitch," to move one way or another, to not back up on ground balls, to be alert to a variety of possibilities. José Oquendo, who became the Cards' regular second baseman in 1989, said that Smith, dissatisfied with the way he made his double-play throw (not enough on it), badgered him until he got it right. "It wasn't ever like he was criticizing me—it was always for the sake of the play," Oquendo said.

Smith somewhat disconcertingly refers to what he does as an "art." That is usually left to sportswriters, but Smith consciously makes this association for himself because it helps him with what he feels are the demands of his position.

From the earliest age, he knew that his agility set him apart from others. But where other highly coordinated kids might have contented themselves with hours on a trampoline, Smith spent

them on a ball field. As he once lay in his room and sought to catch balls with his eyes closed so as to improve the quickness of his hands, he has continued to work systematically at improving his reflexes. These are "scales" for him, and along with his routines in infield practice, they contribute to his art:

—In the off-season, he studies martial arts, most recently *tai chi,* to improve his hand-eye coordination, body control, and alertness.

—He has for years practiced self-hypnosis. His routine is to enclose himself in a dark room, fix his eyes upon a lighted candle or illuminated red dot until he is in a trance, the maximum state of heightened concentration.

—During spring training every year and at other times during the season, Smith has a practice routine where he gets down on his knees in the infield like a penitent and then has a coach, standing fifty to seventy feet away, smash ground balls at him. Smith's goal is not to atone for sins but to use his hands reflexively to flag down the hottest grounders. "It is a terrifying thing to watch," Terry Pendleton says. "No one in their right mind—except Ozzie—would even think of doing that." Nick Leyva, the Phils' manager, who was, when he was with the Cards, most often the coach fungoing to Smith in these drills, notes that "what really gets you is how easily he does it."

When he was growing up, Smith observed a brother of his squander tremendous gifts as a painter. "He had the ability to make the ugliest things beautiful," Smith said, "but he never had the discipline to follow through." Following through has always had this extra dimension for Smith. Discipline meant taking one's gifts to the limit. It also meant having the ability to convey a sense of beauty, to share it with others.

The most obvious way Smith shares his gifts with fans is in the season-opening and -closing (and occasionally in-season) backflips he performs as he goes out to his position. "I know people get a kick out of it and it's fun for me," Smith says, explaining that players are as much entertainers as they are ath-

letes and that that alone makes it mandatory to always give fans their money's worth at the ballpark. If that is a useful mind-set for the long season of 162 games, it is not the one that makes Smith think of what he does as an "art." Lately, he has begun to have second thoughts about doing backflips because, he says, "they tend to make people forget that what I really do is play shortstop." The art is, and always has been, playing shortstop.

The art that Smith most likens to playing shortstop is jazz, which he listens to regularly. "The whole thing in jazz is being free to create, to know something so well that you can improvise. I think of shortstop in the same way," Smith says.

On the field, knowing what he is doing so well that he can improvise or "create" has made Smith the innovative force that he is. If asked he will talk about fielding balls off the left foot, grabbing seams, throwing overhand for accuracy, straddling the base, snapping down rather than reaching out for a tag—but only if he is asked. "The only time I think like that is when I try to explain it to others," he says.

In reality, everything he does is designed to follow the flow of motion dictated by his own body. Less agile athletes would wreck themselves if they took this too far. Smith goes to extremes, to the point where he breaks every rule in the book, but where, nearly always, what he improvises is smoother, easier, quicker than what he might have achieved according to Hoyle. He is able to go to extremes because his body allows him that, and because he knows what he is doing so well.

On fielding certain kinds of grounders, for example, Smith will, like other shortstops, "surround" the ball because he knows he gains an extra step, but then he will take the ball off his right foot and throw from the side or from down under while on the run—not to be flashy but because that is the easiest way to make the play.

Smith thinks of second base not as a home or as a place of danger but as a kind of magic lantern. He does not think of injury when he sweeps across the bag any more than he thinks of

whether his left foot or right should hit the bag first or whether the inside or outside part is the area where he wants to receive the throw. He wants only to keep free enough in his body to create, to respond instantly to *anything* that might happen—bad hop, bad throw, bad runner. In fact, this kind of readiness is Smith's defense against injury. Keeping the bag between the runner and himself provides protection, as does jumping ability—both standard for most shortstops. But Smith, with his quickness, is able to do something else:

"When you talk about coming across the bag on a double play, you've got to be able to improvise," he says, "because that guy bearing down on you is never going to be in the same place two times in a row."

And what he does is fake the runner out of his athletic equipment. "You have to learn," he says, "that if the runner is going to be here, I'm going to go there—and he's not going to know it till it's too late. You have to develop that ability; you have to teach yourself to be unpredictable."

Ozzie Smith, many baseball people say, is the ultimate turf shortstop, the player ideally suited to the newer, faster game on plastic. On one level they are right. He is able to do things faster and from deeper places than others. Several years ago, he suffered a torn rotator cuff, one of the most career-threatening injuries a player can suffer. He rehabilitated himself without surgery—and he let his body compensate for the arm strength he lost. Ball in the hole? Smith became the first shortstop on the planet to slide *toward third base* so he could, even as he caught the ball, be firmly planted as he got up to make his throw!

But Smith is no lover of turf. Since the surface is so true, he says, there is a tendency to be lazy. On natural surfaces, you can't wait for a ball, he says. You must charge; you must be ready for anything. The game that Dickey Pearce came to is actually the one Smith prefers and the one his talents are most challenged by. But then he has done with turf what Dickey Pearce once did with positioning.

"You change with the game, that's all. Four or five years ago," Smith says, "there weren't guys who were throwing on the run— now it's an everyday occurrence. Guys throwing off the wrong foot—you see it all the time today. Of course Astroturf has a lot to do with it because you don't have a lot of time to field the ball, cradle it, get a good motion, look good for the camera—you don't have time for that now because the game is so much faster. I don't have the greatest arm in the world, but you learn to be quick and accurate. All of which takes work. You learn where your release point is—I've been working at that since I was a kid. When I was younger I'd sit down with a bucket of balls, pick a spot to hit, and try to come as close to it as I possibly could. But it's all about changing, being able to go from plan A to plan B [while] being absolutely consistent."

Says Ozzie Smith, sounding as much like a veteran jazzman as a fielder, "I think I've gotten better as I've gotten older. What I set out to do was to be as entertaining as I could possibly be— I wanted to be a player people could enjoy watching play. The one person I never wanted to cheat was myself, and in not cheating myself I think I've never cheated anyone else."

LEFT FIELD

Come, fill your glasses to the brim
With joyous, sparkling wine,
And drink a toast to all that's "Left"
Of the 'riginal First Nine.

(1) **RICKEY HENDERSON** *retrieves a ball in the outfield. His great speed made him a prototype left fielder in the early eighties.*

THE NEW YORK YANKEES

(2) *Fenway at night: The star of the show is the Green Monster, maker and breaker of fly balls—and skilled play in left field.*

THE BOSTON RED SOX

(3) **BARRY BONDS,** *another speedster, one of the game's few "born" left fielders.*

THE PITTSBURGH PIRATES

HISTORY HAS NOT been kind to left fielders. For the longest time the position was reserved for a team's poorest defensive outfielder. Players are "born" to every other portion of the field but no one seriously talks about someone born to play left field.

Then again, left fielders have been phantoms. Ken Griffey, Sr., certainly no phantom, made a pair of spectacular catches playing left for the Yankees in an early 1985 game against the White Sox. One of them, a ball snagged in Yankee Stadium's left-field corner after an impossible run, evoked memories of another day for Griffey's manager, Yogi Berra.

"Reminds me of Amoros," Berra said to Griffey, recalling the great catch Dodgers left fielder Sandy Amoros made against him in the 1955 World Series.

"Who's Amoros?" Griffey asked.

Amoros was one of the phantoms—and did his phantom's thing. Remember?

Early October, brilliant with fall sunshine in the East and across the worst sun field in baseball—left field in Yankee Stadium. Dodgers and Yanks, tied at three games, locked in the old ritual. The Dodgers, in their long history, had never won a World Championship, while the Yanks had won too many times to count, including a tormenting five-for-five over the Dodgers. But in the sixth inning of this game, the Dodgers clung to a hungry 2–0 lead behind Johnny Podres, a smart but hittable lefty. Opening the home half of the inning, Billy Martin walked. With the Dodgers' infield looking for a bunt, the next batter, Gil Mc-Dougald, dropped a perfect one, not for a sacrifice but for a hit.

Two men on, no one out, Berra coming up—this was what the old ritual was all about: winter in Canarsie, springtime on the Grand Concourse.

But who then was to know the folly or wisdom of a move made earlier in the game, shifting the Dodgers' starting right-hand-throwing left fielder, Jim Gilliam, to second base, inserting in his place speedy-but-shaky left-hand-throwing Sandy Amoros?

With Berra batting, Amoros, per instruction from his bench, shifted far over toward left-center field: Baseball wisdom dictated that the defense concentrate on the short field in right, not the sun field in left. But bad-ball-hitting Berra concentrated instead on a poorly served outside pitch by Podres. He lofted it down the left-field line into the corner. Everyone—except Amoros—assumed the hit was at least a game-tying double. Amoros, using all his speed, and seeming to cover a distance as wide as the South Bronx itself, flung out his gloved hand and made a last-second, in-the-web catch of the ball (a right-handed-throwing left fielder more ideally suited to the position—like Jim Gilliam—would simply have been unable to reach out that far). Amoros recovered, wheeled, and threw back toward the infield. The two base runners, one around third, the other passing second, were, after all, not the tying runs but a pair of dead ducks. A relay throw to first nailed one of them, completing a double play that saved the game, Series, and century for the Dodgers.

But as Amoros had come out of nowhere so he disappeared. His entire major league career consisted of 517 games. Within two years, he had become unneeded day help for the wealthy O'Malleys, who had moved west.

Amoros's unlikely moment in the left-field sun actually seems to come with the territory. Al Gionfriddo played half the number of major league games Amoros did. For the catch he made against Joe DiMaggio in the 1947 World Series, he, like Amoros, will be remembered longer than many Hall of Famers. Five feet six, a speck in the vast reaches of Yankee Stadium, he chased down a monumental shot DiMaggio hit with two out and two on in the

sixth inning of a game in which the Dodgers led 8–6, trailing the Yankees in games 3–2. Gionfriddo seemed to race across the entirety of the Stadium's "Death Valley," arriving at the bullpen fence 415 feet from home plate at precisely the moment Di-Maggio's ball was about to disappear. With a twisting, staggering leap, Gionfriddo caught the ball, turning his rump into the low railing of the fence. Gionfriddo, whose nicknames were all diminutives, saved a big game and extended a Series against America's Hero and team—though what remains of that moment, for most fans, is a vintage film clip of DiMaggio kicking the dirt—gracefully—in disgust.

Many other obscure players, late-inning fill-ins, have made catches in left field equal to or even better than those made by Amoros and Gionfriddo, but because they were made in less dramatic circumstances they have faded with the newspaper accounts describing them. The point is that obscure players who make these plays are often in their position not by accident but by design.

The skills of the position are, in the main, generic outfielding skills. The ability to get a jump on a fly ball and then catch it is fundamental. This begins with positioning and anticipation—the ability to read a situation and then take a routine set, forward on the feet, ready for action.

It is as crucial for the left fielder as for other outfielders to know *how* to move on different kinds of balls in the air: On balls over a fielder's head, for example, it is important not to drift, but to move decisively to an area where the ball will be coming down (the best outfielders can do this with just a quick look over their shoulders or not at all as they go), and then—this is still standard teaching—to make the catch, if possible, with two hands. If a runner is on base and likely to advance, then the catch should be augmented by taking a step or two back and then into the ball for better throwing momentum.

Left fielders, like all outfielders, know that a line drive hit directly at them is harder to play than a ball to either side, where

there are better sight lines for tracking, so they are taught to take a beat before committing themselves on these. On balls hit deep overhead, the basic teaching is to make a turn toward the glove side rather than toward the side of the throwing hand, where a lurching movement coming back across the body for the catch is more likely to cause problems.

Similarly, left fielders are taught a generic method for approaching sinking line drives: Stop and allow a manageable bounce or, if going for a shoestring or diving catch, come in low to the ground, eyes on a line nearly level with the ball; if a dive is to be attempted, then roll, if possible, to avoid injury and to keep the ball from jarring loose. If the dive is made fully extended, keep the glove slightly raised.

Left fielders also follow all-purpose instruction on grounders: Get to them as quickly as possible and field them—hard ones in front of the body or down on one knee, depending on whether runners are on, off the left foot if a throw has to be made, and then, if the ball is softly hit, rounding or angling into the ball to be sure not only of a clean pickup but of gaining control for an immediate throw. Controlling the body is an additional outfield fundamental; no play, the easiest or the most difficult, can be made unless the body is under control. Angling toward balls is a form of control and slowing the body at the last second, even when in full flight, is another. On a ball skipping to the gap, pursuit is not direct but at an angle, the play made with a sudden, shuddering slowing of the body so that the ball can be caught, momentum altered, the throw made. Even on balls that have stopped dead in the grass, the approach requires control—again rounding or angling into the ball, shortening the steps at the last second to gain a fluid rhythm for the pickup and quick throw.

Throwing technique—overhand, opposite shoulder and eyes toward the target, throwing on a line, with adequate momentum and a launching "crowhop" is the same anywhere in the outfield. The throws made must be low and hard, so they can be handled by relay and cutoff people and so they will be harder to "read" by

opposing base runners and coaches. All outfielders know that communication between themselves and any infielders involved in a play is essential: Relays must be accurate, collisions avoided, fences used rather than abused.

Where left field finally becomes different, however, is in its geography. The certain plays and requirements exclusive to left field begin with an ability to cover left-side territory—down the lines, in the corners. The strategy of the position is simple: Catch what can be caught and limit everything else. Wherever possible, the left fielder tries to hold the potential double to a single, triple to a double, to take away any extra base from base runners. Like the right fielder, he pursues balls that will be either hooking or slicing away from him. But in the left-field corner, whether because of the dimensions of the park or because the left side is just different from the right, the movement of the ball creates its own set of problems.

The long-held belief that compromises could be made in left field was based on several criteria, beginning with the happenstance of ballpark construction, which placed most sun fields in right rather than left field. And then there was not that much play in left field (left fielders in the modern period have averaged about two total chances a game and can often go for games at a time without seeing a single play). And most important, left fielders do not have the long, important throw to third that center fielders and, particularly, right fielders have. Left field inevitably became a Switzerland for heavy hitters.

But for some time now things have been changing, as even a cursory glance at the box scores on any given day will suggest. The familiar names in left these days are not Greg Luzinski or Dave Kingman but Kirk Gibson, Rickey Henderson, Tim Raines, Dan Gladden, Bo Jackson, Barry Bonds, Vince Coleman, Kevin McReynolds, Luis Polonia. The common element among these different players is *speed*—flat-out, warp-speed running ability. There have been speedsters in left before—Lou Brock and Ralph Garr come to mind—but never in such profusion. And the

reason is clear: After shortstop, the one position on the field that has been transformed by Astroturf and its demand for quickness is left field. Most curiously, however, this is a change that looks backward as much as forward. Once upon a time, left field was no Switzerland.

As early as Chadwick, we are told that left field, among all the outfield positions, was the most important. "This position," states my 1865 edition of *Beadle's Dime Base Ball Player,* "requires a fielder who occupies it to be a good runner, a fine thrower, and an excellent and sure catcher." The reason that running ability was mentioned first, absent Astroturf, was that in baseball's early days, prior to hard, overhand pitching, most of the action in a game was in left field. The single-season marks for both outfield assists and total chances per game, more than one hundred years after they were made, still belong to left fielders. With most hitting from the right side and platooning unheard of, Chadwick, without the aid of charts and computers, stated the obvious: "Three out of every six balls hit were sent to the left side."

Even after overhand pitching became uniform, the left fielder played a central role. Alfred Spink, describing the position in 1911, noted:

> Left field has always been considered the hardest place to fill in the outer works. It was especially hard in the early days of the professional game, when the pitching was slower than it is now, when the ball contained more rubber than the ball used at the present time.
>
> So it happened that in the earliest days of the professional game the fleetest men on each team were assigned to positions at left field.

Spink's model left fielder was a player of the seventies and eighties named Edgar "Ned" Cuthbert, converted to the more difficult position from center field. Cuthbert epitomized what it was early managers looked for in a left fielder. A great fielder, runner, and hitter, Cuthbert, said Spink, "was a short, stout-built man, a modern athlete in muscle and strength."

There were some Cuthbert types around in Spink's time—
Fred Clarke, Shoeless Joe Jackson, Zack Wheat. Just as in today's
game, left fielders are once more preeminently great athletes.

Fred Clarke, player-manager of the same Pirates team that
included Honus Wagner, did not begin as a left fielder. Bright
and innocent, he was an amateur first baseman and part-time
pitcher. He put an ad in *The Sporting News* one day offering
himself to the upper reaches of the game. He actually got a reply
from a team in the Nebraska State League—$40 a month and a
chance to play the outfield.

"I still wonder why they kept me," he said years later. "They
stuck me in the outfield, then a new position for me, and I was
lucky to catch half the balls they hit me."

Lucky indeed. Clarke regularly turned up at 8 A.M. and
worked at his fielding till game time in late afternoon. By the time
he reached the majors four years later, he was accomplished—
and just as cocky. His first day in the majors, in 1894, turned out
to be memorable—he had five hits, and played flawlessly in left.
He recalled the day himself in a letter to the Baseball Hall of
Fame, written over half a century later:

> When I walked in the clubhouse [that day] with my little bat,
> one of the players asked me what I was going to do with the bat and
> informed me that the pitchers in the league would knock that out of
> my hand . . . I really believed them as I thought players in the big
> leagues never made an error and made hits every time they came to
> bat. I had a telegram that I was to get $100 on arrival and when
> Billy Barney told me to play I showed him the telegram and he said,
> "Oh, that's all right, I'll get it for you after the game." But I did not
> think there would be any after the game for me so I insisted and got
> the money pinned to my baseball pants pocket and went out and
> had that lucky day that made it possible for me to continue in the
> league. After the game, I got my little bat and when I went into the
> clubhouse all the players was looking at me and I walked over and
> threw it in the bat box with the remark that they had a hell of a time
> knocking it out of my hand today.

Fred Clarke was just as opportunistic and smart when he played left field for the next twenty-two years. A base stealer and hitter as well as a manager, he looked for every advantage. He invented perhaps the first prototype of flip-up sunglasses (they nearly took out an eye but he was still far ahead of his time), and he systematically established criteria for outfielding that were based on his own experiences as a left fielder. Left field was his way to the Hall of Fame.

Big players have made their share of big plays at big moments in left field. Babe Ruth made a spectacular catch in left to end the 1928 World Series when he raced from deep to short left field to snare a ball at the box seats down the line from third base.

Zack Wheat made an even more memorable catch in baseball's longest game, the Dodgers and Braves' twenty-six-inning marathon in 1920 that ended in a 1–1 tie. In the sixteenth inning, Braves pitcher Joe Oeschger surprised the world by unloading a drive to the wall in straightaway left field. Wheat, playing shallow, somehow caught up to the ball and made a leaping, twisting, game-saving catch—400 feet from the plate! (Until 1928, when temporary stands were erected, it was 402 feet down the line in left in Braves Field.)

More than anything after hard, overhand pitching, what changed things in left—and across the outfield—was the rule abolishing spitballs and mandating new, clean baseballs for play in 1920. With balls rocketing to the far reaches of the field, it was no longer possible to routinely play shallow. Having to back up, outfielders could not be expected to make regular unassisted throws. As the relay gained in importance, the need for long, strong throwing was drastically altered—and all but eliminated in left field, making it possible to hide a weak arm there. As ballpark construction changed, particularly as fences were brought closer to make the newly discovered home run easier, it became possible to hide slow feet in the corner as well.

The defensive skills of left fielders for much of the period that followed, were, as always, bound to the parks in which they were

exercised. With the need for speed and throwing power cut back, with hitting an ever-growing demand at the position, how slower, weaker-throwing outfielders played the nooks and crannies of different parks became crucial. It wasn't the ability to throw four hundred feet but the ability to judge a forty-foot carom that counted. In a decade-by-decade survey of the game's best fielders by position conducted by the Society for American Baseball Research, only two left fielders, Al Simmons and Carl Yastrzemski, were among the top outfielders named between 1920 and 1970.

Yet the work of the game's slower cornermen was still about the basic task of making the catches and limiting damage—so much so that it is too easy to overlook the odd and beautiful skills matched to those odd and beautiful parks now fallen to the wrecking ball. Those parks, perhaps more than we realize, created even more challenges than they took away.

In Cleveland's League Park, left fielders had to guard a line 375 feet long and a bleacher wall in left center that had little three-step stoops jutting out; Crosley Field and Fenway Park had slopes going up to the wall in left ("Duffy's Cliff" existed long before the Green Monster); Forbes Field had a scoreboard on the playing field. Wrigley was longer down the lines than in the alleys; the Polo Grounds, with its high concrete walls bent at horseshoe angles, was 279 feet down the left-field line but 457 feet in the bull-pen area (open to the field of play) in left center; Shibe Park and Ebbets Field had their concrete walls, while Sportsman's Park had its wide foul territory that suddenly narrowed along a low barrier—a perfect carom target—to almost nothing in the left-field corner.

When you talk with some of the left fielders who learned their trade in these old parks, you get a sense not of past deficiencies but of skills that are disappearing from the game.

Ralph Kiner, like most left fielders of his era, was little known for his glove. He had a relatively brief career—ten years—spent mainly with the Pirates in the days when the whole team was

laughable. But in that time he forged a place in the Hall of Fame for himself. It was done almost exclusively with his bat. Kiner hit home runs at a greater per at-bat ratio than any player in history save Babe Ruth. Had he played twenty instead of ten years, he might have matched or surpassed Hank Aaron—and he would surely have become a legend in places beyond Pittsburgh.

Kiner was slow, he made errors, and he had an average throwing arm at best. But he threw accurately, and always knew where he was on the field. One year (1947) he led the National League in outfield putouts (aided undoubtedly by a pitching staff with a 4.68 earned run average), and if you listen to him today, abundantly clear is that he took defense seriously. During his years, Kiner happened to play more games in left field than anyone else in both leagues. He was a survivor at his position not just because of his bat but because he made a real point of improving himself defensively. "There was always someone in the minors ready to take your place if you didn't do your job," Kiner says. He did his job.

He studied hitters thoroughly; there were no elaborate scouting reports in his day. He turned up early at each ballpark he went to because part of his job was to take balls off the different walls. The lost part of Kiner's career was how he played these old ballparks.

Much of it, he says, depended on positioning. At Crosley Field, with its slope, "the trick was to plant yourself about three feet from the incline and then when you broke back, you counted those three steps to yourself. If you didn't you'd stumble and fall every time." Wrigley Field, where Kiner finished his career, besides being deeper down the lines than in the alleys, had no warning tracks then.

Concrete walls and the absence of warning tracks is almost unimaginable to most of today's left fielders. A few seasons ago, the Angels' Brian Downing, playing left, and Fred Lynn, playing center, combined on a truly spectacular play, but one that could not have taken place in Kiner's day. On a hit headed toward

home-run territory in left-center field, Downing, after a long, all-out run, leaped high for the ball and missed it, but knocked the collapsible canvas fence nearly to the ground; Lynn, soaring over Downing, aided by the extra foot or two of bulldozed space, made the catch, coming down on top of Downing. Had the wall been concrete—as it still is in Wrigley—Downing and Lynn would have been Angels of another sort.

"In Wrigley," Kiner said, "there was this well area in left, and that little area has about an additional forty-five feet, so you really had to know where that fence was, where it comes back at you. As a matter of fact, the best way to play that field," he added, "was to position yourself right off the corner of the angle where the wall comes out so you know that if you turn to your right you're going to the deep part, if you turn to your left you're going to the short part."

Charlie Keller was another heralded bat in the corner. As a rookie right fielder with the Yankees in 1939, he hit .334, seven points higher than a rookie left fielder named Ted Williams. A year later, to make way for the stronger-throwing Tommy Henrich, Keller was moved to sunny Switzerland, where he remained until he retired in 1952. War and a later back injury took enough of his bat to ultimately reduce him to part-time play, but left field in Yankee Stadium might have taken something from him too.

Keller, like Kiner, remembers that left field was very much a challenge. In the old stadium it not only had a vast playing area, but it was also bordered by a low, tricky concrete barrier. Joe Medwick, then with the Dodgers, hoisted himself on that low barrier in the opening game of the 1941 Series to take a home run away from Joe DiMaggio (who else?).

Keller believed in defense—believed his old team played something called "a nine-man defense" that won more games for the Yanks than their hitting. He learned his position, like Kiner, through longevity. He made it a habit to spend the entire length of batting practice—save for when he was hitting—taking balls off the bat, measuring spins, angles, and caroms.

Keller observed that visiting left fielders took three quarters of a season to figure out where to stand in vast reaches of the field —it took that long to wear down a bald patch in the grass. But he played slightly deeper than other left fielders, several paces back of the bald patch. What he was up to was relatively simple. He counted on his pitchers and adjusted accordingly. "Guys like Red Ruffing, Lefty Gomez, Spud Chandler put the ball where they were supposed to," he said.

Keller also had a way of domesticating Death Valley. "What you had to do was get yourself between the ball and home plate so you could be sure of playing the ball," he said. It was a little like learning a pool table. "A ball came off the wall a certain way thirty feet from the foul pole, another way forty feet from the pole. If you didn't have the angle exactly right, the ball would kick around the wall and be by you for a triple."

Keller had the same approach to the sun field. "The trick there," he said, "was *when* you got your sunglasses down." Most left fielders snapped their glasses down as soon as they saw a fly ball hit in their direction, he explained. Mistake. You had to watch the ball till it cleared the sight line of the grandstand roof before going to the glasses, because it was not the sun but the deep shadows of the old stadium that caused the most trouble.

THE OLD YANKEE STADIUM, of course, is gone with most of the other old parks. The newer stadiums, along with new league rules mandating uniform distances down the lines, have changed the game and nowhere more so than in the corners of the field, where uniformity and the efficiency of space have replaced nooks and crannies. "There's no question," Ralph Kiner says, "the biggest difference in playing left field then and now is that today most parks are symmetrical; it's the same wherever you go." Add artificial turf—six plastic tops in the National League, four in the American—and you have the sort of urban renewal that makes for a new breed of left fielder.

For now, though, we are in the midst of change, not at the

end of it. There are enough old parks and traditional sorts of left fielders around to see this corner game as a kind of palimpsest of generations. Whatever finally happens, there is something living, as Wordsworth might say, in the embers.

Toward the end of the 1988 season, in the midst of what was then a tight pennant race, I watched a weekend Yankees–Red Sox series at Fenway. The games featured a matchup of two big-name left fielders, Mike Greenwell of the Red Sox and Rickey Henderson, then with the Yankees. Both players are young but have been around for a few seasons, both had struggled in the field in recent seasons, and both, in this series, illustrated the difficulties of playing the old parks.

In the course of this series, there were some significant plays in left field. For example, in the opening game, Greenwell, a champagne hitter no matter what he does in the field, chased a high fly ball into the treacherous corner in left, where high walls meet a foot from the foul line. He seemed to stagger under the ball as it fell behind him for a double, an important hit in a 5–3 Yankees win.

The next day, the Yanks got off to a quick start when Greenwell leaped for and missed a ball just over his head at the scoreboard in left, leading to two runs. Rickey Henderson later chased a hot smash into the corner but seemed to get there late and then retrieved the ball tentatively. This allowed a critical run to cross the plate during a Red Sox rally that pulled them back into the game, and they went on to win. In the third game of the set, Greenwell turned a line drive into a diving catch in left. He seemed out of position, though, playing too shallow, disadvantage turned to advantage. Henderson subsequently made a shaky catch down the left-field line as fans leaned over to interfere with him, but the Sox won it 3–1. In the opening inning of the fourth and final game, Greenwell, again seeming to play shallow, got to a sinking line drive he shouldn't have, but then misplayed it into a double. Henderson made a snow-cone catch of a soft fly down the left-field line in the home half of the inning and then an inning

later misplayed a carom on a double into the corner by Marty Barrett, the Boston second baseman, as the Red Sox won again, 9–4.

The performances of both these left fielders were noticeable enough to draw criticism from TV announcers and writers alike. But the games also underscored the difficulties of playing left field in Fenway Park, everyone's living baseball museum. For Rickey Henderson, the difficulties added up to a twice-a-year annoyance; for Mike Greenwell, it was something else.

Greenwell, at first glance, is a traditional left fielder, another bat in the corner. But in Fenway Park there is a complication. There have been only three left fielders prior to him in fifty years, two of whom are in the Hall of Fame, and the third a possible candidate. Greenwell, at twenty-six, is standing where Ted Williams, Carl Yastrzemski, and Jim Rice stood before him—and knowledge of that is never far from him.

"I think everyone gets labeled in this game," Greenwell says, "and because I've been a hitter no one really looks at my fielding. But that's just what happened to the guys who played left here before me. There have been three left fielders in a half century, and for me to be the fourth is a great responsibility."

The three great hitters before Greenwell were all initially derided as fielders and all overcame their critics and many of their shortcomings with responsible efforts to make themselves better defenders.

Ted Williams, just because he set so many marks as a hitter, is almost completely overlooked as a fielder. But with his long, loping stride—which was sometimes mistaken for loafing—he covered more ground than anyone realized. He learned the wall with the same diligence he learned the strike zone—and for roughly the same reason: pride, a fierce, finicky desire to be the best at what he did. In his time, he made some plays in the field, plays he himself talked down or around, out of shyness or pain or pride.

On Joe DiMaggio Day at Yankee Stadium in September

1948, Williams made a catch of a DiMaggio drive at the bull-pen fence that had fans buzzing for innings afterward. But because he was thrown out trying to score in a later inning, the papers the next day, said baseball historian John B. Holway, "were full of Ted's loafing and getting nipped at home." Williams referred to the catch afterward as "my Gionfriddo catch."

A year later, in the All-Star game in Brooklyn, Williams made an incredible bare-handed catch of a slicing line drive hit by Don Newcombe—but the catch was lost in an avalanche of hits and history; the game, won by the American League 11–7, marked the first time black players appeared in All-Star competition.

The following year, in Chicago, Williams made another, far more significant catch in another All-Star game. In the first inning, Ralph Kiner hit what looked like a home run to left center. Williams, shifted far around to left, made a leaping, crashing catch against the concrete wall in Comiskey Park, shattering his elbow. He remained in the game for nine innings, however, even managing a sharp fifth-inning base hit. The injury ruined what Williams said was his best season, but more important, threatened his career. Delicate surgery and a long recuperation followed. In *The Picture History of the Boston Red Sox* by George Sullivan, Jack Fadden, the Red Sox trainer at the time, recalled Williams's injury and recuperation—and, incidentally, why Williams never settled on being a bat in the corner:

"There were seven distinct fractures in Ted's elbow, a disaster. There was a serious question he'd ever be able to swing a bat normally again. The most you could hope for was eighty, maybe eighty-five percent normal freedom.

"That wasn't good enough for Ted. His dedication to therapy, his application, was amazing. Home or away. Morning, noon, and night. He'd even exercise in the dugout between innings. And it paid.

"Williams attacked his later injuries with the same perseverance—the broken collarbone, the fractured ankle, the pinched neck nerve.

"The man was truly remarkable in every way, one of a kind. He had the greatest approach to his job of anyone I've ever seen —total dedication."

Which was the way Yaz went at it too. Ralph Kiner remembers a play Yastrzemski made in his rookie year, when he wasn't supposed to be a fielder. "It was one of the great plays I've ever seen," he said. "It was at Fenway, I don't remember exactly when in the season. Minoso hit one towards the fence and Yaz positioned himself to play the rebound—only there was no rebound. At the last second, Yaz turned around and caught the ball, completely fooling the runner and everyone in the place, who thought for sure the ball was well up on the wall. He threw into the infield for an easy double play. How was he able to do that? Because he knew the park so well and because he had to be thinking about it ahead of time."

Yaz thought and worked his way to seven Gold Gloves and a major-league-record seven league-leading years in assists. The play he is proudest of came in a pennant-clinching game against Oakland in the 1975 playoffs, when he made a diving stop of a ball hit by Reggie Jackson in left-center field with two men on. Instead of a two-run triple, Jackson was held to a single, a double play followed, and the victory was preserved. Jackson said afterward, "There were only two people who could have made that play, Carl Yastrzemski and God."

Greenwell says that he did not speak much to Yaz or Ted Williams about playing Fenway; they just were not around that much. But his teammate, Jim Rice was. And Rice passed on to him essentially what Yaz had passed on to Rice and what Williams had passed on to Yaz.

At least once every home stand—just as Williams, Rice, and Yaz did—Greenwell goes to the wall and has a coach hit fifty to seventy-five balls off every part of it — off the corner by the foul pole, off the scoreboard, the low concrete base, the midsection of padding, the upper layers of metal stripping. The wall's construction is more uniform today then it was in Williams's time or even

Yaz's, but the ball ricochets off each section differently. It is as though there are three different walls.

The angles of balls coming off the wall are also critical. "The further down the wall you go towards center," Greenwell says, "the more the ball caroms away to the right, so it's never a question of simply turning and taking a ball off the wall, but of where you are and of knowing when and when not to get caught on the wall."

Williams, Yaz, Rice, and now Greenwell have made routine the taking of a wall carom with a bare hand, turning, and throwing to the appropriate base or relay man. It is actually four separate movements—setting, catching, whirling, and throwing—done so often and to such a point of muscle memory that it seems like a single, fluid movement. The key, under pressure of a game, Greenwell says, is being absolutely clear-headed about when the play is to be made bare-handed. It is risky. There is always the chance the ball will be dropped. Thus, prior to a pitch, the decision to take a ball bare-handed—like Yaz's play on Minoso—must be calculated. The risk is taken because there is actually the chance, when it counts, to hold a batter to a single that in any other park would be a double, triple, or homer. "Knowing that makes it a lot easier to put aside the sense of risk," Greenwell says. "Guy hits it that good—my hat's off to him—pay him respect by taking a chance on nailing him."

Fenway Park is notoriously booby-trapped. In the left-field corner, there is a doorway facing out to the field. When a ball catches the far corner of the doorway, it can carom directly backward, hitting the opposite side of the doorway, which will then bumper-jump the ball to the wall, where it will take yet another carom. And behind third base is an angled low railing that serves to bumper-jump balls heading down the left-field line out to the grass behind shortstop.

These quirky features, though they have been excessively represented as charms, are something else to play.

"I've seen fielders go nuts because they just didn't know what

to do with the wall," Greenwell says. "They'll try to guess where a ball's going to wind up and instead of going to the ball they'll be standing someplace else looking foolish."

The secret to playing the booby traps, Greenwell says, is to ignore them—to go where you think the ball is going to be hit, and then to be "reactive, like a third baseman." Again, experience counts. A fledgling left fielder in Fenway will measure the angled barrier behind third base and see doubles coming off it. Greenwell, like his predecessors, knows this is wrong. "Singles come off that railing—not doubles—so you are giving up nothing when you ready yourself for a ball you think will go down in the corner," he says.

Most observers have noted that the wall both gives and takes away. Bucky Dent's bloop homer in the 1978 Yankees–Red Sox playoff game has been matched by any number of 350-foot line-drive singles. So an experienced Fenway left fielder knows that, despite the shadow of Bucky Dent, he has a tremendous advantage in the field. He can play shallow—as Greenwell did, still uncertainly, in that Yankees series.

"That's the most interesting thing about the wall," Greenwell says. "I'll steal hits off left-handed hitters that slice line drives over the shortstop's head that in every other park in the league would fall in. In Fenway, if you've learned positioning, you get to those balls. The real secret of Fenway, the one nobody quite understands," he adds, "is that it gives more advantage to the defense than offense."

Whatever its charms, Fenway remains one of the great schools for left fielders. It demands constant attention to detail, a willingness to make the do-or-die play, something that goes beyond the park to the heart of what good left fielders do anywhere. It is not the leaping catch over the wall or the throw that cuts down the game-winning run at home plate (these are actually few and far between) so much as the quick play—the steps to the line or gap, the way a carom is taken, the movement from a correct set position toward the flight of a ball, the accurate throw to a cutoff

man or all the way through to hold a runner at his base—that is the basic work of left fielders anywhere. It is no accident that Ted Williams and Carl Yastrzemski made great plays in other parks. They made them because they learned the routines of their position so well in Fenway.

In other parks, however, in the uniform, elephantine salad-bowl stadiums, with their expanses of wide, slick surfaces, the task of limiting damage requires one more dimension. Enter Rickey Henderson—or the idea of Rickey Henderson.

Until the Yankees temporarily made a center fielder out of him, Henderson thought of himself as many others did—as the best left fielder in the game. While other base stealers were being planted in left in the same period, he got to balls that other speedsters couldn't touch. *The Baseball Encyclopedia* has this intriguing career fielding stat for Henderson: He has averaged 2.7 putouts per game through 1988. Though the number is qualified by the year and a half he spent in center, where there are more balls to catch, and by variables such as pitching staffs and outfielders he played with, he still ranks ninth in the category among *all* outfielders. Among the top fifteen listed in the category from the beginning of the game to the present, he is the only non–center fielder, the only cornerman—left or right—to make it.

Henderson gets to balls others can't because his quickness is as spectacular as his speed. Those first two explosive steps he makes as a base stealer power his outfield shoes as well. Henderson knows this, and it is the basic reason he prefers playing left to center field, a position where command and authority (which Henderson really does not have) count just as much as speed.

"I'm more into the game in left field than anywhere else because everything moves so much faster," he says. "I was talking about this with [José] Canseco as early as the 1987 All-Star game. He said he wanted to move from left to right [he did in 1988] because everything was on him too fast in left. But that's my game. In center field, everything's in front of you. I wound up making errors there because I'd be going full speed for a long

way and couldn't slow down. In left, I never had that problem. You have to be quick, on your toes, ready for anything . . . it fits me more. I move fast, my feet are quick, everything I do is quick. Left field is just more exciting."

But Henderson, who won a Gold Glove with Oakland in 1981, when he may have been the game's best left fielder, seems more like a prototype than an advanced model these days. In 1988, he made more errors in left—twelve—than in any single season of his career. Playing in the media-glutted market of New York was probably responsible, along with Henderson's own attitude, which, it has been frequently charged, is an unpredictable mix of fire and boredom. It is hard to tell.

Like a lot of big-money players, Henderson seems reluctant to play while injured. Then again, his game, so much of which is based on speed and quickness, does not easily bear injury. He was ridiculed a couple of seasons ago for excessively nursing a hamstring injury, but no one in the Yankees' official family or the media bothered to acknowledge the severity of the injury. It was located at the top of the hamstring, in the groin area rather than midleg, which made it inaccessible to the usual therapies of ice, heat, taping, and the progressive strengthening of the quadriceps. Because Henderson is so aggressive and productive on the base paths, his body takes an especially heavy battering. His shoulders, legs, and hands are bruised and painful by midseason every year. And by September, his bat is slower and the times he must play through pain more frequent.

On the field, Henderson lends fuel to his critics by seeming to look indifferent and distracted. Between pitches, he often stretches, squats, rolls his head on his neck; when pitchers are changed he sometimes goes to the left-field wall and carries on conversations with the fans, and occasionally the conversations are carried on between pitches as well. But this behavior, too, is misleading.

Inactivity and a sense of isolation are common problems for outfielders, and players solve them in different ways. Henderson,

a heavily muscled man, needs to stretch constantly to keep loose. Other outfielders do this as well, but perhaps less obviously. He also apparently needs to yak to overcome his sense of isolation. There are other yakkers in the game.

Tim Raines acknowledges that he loves to talk to fans, particularly in Chicago, where crowds are often hostile and where they throw back enemy home-run balls. "I'll talk to them about anything they want to talk about," Raines says. It is a game for him, but far from distracting him, it keeps him energized during those stretches of inactivity when more than anticipation is required to stay alert. "The fans don't know it, but I'm using them more than they're abusing me," Raines says. "They work me over and I start to laugh. They'll think, 'Why is this guy laughing?' They'll start to chant, 'Fee-Fie-Fo-Fum, Raines you're a fucking bum'—and I'll enjoy 'em and talk back to them and whaddaya know, they'll say, 'Why don't you come to Chicago and play—you for Leon Durham straight up'—or whoever they're getting rid of that month. 'Come on to Chicago and play real baseball—Canada's a hockey town.' Even when they throw things—which I don't like —I'll answer 'em. 'How could you miss?' I'll say, and all the while it's me using them, which they don't know, so I can stay loose and relaxed and ready to go."

Introversion and reticence may look more dignified in the outfield, but looks can be deceiving. The problem of staying in the game remains. Kevin McReynolds, the Mets' left fielder, a celebrated nontalker, castigated, at times, by the New York media for his seeming indifference, imagines duck hunts while he waits for action to come his way. Unbeknownst to fans, McReynolds turns on an inner movie camera and puts himself in the marshes and fields of Arkansas, far from the noises and distractions of New York and Shea Stadium. "The less distraction I have, the more my head's in the game. It's easy for me to concentrate—just wander around out there thinkin' about duck huntin'. It keeps my mind relaxed between pitches and as soon as the pitcher's ready to go, so am I," McReynolds says.

Vince Coleman's way around the problem may actually be the most bizarre of all. The Cards' high-flying base stealer is *all* intensity and attentiveness. Not a second to spare, not an inch to give. "The second you let up," he says, sounding like the infielder he once was, "is the second you mess up." The notion of being lonely or inattentive in the outfield is as unthinkable to him as falling asleep behind the wheel of a car.

For Coleman, some of this may have to do with playing on a team that prides itself on defense. His manager, Whitey Herzog, says that initially Coleman was more interested in stealing bases than defending turf, and has had to improve his game. A weak thrower to begin with, he has worked for years on strengthening his arm in a team-wide program of long toss. And he has learned to make up for what his arm cannot do by what his legs can. He charges hard so that he can unload sooner and closer in and he "cheats" to a shallower position whenever he can. In addition, because he does not have Rickey Henderson's explosive first steps to the ball, he has had to work especially hard to train his feet. "I have a tendency to not read a ball right, particularly when it's hit right at me," Coleman says, "so I had to learn *not* to move, to keep my feet planted for a second before going." His speed allows him to outrun his mistakes, he says, but it is this unrelenting infielder's intensity that has allowed him to keep on top of things as a left fielder—to the point where he is now regularly among the league leaders in outfield assists.

"If you look at Ozzie," he says, "you see that he moves with every pitch into a balanced position where he can attack the ball —and not just lay back. That's what I need to do—every minute, every pitch. I never want to be caught with my hands on my knees, never in a position where I'm just standing there. If a runner's on first and a ball's hit in the alley, I want to keep the hitter from getting to second; if the runner's on second and it's hit to me, I want to throw him out at the plate. And if no one's on base," Coleman says, "I anticipate that it's going to be hit to me anyway—left, right, over my head, or in front of me, so I'm never out there wondering."

Rickey Henderson, who is more easygoing and far more experienced, isn't out there wondering either. But his game in the field decayed in recent years and the principal reason may not have to do with his personality so much as the team he played for. The most effective left-field play is almost always done within a unit of outfielders. There was little unit play on the Yankees in the years Rickey was there. It was neither Henderson's nor any of his teammates' fault that constant personnel changes left the Yankees' outfield, like the rest of the team, a way station along the road.

In Oakland, where he did just as much yakking and stretching in the outfield, Henderson was part of an outfield unit, considered the best in the game. Dwayne Murphy, Tony Armas, and Henderson came up through the Oakland system and trained together in the minors. The minor league outfield coach, Lee Walls, was a drill master who worked his troops fiercely but imaginatively. "Lee had drills for quickness like you've never seen," Henderson says. "He'd line us up behind each other and then he'd flip balls to us—this way, that, over our heads, to our side. We'd have to be perfect with our reflexes, learn each other's movements as well as our own; we even wound up practicing diving in this drill—man, nobody ever practices diving—but we did."

In addition to teaching their outfielders to move as a unit, the A's, in those days of Billy-ball, also left positioning to the players themselves. This encouraged aggressiveness—and communication, absolutely essential in outfielding. The players moved from batter to batter, pitch to pitch. They talked to each other. On balls to the wall or hits to the alleys, they not only backed each other up, but telegraphed instructions to each other on tough plays, keying all the while off center fielder Dwayne Murphy. "He was the boss," Henderson said.

The Athletics' outfield Henderson returned to was different but offered some of the stability missing in New York. With a unit built to key off Dave Henderson, Rickey Henderson was able to provide as well as to receive support.

"Rickey lets me cheat the other way because he gets to balls no one else can," Dave Henderson says.

"I don't know what happened in New York," Tony La Russa, the Athletics' manager said, "but to me, Rickey is a great four-direction outfielder, which means he can go anywhere to make any play. He's the best in the game."

For Rickey Henderson, a veteran now rather than a rookie with the Athletics, his homecoming represented not so much a remembrance of things past as a going back to the future.

"You have a set outfield here," he said simply, "and that makes you more confident. You can do more." Like lead a team to a world championship.

The new breed of left fielders in the game have fared somewhat better than Henderson did with the Yankees. Vince Coleman, from his first days in the majors, has played alongside Gold Glove center fielder Willie McGee, with Ozzie Smith and Terry Pendleton playing in front of him; the outfield partner in immediate proximity to Minnesota's Dan Gladden has been Kirby Puckett; Bo Jackson broke in playing alongside Willie Wilson; Barry Bonds has been playing alongside Andy Van Slyke.

A talk with any of the prime left fielders in the game makes clear just how important their position has become in the defensive scheme of things. Kevin McReynolds began his career as a center fielder but was switched to left not because he was slow or weak-winged but because both the Padres and Mets, the two teams he has played for, needed to shore up their left-side defenses. McReynolds brought his center fielder's speed with him as well as a powerful throwing arm. A couple of seasons at the position were, in personal terms, something of a surprise. McReynolds discovered (a) that left field was the more difficult of the two positions to play because, he says, "you don't see the ball as well in left—every ball there seems to be moving away from you—you have to react more quickly"; and (b) that when he did have the opportunity to move back to center field for one game during the 1988 season, he didn't enjoy it. "As a matter of fact, I

was so uncomfortable I would have rather been playing behind the fence," he said.

McReynolds's game is simple, aggressive, and effective. He is fast, much faster than his large, almost bulky frame suggests. In 1988, he stole twenty-one bases without being caught, the best stealing percentage in the majors, and one that indicates that beyond having speed, McReynolds is also quick and smart.

He tries, when he can, to play shallow in the deepest-playing outfield in baseball, convinced that the majority of hits in a game will fall in front of him rather than over his head. The dramatic over-the-wall catch, while noticed as a "great" play, doesn't happen that frequently. Playing walls depends on knowing them— are they plywood, concrete, chain link, padded? Do they have oddities to account for, like the little projecting screen down the left-field line at Three Rivers Stadium in Pittsburgh, the "well" in Wrigley Field? Playing walls means learning how to play the warning track, reaching back with the hand, if there is time, to "feel" for the wall, moving sideways along the wall, when possible, in setting up for a catch, being aware, before a ball is hit, of where the wall is and how a ball will come off it.

But McReynolds does not think too much about walls. Good fences, to him, do not necessarily make good left fielders. Catching up to baseballs does. With no one on base, the goal, McReynolds says, is just to catch the ball: "I don't care if I stumble or look bad, just so long as I catch it." It is harder for him to go back and to his left than to his right, so he will cheat just a bit in positioning depending on the hitter.

He has worked hardest, perhaps, on his footwork. In college, where he was well coached in outfield fundamentals, he was taught to limit the number of steps he took after retrieving a ball and throwing it. "I worked on footwork in college, but much more since," McReynolds says. "The most I want to take is two steps, that is, two controlled steps—if I take that many. A lot of times, I can get rid of the ball quicker than that now—like an infielder, a step and a throw—that's what I've been working for."

The left fielder saves games more by what doesn't happen than by what does, McReynolds says. "You go all out on a ball down the line, and the worst that can happen is it's going to be a double —ball down the line *should* be a double. If by some chance you get there and keep the runner from going to second or throw him out, so much the better. A lot of times if you get to the ball quick enough, the runner won't even attempt to go to second. That's the real payoff. You don't wind up throwing that many guys out. But when you can hold the runner, you keep the double play in order, and that counts because you may have stopped a big inning."

From the time he has taken up playing left field, McReynolds has led the National League in outfield assists as well as quickly becoming a Gold Glover. Uncomfortable in the limelight, McReynolds says that each position player on the field contributes as much as any other—including the left fielder. His view of what left fielders contribute, though, might have been laughed at twenty years ago:

"I've heard that left field is called the idiot position. For the most part, left fielders don't get any respect, but somebody has to take up that position, and it helps to have somebody that plays the position and can do certain things—get to a ball and get rid of it, maybe keep a guy from getting a double, maybe get to a ball quick enough to keep a guy from scoring from second, force the other team to do it with two hits instead of one—certain little things like that that don't show up in the box score but that count at the end of the game and which, I'm sure, managers and teammates notice."

PERHAPS THE MOST intriguing if underrated newcomer in left these days is a third-year man, Barry Bonds of the Pirates. Barry is the son of Bobby, the second player ever in baseball's 30-30 club (30 home runs, 30 stolen bases in the same season; Willie Mays was the charter member, and others now include Howard Johnson, Darryl Strawberry, Eric Davis, and José Canseco, sole proprietor of the 40-40 club). Barry has been touted as another

30-30 player and the thought of it is pleasing because he makes no bones about wanting to follow in his father's footsteps. What might make him even more unusual, though, is that he has always been a left fielder. Though he spent a year in center for the Pirates, his heart has always belonged to left. "I am a natural left fielder," he says—perhaps the only person on the planet who had ever acknowledged such a thing.

Bonds believes he is so well suited to his position because he has been fully trained for it. Growing up in a baseball family, with his father playing an outfield corner—right field—for many years and his godfather, Willie Mays, playing alongside his father, Barry was tuned to outfield thinking from an early age.

"I used to travel around with the team," he says. "I would have loved to hit but no one would let me. Instead, they let me play the field."

Father and godfather, though, were reluctant to provide technical pointers. Instead, they were more concerned that the youngster learn to think like an outfielder. "Over and over again, they both impressed on me the need to think about hitters, to study them and learn them like tables in math. They taught me about who was running, who was pitching, what was happening in the game at the moment. You had to be ready for each moment and each moment had to be taken for itself," Bonds said.

The younger Bonds also learned early about outfield communication. His father and Mays talked about it all the time and demonstrated it on the field. Each player knew where the other was at all times, and each helped the other out in positioning, backing up, directing throws, and even pursuing fly balls. And in one dramatic instance when communication between them broke down, there was a lesson, too. In a 1970 game at Candlestick Park, Mays and Bonds *both* went for a ball headed out over the chain-link fence in right center. They simultaneously leaped for the ball, Mays soaring up over Bonds, then landing on top of him as both fell in a heap at the base of the fence. Mays, somehow, had managed to hold on to the ball.

For Barry, the risk-taking, the aggressiveness, the sheer élan

of the play, stayed in his memory. "I've known from a very early age," he said, "just why I love left field. It's exciting out there—diving or going over a wall, charging a ball, challenging someone by playing shallow, telling them they can't hit one over your head and if they do you go back and take it away from them and if they hit a ground ball you're gonna throw out the runner. I remember what Willie and my dad used to do, the catches they made, the times they got up on the wall, sometimes together, the diving plays they made—that was baseball. My dad sits there today and says we play Hollywood baseball, and maybe we do, but I love the game they taught me."

But Bonds's grounding in fundamentals, in learning how to do technically what his imagination was already primed to do, did not come until he went to college, when he played left field for Arizona State alongside center fielder Oddibe McDowell.

There Bonds learned firsthand the advantages of good communication. He was drilled on a variety of plays and moves he would have to make. On tracking fly balls, he worked with pop-fly machines, chasing balls behind him and over his head until he could make his pursuit with just the quickest of looks as he went to the area where he knew the ball would be coming down. He threw every day, often into a spring-frame netting that would propel the ball back at him in such a way that he could measure the quality of his throws. He worked endlessly on cutoffs—who to throw to, under what circumstances, and why. He had to hit his cutoff man—this was primary. But the strength of his own arm and that of his cutoff man determined where in the field the other would be standing. The stronger the arm of the cutoff man, the deeper he could come out to set up. Communicate with him, know where he was going to be, get the ball to him properly (about shoulder-high, glove-hand side), and the job was done.

But on throwing to the base, more was required. With no one on and a single to left center, obviously the throw went to second. With a runner on and a single to left, the throw was to third. With two men on or with the bases loaded, the priorities

became more complex. Do you have a chance for a play at the plate or at third? Is an aggressive attempt to get a lead runner foolishly going to allow a trailing runner to advance an extra base? These decisions are left to a fielder's precise knowledge of situations. The decisions have to be made prior to the play.

"Sometimes," Bonds says, "you know there won't be a play at a lead base—the guy on second won't try to score on a single to left—so your throw can go to third; you might catch the runner rounding the base just a step too far. But you have to know what you're doing."

Backing up other fielders involves advance preparation as well. "Backing up begins with communication. You've got to know what the other guy wants to do, what his range and abilities are, how you can help out—who calls the ball, where you're supposed to be. When you back him up," Bonds says, "you're giving the other guy room, you're letting him know that you're there for him if he misses the ball—he can be more aggressive—and you've found another way to hold runners too."

When Bonds blossomed as a college star, his father and godfather were much more willing to talk shop with him, satisfied that the earliest, most important lessons about attitude and situations had been assimilated.

"Willie and my dad . . . taught that your job is done when you get the ball to the cutoff man," Bonds said, "but therefore you've got to get it to him as quick as you can. That means proper footwork, hand speed, hand-eye coordination, and release point in throwing. Each person's taught differently—they'll teach you if the ball's hit to the wall and stops, pick it up with your hand. A lot of times you'll pick it up with your glove and it'll fall out or you don't have it and you take an extra step, and then have to come back. Or you're taught to take a carom with the bare hand so you're going with your momentum into the throw."

Bobby Bonds and Mays refined the teaching so that by the time Barry began playing major league parks, his thinking, deeply schooled in batters, runners, game moments, would enable him

to do things he might not have done if he was just simply a good athlete.

"Now I vary it," he says. "On balls at or off the wall, it depends entirely on where I am and what's going on. If we're playing on turf and the ball's going to carom right at me, I'll take it with my glove, and *boom*. But sometimes on grass, like in San Francisco, the ball is either dead or has nothing on it and I'll take it with my bare hand and throw it—it doesn't do you any good to pick it up with your glove, change hands, and then throw. So it varies from field to field and situation to situation. For instance, if someone slow, like Jody Davis, is running and if I know he's got a double, I'm just going to pick the ball up, without worrying whether or not it's bare-handed, and get it to my cutoff man because I know he's not going to get a triple. But if Eric Davis is running, I'm going to get it with my hand and get it in as fast as I can because I know he can stretch it to a triple."

At twenty-four, Barry Bonds is not a grinder like Vince Coleman, a yakker like Henderson or Tim Raines, a stoic like McReynolds. Clubhouse people will tell you he is moody—effervescent one moment, withdrawn the next. He wears a small gold earring (as does another left fielder, Lonnie Smith) and he wears a headset to close himself off from the excessive noise that accompanies him to and from the ballpark every day. But as young as he is, experience and training have led him to an actual philosophy of playing left field.

Bonds, like his father and godfather, wants to take the play away from the other team wherever and whenever he can. This begins, for him, with an acknowledgment that his arm is not so powerful and that his center fielder, Andy Van Slyke, is an active and superb communicator.

Bonds plays shallow whenever he can. He does it because it makes sense but also because he knows it can sometimes change the intention of a hitter at the plate—as if a third baseman were playing close. "With a third baseman, you actually don't want a hitter to bunt; you challenge him to hit it by you," Bonds says.

"It's the same thing in the outfield. Have a guy looking out there saying, 'He's crazy to be playing that shallow.' So I'm forcing him to change. I think the guy I've really gotten to that way is Tony Gwynn. He wants to hit to left so badly, ninety-nine point nine percent of the time he'll just eat that line up, which is why he's a three-seventy hitter. So I play him shallow and dare him to hit it over my head. And I know Tony Gwynn can hit home runs and is a great gap hitter but he's going to *have* to hit it far because I'm going to take everything else away from him. I'm forcing him to play with his game."

Cocky as he is, Bonds is not obdurate about this. The game he plays is subtle and smart, perfectly matched to his great speed and superb grounding in fundamentals. He knows parks, knows that the ball kicks unpredictably coming out of the corner in Pittsburgh, that it comes off the wall with pace in Cincinnati, that Chicago, long down the lines, shorter in the gaps, has to be played differently; unlike Ralph Kiner and some other present-day left fielders, Bonds does not play on the invisible seam between the well and the alley. As he does in every park, he measures the distance between the wall and where he is standing *with each new batter*. So in Wrigley Field, he says, "I vary it. It depends completely on who's hitting. Sometimes I'll play really shallow, sometimes straight where the deep part is. Sometimes I'll play over—it's always who's hitting and what the situation is. If it's early in the ball game and there's a man on second, you can play deep and give them a run—or take a chance and play shallow— but it depends on who's hitting. If Andre Dawson's the batter, you just don't play shallow. Give him the hit—don't risk having him beat you over your head. But if Casey Candaele or Doug Dascenzo is up, let them take a shot at you, because the chances of them doing that are small while they do have a better chance of putting one in front of you. But now if it's a close game and it's late, I won't take the chance of Candaele or Dascenzo hitting one over my head—if we're three runs up I sure will, even then —but it's all situation, and situation includes everything, the hit-

ter, the score, the inning, the park you're playing in, the wind, the sun, even the lights at night."

His first year, Bonds played center field for the Pirates. But when Andy Van Slyke arrived in 1987, manager Jim Leyland put him in center because he had a stronger arm and was more willing to play deep than Bonds was. In making the move, though, Leyland had something else in mind. Bonds had covered center well for the Pirates, but he wanted him to play left. Leyland, a new manager, had some feeling about left field.

"In my opinion, first base and left field are the two most underrated positions on the field," he said. "First base handles more throws than anyone, and in left you have to get to balls and make plays quicker than anyone realizes. Even if you don't have the strongest outfield arm, you have to know how to cut down the distance and to make the shorter throw. Its actually good if you don't have the greatest arm in the world because you can cut down the distance you have to throw by the way you charge and unload. I think right now Bonds and Kevin McReynolds are the two best defensive left fielders in the league. They get to the ball quicker and they have great instincts about who's running, what the situation is, how to charge, when to charge, when not to charge."

What Leyland is talking about hasn't been seen in the game since the days of slow pitching a century ago: players born to play left field.

RIGHT FIELD

He knows the place, he plays right well
To none the palm he'll yield;
He's bound you shant catch "Moses Grant"
A "napping" in right field.

① *Good fences make for good right fielders. Playing in an era when outfield walls were typically as challenging and as unyielding as Wrigley Field's ivy-covered concrete barrier,* **ROBERTO CLEMENTE** *was the game's most formidable right fielder. He possessed one of the most powerful arms in baseball history, and won twelve Gold Gloves in his eighteen-year career with the Pirates.*

UPI/BETTMANN NEWSPHOTOS

② **RUBEN SIERRA,** *the twenty-four-year-old right fielder on the Texas Rangers, reminds some observers of a young Clemente. But Sierra's throwing power comes from the specific way he charges a ball in the outfield rather than from great natural arm strength.*

THE TEXAS RANGERS

③ **DAVE WINFIELD,** *in a perfect imitation of an NBA power forward, makes a spectacular catch, reaching above a ten-foot barrier in Yankee Stadium. Key to the catch: a willingness to challenge* anything *plus a well-placed spiked shoe in the middle of the wall's plastic padding.*

© 1981 NEW YORK NEWS, INC. REPRINTED BY PERMISSION

④ **DWIGHT EVANS** *has been setting standards in right field for the last decade and a half. Slower afoot than some of his contemporaries, Evans has more than compensated with intelligence, unmatchable work habits, and one of the strongest outfield arms since Roberto Clemente.*

THE BOSTON RED SOX

SEVERAL SEASONS AGO, I went to a college game to watch a pitcher I had heard a lot about. The pitcher, who has since graduated and worked his way up to the majors, didn't have it that day. But the most interesting part of the afternoon occurred before the game even started. A scout I knew had set himself up in a corner of the bleachers, away from his brother scouts, who were exchanging pregame pleasantries.

An hour before game time, this scout was working, paying careful attention to a group of players taking fungoes in the outfield. After each catch and throw, the scout made entries in a notebook he was carrying. When the round of flycatching was over, he closed his book and started to leave the field. I asked him jokingly if he had seen enough.

"Oh yeah," he said. "I got an outfielder today."

I thought he was kidding so I asked about the pitcher.

"Everybody knows about him—who needs to see him again?"

He wasn't kidding. But I was confused. What could he have turned up watching fungoes? He smiled.

Outfielders didn't necessarily have the chance to throw in an actual game, he said. But just because of that, they would regularly unload in practice. "They have this seventh sense of things," he said with a wink. "They know when scouts are in the stands—especially when you make yourself obvious, the way I do—know what I mean? Outfielders are smarter than anyone thinks because they constantly have to find ways to let people know they're there."

A couple of seasons later, I remembered this pregame mind-game when I was speaking to Dwight Evans, the Red Sox eight-

time Gold Glove right fielder. Evans, who has played over two thousand games in right through a magnificent seventeen-year career, was talking about how from the time he began playing, he always believed in practice. "I tell young players that practice doesn't make perfect but that perfect practice does," he said. But Evan's pregame routine, consistent and intense as all his other work habits, had one other purpose to it: attracting the attention of managers and coaches on the other team. Just as if they were scouts.

Evans did everything game-high, he said. He made a point of taking infield—to work on his hands and reflexes but also to throw across the diamond from as close a position to the other team's bench as possible. Just as purposefully, he charged balls, picked them up, and threw them with the same intensity he did when taking fungoes in the outfield.

"I want people to see me do that," Evans explained. "A lot of times the other team watches you—especially the third-base coach—and they'll see that you're throwing, and it'll stay in their head. You want to plant that seed. Let them think about it so when the game comes, the runner peeks at you as he's going, the third-base coach's arms will somehow go up, stopping the runner. So you charge hard in practice and throw well—just as if it's in a game. In a game, you might make a bad throw, but the runner will have held."

Like the scout, he was smiling. "It's like a chess game in right field," he said, "and you always want to be one move ahead of your opponent."

Right field isn't normally considered one of the chess-playing positions. The usual criteria for this cornerman involves an ability, as with the left fielder, to limit damage—to get to balls quickly, whether in the corners, alleys, in front, or overhead, and to turn them in time to keep runs off the board and runners unable to take the extra base. With Astroturf surfaces, speed as well as quickness has more recently been emphasized, but, above all, right fielders, because of their place on the field, are required

to make the longest, most crucial outfield throw—from right field, sometimes from deep in the corner, to third base. Thus it is almost mandatory that the right fielder, whatever his arm strength, have a keen sense of strategy, since a variety of important plays can develop from the deep field. From the time of Babe Ruth, right field has been a glamour position. Showstoppers play there, those who *know* how to display the merchandise. Sometimes, money and candy-bar wrappers shower down on them: They hit home runs, they have cannons for arms. Less frequently, these cornermen, the ones who have the ability and who pay that much attention to detail, become masters of the subtler game.

The physical demands on a right fielder, while not absolutely daunting, are tough enough. Catching a ball in right field is tougher than it is in center, where the sight lines make it easier for a fielder to see what his pitcher is throwing and to see the ball off the bat. It is also tougher than left for reasons that are not so clear-cut. In both corner positions, the usual flight of a ball is a hook or slice. For some reason, these, and even the angles of pursuit on grounders, seem harder to follow.

Right fielders, because most of them are right-handed, also have a more difficult play coming out of the corner than do left fielders. Pursuing a ball down the line, the right fielder will often make his retrieval and throw with a counterclockwise spin, going with rather than against the force of his momentum as he reaches across his body, turning almost 360 degrees before unloading to the infield. Not all right fielders can do this, and some who attempt it give up accuracy as they spin. Right-handed left fielders (the majority of all outfielders are righties) don't have the corner spin to worry about at all, while their spin going left into the gap is unobstructed by railings or barriers.

As well as the long throw, it is the greater danger of the extra base and the more inviting challenge of first base, the closer base, that makes right field physically and mentally more challenging. The right fielder, more than his counterparts in left and center, who usually have no play at all, is challenged by the hit with a

runner in scoring position; the right fielder *assumes* runners on
first will be looking to advance to third on a hit—left fielders
don't. On a simple single with no one on, right fielders are taught
to look toward first before they throw the ball back into the
infield. The look is intended as a check both to the runner and to
the right fielder, who may have an opportunity to throw behind
the runner if he rounds the base too far or, in an extreme case, to
actually throw out the runner if he is too slow getting down the
line. Carl Furillo—who made the play almost routinely—once
forced a runner at first base with a no-hit game still in the works.
Enos Slaughter, the former Cards right fielder, once caught the
Braves' Connie Ryan rounding first on a ground single after Stan
Musial had completely taken himself out of the play trying to field
the ball as it went through the infield. Slaughter threw to the
catcher, who had come down the line to back up first on the hit.

The backup responsibilities of right fielders also add a dimension to their game that left fielders don't have. For the most part,
left fielders move to back up third base on any plays involving
throws coming up the line—pickoff throws from the catcher,
force throws on bunts and swinging bunts. They also can move
to back up third on plays coming from the right side of the
diamond. But right fielders, as well as having to back up many
first-base plays, also move into the middle of the field to back up
on a variety of plays at second base coming from the left side of
the diamond. With runners on first and second on a double-play
grounder to third, it is absolutely essential for the right fielder to
quickly move in line behind the second baseman. If he doesn't,
an overthrow will usually mean a run scored. On a single to left
with a runner on second or with runners on second and third,
the right fielder *must* be in position behind second base in case
any play develops there. On a certain extra-base hit down the left-
field line with a man on base, the right fielder is most often the
man who will move in to cover the second-base bag while the
middle infielders have moved off to work the relay from left field.

For all the strong-arming done in right, a glamour player with

a big arm but with little or no interest in the subtle game produces only limited benefits. Reggie Jackson, who had speed as well as arm strength to go with his home-run bat, seemed to lose defensive ability through his career in direct proportion to the number of home runs he hit. Darryl Strawberry, the Mets' superstar, has great ability but is, at best, an indifferent fielder. His throwing is powerful but erratic, his positioning immobile. Hometown announcers refer to a square yard of worn grass in right field from which Strawberry rarely strays as the "Strawberry Patch."

Right field, it turns out, is the most surprising of positions because its beauties are veiled even as its power is revealed.

Once upon a time, this was not the case. In the beginning, right field was not for the beautiful, the powerful, or the smart. It was the last refuge on the field, the last grasp of the bat handle for sandlot captains choosing up sides for a game. In the words of my trusty 1865 Beadle:

> [Right field] is the position that the poorest player of the nine— if there be any such—should occupy; not that the position does not require as good a player to occupy it as the others, but that it is only occasionally, in comparison to other portions of the field, that balls are sent in this direction.

Just so. As left field got the action in the days before overhand pitching, right field did not. In 1876, Art Allison, the regular right fielder for the Louisville Colonels in the National League, made a grand total of 34 putouts over the entire season. The most any right fielder in the National League had that year was 73 (the top total for a left fielder, by contrast, was 202). In 1884, the first year in which overhand pitching was considered legal, Jim Lillie of Buffalo led all National League right fielders with 190 putouts. By the turn of the century, right field had not only become a more lively place but it may also have become the outfield's marketplace. Not only were right fielders recording more putouts,

they were racking up assists as if they were infielders, averaging between 20 and 40 outfield assists a season, most on force plays from the short field. In one National League game during 1905, Dusty Miller of Cincinnati nailed four Philadelphia runners at first. It was record-tying, but in that same year left fielder Fred Clarke got four outfield assists in a game—one at each of the different bases—a far more impressive feat. Spink noted toward the end of the dead-ball era that in these early, shallow-playing days of the game, the men of right "were asked to pick up right field hits rapidly and try and throw out the batsman before he reached first base.

"This play . . . in the earlier days of the professional game . . . was pulled off three or four times in each and every contest."

There were few lasting stars among early right fielders—Lipman Pike, Tom McCarthy, and Hugh Nicol were considered noteworthy, but of these only McCarthy made baseball historian William Akin's survey list of nine top-fielding pre-twentieth century outfielders in "Bare Hands and Kid Gloves: The Best Fielders, 1880–1899." Yet a great change was under way in this period, a change that eventually turned right field into a marquee position (but one that also tended to obscure some of the skills these early performers brought to the position).

Of course, right fielders made catches, some of which to this day still have vapors of make-believe and controversy clinging to them. Wee Willie Keeler of the 1890s Orioles was reported in one game to have used a loose plank in an outfield fence to seesaw himself into the air to make a catch before disappearing into the crowds behind him. However, the same yarn was told about Joe Kelley, a contemporary of Keeler's.

In the 1912 World Series, the Giants and Red Sox played a Series-concluding eighth game at Fenway Park. With the score tied at 1–1, the Giants, behind Christy Mathewson, moved ahead 2–1, only to have the Red Sox come back to tie and eventually win the game following a celebrated dropped outfield fly by Fred Snodgrass in the last of the tenth. But until then the game had

been preserved by another kind of outfield play by Harry Hooper, the Sox right fielder, one of the first big star right fielders in the game and a member of the famed outfield unit that included Tris Speaker and Duffy Lewis. In the top of the fifth with the Giants leading 1–0, they got their lead man on. The next batter smashed a deep fly toward Hooper—some say in right center, some say near the foul pole down the line. Somewhere between Lansdowne and Jersey streets, Hooper, pushing off with one hand on the fence (or foul pole), the other reaching for the ball, vaulted two, five, ten, fifteen feet (depending on the storyteller) over the barrier between himself and the fans, winding up stretched horizontally across the heads and shoulders of the crowd—with the ball in his possession. The catch was a game saver—and a mythmaker. Hooper himself, in one history of the Red Sox, was quoted as saying he made the catch bare-handed.

Lest anyone be concerned that Christy Mathewson, the game's avatar of clean living and high sportsmanship, had been capriciously victimized, consider the literal bolt of heavenly support he received from a right fielder three years earlier. In a late-summer game in Pittsburgh, Mathewson had run into a jam in the last of the eighth. The Pirates had two men on, there were two out, and a gathering storm overhead had turned the long shadows of late afternoon to inky darkness. The distance between the mound and plate was barely visible and—so the story goes—Mathewson had to walk halfway in before each pitch to pick up the catcher's signs. Somehow, Dots Miller, the Pirates' rookie second baseman, was able to do in darkness what other, better hitters were unable to do in broad daylight: He smote a Mathewson pitch to the far corners of the field. The storytellers argue whether anyone saw the direction in which the ball was hit, but there was no argument about what followed: Suddenly there was a terrific, Roy Hobbsish snake of lightning across the sky that illumined all of Forbes Field just long enough for the Giants' startled right fielder, Red Murray, to throw out a bare hand, catch the ball, and save the game. Of course what followed was pre-

dictable. "Moments later," wrote Lowell Reidenbaugh of *The Sporting News* in 1983, "a torrential downpour washed out further action."

But perhaps the most magical and/or fictional catch ever made in right occurred in the 1925 Series between the Senators and Pirates. With the players of both teams wearing black armbands for Christy Mathewson, whose death on the eve of the Series had shocked and saddened the baseball world, the Series switched to Washington tied at one game apiece. In the top of the eighth, just after the Senators had moved into a 4–3 lead, future Hall of Famer Sam Rice, who had been playing center field that day, was shifted back to his usual spot in right. With two out and no one on, Earl Smith, the Pirates' catcher, appeared to hit a game-tying home run to right. Rice raced to the barrier in front of the temporary bleachers, erected just before that game. As the ball descended toward the stands, Rice leap-frogged into the ocean of Senators fans watching the play. When he emerged from the surf many minutes later and only when an umpire approached the barrier, he was, somehow, in possession of the baseball. The controversy that followed the ump's out call and the baseball commissioner's subsequent ruling that a valid catch had been made continued throughout Rice's life—and beyond. In 1965, Rice wrote a letter to the Hall of Fame (to be opened only after his death), attempting to settle the question once and for all. All he did was raise the art of tall-tale telling to new levels:

> It was a cold and windy day, the rightfield bleachers were crowded with people in overcoats and wrapped in blankets, the ball was a line drive headed for the bleachers towards right center. I turned slightly to my right and had the ball in view all the way, going at top speed and about 15 feet from the bleachers jumped as high as I could and back handed it and the ball hit the center of the pocket in my glove (I had a death grip on it).
>
> I hit the ground about 5 feet from a barrier about 4 feet high in front of the bleachers with all the brakes on but couldn't stop so I tried to jump in to land in the crowd but my feet hit the barrier

about a foot from the top and I toppled over on my stomach into the first row of bleachers. I hit my adam's apple on something which sort of knocked me out for a few seconds but [center fielder Earl] McNeely arrived about that time and grabbed me by the shirt and pulled me out. I remember trotting back towards the infield still carrying the ball for about half way and then tossing it towards the pitcher's mound. (How I have wished many times I had kept it.) At no time did I lose possession of it.

What all the storytelling conceals, however, is how much right field changed as a position over the years. When Sam Rice tumbled into the seats in 1925, right-field defense was very different from what it had been years before. In the first decades of the game—until hard overhand pitching was established—right fielders did little. Then, from the mid-1880s until the end of the dead-ball era (1920), they did a lot, usually in close toward the infield rather than back toward the walls. Defending deep came with power hitting, in just that period when Sam Rice was leaving the game and Babe Ruth was taking it over.

Ruth himself noted some of the changes. Writing in 1928, he observed:

> Outfield play has changed a lot in the last few years. Fifteen years ago, before the rabbit ball came into existence, and in the era when hitters choked their hits and tried for direction more than distance, the outfielders ranged close in. They took more chances on a ball going over their heads than they do now. And they were called upon to do a lot more throwing. A strong throwing arm was absolutely necessary to an outfielder ten years ago—and many a run was cut down at the plate by a good throw.
>
> Now, however, since the rabbit ball has come into being and hitters are aiming at the fences, the outfielders play far out and the throwing end of the game is not as important as it once was. The distances are so great that a throw home from most outfield positions is almost impossible. And centerfielders in particular have little or no chance to nail their man on a long fly. And by the way, that explains

why managers arrange their outfielders to put the weak thrower in center field, if possible.

In other words, from the time right-field play came into prominence—around 1884—till the beginning of the rabbit-ball era, great throwing ability and speed were essential. Playing in parks where outfield boundaries were often open or bordered by standing crowds that would part like the Red Sea to allow additional space, outfielders simply had to be able to cover ground; and because they played shallow, the long, strong throw was emphasized.

An objective measure of what kind of skills these middle-era right fielders possessed was provided in 1896, when Baltimore newspapers reported on a season-ending field contest held among members of the old Orioles. The players competed in six different events, including distance throwing, circling the bases, and the 100-yard dash. Willie Keeler, five feet four and 140 pounds, the only man in the history of baseball to hit more than two hundred singles in a single season (most of them placed "where they ain't"), finished first in the bases tour—it took him an astonishing fifteen seconds; he tied with a teammate in the 100-yard dash— at 10.2 seconds! And in distance throwing, Wee Willie finished second. Joe Kelley, the left fielder (like Keeler, eventually a Hall of Famer), heaved a baseball 388 feet and 10 inches. Keeler's throw went 371 feet, 11 inches *on the fly!*

While the lively ball surely changed both the nature of outfield play and the skills that went with it, ballpark construction did too. Between 1909, when Forbes Field and Shibe Park were opened, and 1923, when Yankee Stadium was completed, new stadiums proliferated. As noted earlier, instead of limitless space in the outfield, there was particular space, quirky, different, challenging. Right-field areas, in particular, even before the Babe, were usually shorter, trickier, nastier to play. A list of the new parks, when they opened, and their dimensions (some were altered in years following) suggests just how extensive the influence of ballpark construction might have been:

PARK	LF	CF	RF
SHIBE PARK (1909)	360	420	360
FORBES FIELD (1909)	360	462	360
COMISKEY PARK (1910)	363	420	363
CROSLEY FIELD (1912)	360	420	360
FENWAY PARK (1912)	315	410	301
EBBETS FIELD (1913)	352	407	297
TIGER STADIUM–NEVINS (1913)	340	440	320
BRAVES FIELD (1915)	402	550	319
WRIGLEY FIELD (1916)	355	400	353
YANKEE STADIUM (1923)	301	461 (LCF)	296
POLO GROUNDS (OF ENCLOSED—1923)	279	483	257

The new parks took some getting used to. But beyond the usual shakedown cruises, there remained the problem of having to go out and master spaces, to play these parks, each with its own set of very peculiar features, with skills matched to them. As with the left-field wall in Fenway, it was no easy task.

In Shibe Park, the scoreboard at field level, just above a low barrier in right center caused all kinds of problems. A ball hitting any of its innumerable angles could carom almost anywhere. "It was as tough a place to play as there was," remembers Bill Virdon, who played alongside Roberto Clemente. "Not only did you have those angles but there were also these hooks where they hung those hand-lettered scores. The ball could hit those hooks—and so could you."

The right-field wall in Brooklyn, remodeled in the 1920s to add height, was concave with a screen on top of it. A ball hitting one part of the wall would carom back to the infield, but another might bounce almost straight upward, and a ball hitting the screen could come straight down, as though shot from the sky. Whatever the pleasure these parks provided, playing them involved ceremonies of danger and skill.

"There was nothing like playing those old parks," says Al Kaline, who forged a Hall of Fame career for himself by playing right for over two decades in Tiger Stadium. "All the new parks are three hundred and thirty feet down the lines and they're all four hundred feet in center—so when you play one park you play them all. That takes away from what you do."

Because it had become a shorter field where shallower play was possible, because it was bordered usually by concrete and by peculiar architectural features, and then because the action of the game at the position had become so standardized, right field underwent yet another change. Between the ages of Babe Ruth and Astroturf, speed became less important, throwing power more important. It became customary to place the strongest-throwing outfielder (not necessarily the most skillful) in right field to take advantage of opportunities not available in center or left. Playing for the Phillies in 1930 in tiny, rickety Baker Bowl, with its pop-fly-close right-field wall, Chuck Klein racked up forty-four outfield assists, the most since old-time right fielder Tom McCarthy had the same number in 1888. Ostensibly, a good percentage of Klein's assists—as McCarthy's—were on rifle-shot throws to first for force-outs.

By the time Al Kaline began playing in the early 1950s, right field was a place for not only strong arms but sharp minds as well. Across the leagues, the position was filled by players who could both throw and think. Hank Bauer, Jimmy Piersall, Wally Post, Stan Musial, Jim Rivera, and, of course, Carl Furillo were all playing right in 1954, Kaline's first full season.

Furillo, in particular, caught the attention of base runners and fans. With an arm and a will to match, he made an engineer's study of the right-field wall at Ebbets Field.

"Carl Furillo was the best at playing Ebbets Field's right-field wall, which was the craziest wall in baseball," longtime Dodger-watcher Bill Reddy told Peter Golenbock in *Bums*.

The right-field wall was thirty feet high, with a twenty-eight-foot screen on top of it. The scoreboard was in the middle of the wall,

between center and right, and on top of the scoreboard was the Bulova clock—they made a big thing about "Baseball time is Bulova time." There was a Shaefer beer sign and the "h" in Shaefer lit up for a hit, and the "e" lit up for an error. The scoreboard took up a good portion of the wall. . . .

A fly ball or a ball bouncing once or twice before it hit the wall . . . never seemed to go in the same way twice, and it used to give enemy outfielders fits as Dodger runners would fly around the bases. Furillo, though, knew the wall like the back of his hand. He was always in the right place to pick that ball up. So he nailed more runners going into second and third base, because he had a terrific arm.

Furillo himself described how he learned to play the wall. A man who did not like to give interviews, who prided himself on hard-nosed but quiet play that occasionally erupted into fighting or, in later years, into a more muffled sort of bitterness against those he felt had either betrayed him or undervalued his career, Furillo's memories of the wall are almost an epitaph to a career and to an era:

I worked at [playing the wall]. I'd be out early and study it. Players would go out there and hit fungoes with me. When the ball came out, you had to imagine where it was going. Will it hit above the cement and hit the screen? Then you run like hell toward the wall, because it's gonna drop dead. Will it hit the cement? Then you gotta run like hell to the infield because its gonna come shooting out. I can't even tell you if it's gonna hit the scoreboard. The angles were crazy. I had to work. I studied every angle of that fucking wall. I'd take that sight line and know just where it would go. I worked, that's how I learned it.

Kaline had no walls to learn like Ebbets Field—but he had to learn those in Shibe Park, Comiskey Park, Griffith Stadium, Fenway, Sportsman's Park, Memorial Stadium, Yankee Stadium, and, for half of his team's games, Tiger Stadium, with its steep overhang in right, its cement walls and raised hard-wire screens.

None of those walls were easy, no matter the angles of balls coming off them, because all of them were cement and Kaline happened to be a wallbanger. Playing in the days before warning tracks, padding, or collapsible barrier frames, Kaline had, in addition to learning the fine points of wall play, a more fundamental educational challenge: survival. He could have learned to pull up shy of walls as many outfielders did, to surrender close or borderline plays to a ricochet rather than a crash. But his game would not permit it.

"The toughest play for me, always," says Kaline, who managed to avoid a serious run-in with a wall for twenty-two years, "was timing the ball with the wall. Would you get there in the air or get there and stop? Because the walls were concrete in those days, you had to know what you were doing. It hurt when you hit those walls. I was a wallbanger all right—I used to bang up my knees a lot—but I worked at what I did. I learned to go in softly. I deliberately tried to relax when I went into walls so I wouldn't be stiff and wind up breaking an elbow or something—and that was hard to do when you approached a wall full speed. Till warning tracks came in, all you could do was peek. You knew where the ball was going—sort of—and you peeked to see how close you were to the wall as you approached it."

Kaline could catch a ball well enough and had the kind of strong throwing arm that would have enabled him to cover a multitude of mistakes in right field. But he had an even stronger sense of his position, so he worked at those areas of his game—like going into walls—that he felt were his weakest.

"I studied the game, studied techniques," Kaline says. "I did it from the time I was a kid and I kept it up." In the big leagues, he learned pitchers and hitters till he knew them in his sleep. He learned the walls in Tiger Stadium and elsewhere not because he was a tough guy but so he could play them. If you misjudged a ball off a wall at Tiger Stadium, the ball would kick all the way back toward the infield, so the ability to move back from the wall was as important as the willingness to go into it full tilt.

Kaline was one of the first right fielders to perfect the right-handed spinning move coming out of the corner. The base denied was a potential run denied, the runner held at first was a potential double play, the accurate throw to a cutoff man was better than the big throw that missed him—and missed the possibility of cutting down a runner.

Kaline was a great defensive right fielder for the same reason Carl Furillo was—his natural gifts became an extension of his thinking. He was just as likely to throw behind an unsuspecting runner as ahead to try to catch a runner he had no chance for. Similarly, where other right fielders might more reasonably have thrown to second on a single to right with a runner coming around to score from second, he might risk surrendering an extra base to catch the runner at the plate. Each situation in a game carried its own inner set of instructions, and being able to perceive and execute them quickly were what the position was all about.

"The point was that I practiced the way I played," Kaline said, "even in spring training. I always played games with myself. For instance, the way you charge a ball really matters. You have to get there quickly; your footwork has to be precise so you get a throw off taking one or two, not four or five steps. You have to do it right and then you have to repeat it over and over again. But repeat what? You repeat what you do in a game, not what you do in practice. You can't practice in one way and then expect to do it differently in a game, so you do it right all the time."

This approach to practice was something Dwight Evans, early in his career, saw and admired in Kaline, who in turn has since seen and admired it in Evans, the best right fielder playing, in Kaline's opinion. But game-high practice is the hardest of all things to teach, Kaline believes, because of the intense concentration and effort required and then for more subtle reasons. "A lot of guys shy away from it because they think they'll get tagged as hot dogs or showboats, never realizing that what it's all about is doing things right. Who cares what people think," Kaline says,

apparently innocent of scouts or third-base coaches on other teams, "so long as you do it right?"

AMONG PEOPLE in the game, the consensus is that no one ever played right field better than Roberto Clemente. Clemente won sixteen Gold Gloves, led the league five times in assists, wound up with a lifetime .317 batting average, and earned almost immediate election to the Hall of Fame following his death in a plane crash in 1972 while taking part in a relief effort for earthquake victims in Nicaragua.

Clemente's natural gifts were extraordinary. He simply startled scouts with his running and throwing ability. Jim Kaplan recalled the now legendary story of how Al Campanis, then a scout for the Brooklyn Dodgers, saw Clemente at a tryout in Puerto Rico. Campanis had seventy-two hopefuls in camp and, following formal routine, first had the players practice throwing. Clemente uncorked a throw from center field all the way to the plate that Campanis simply did not believe. "*¡Uno más!*" he said. Clemente repeated the throw exactly. Then Campanis had the young players run 60-yard dashes. Clemente, in full uniform, ran his in 6.4 seconds. "*¡Uno más!*" spluttered Campanis. One more time: 6.4, over and out.

Clemente, though, was never content with his own ability. He had a routine for everything. For throwing accuracy, he had a basket set up at second base in practice and would try to wing balls into them from every point in his position; at each park, he had coaches hit balls off every angle, hook, overhang, and crevice in every wall he might have to contend with in a game.

Clemente made errors pushing himself to the limit. Through much of his career, his fielding average lagged as he regularly committed in excess of ten errors per season. But he made plays no one else did. He practically perfected the sliding catch, unseen in the game since the time of Harry Hooper, for a new generation of Astroturf outfielders.

Clemente spun out of the corner so dramatically, and with

such good results, others copied him. He went for balls off walls, screens, and scoreboards as no one else did.

Darrell Mack of the UPI led his June 6, 1971, game story with this:

> Roberto Clemente of the Pittsburgh Pirates made the greatest catch in the history of the Astrodome and as good a catch as he ever made in his 17-year career to save Steve Blass' 3–0 shutout over the Houston Astros Tuesday night.

Actually, Clemente made two amazing catches in that game —both in the same inning. With the Pirates leading 1–0 in the eighth inning, one out, and the Astros' Joe Morgan on first, César Cedeño hit a low line drive to right that Clemente lost in the lights. He charged the ball, became blinded, slid, sighted the ball again, *then* put out his glove and caught it—one, possibly two runs saved. The second catch followed immediately:

> Then Clemente was playing in the same spot in medium deep right center when Bob Watson cracked a liner toward the right field corner. Most right fielders would have played it off the wall and Morgan would have scored the tying run, but the 36-year-old Clemente took off after the ball.
>
> He caught up with it at the wall, leaped high and caught it as he crashed into the boards at full speed. He said it was above the yellow home run line which runs across the wall 10 feet above the ground. A homer would have put Houston ahead 2–1.

The catch was so spectacular everyone was talking about it afterward. The Astros' manager, Harry Walker, who had been in the game for thirty-four years, and a coach, Buddy Hancken, who had been around longer than that, both said it was the greatest catch they had ever seen. But Bill Mazeroski, a teammate, remembered one better: a catch Clemente made off Willie Mays, going full tilt into the right-center-field wall at Forbes Field. That catch,

which preserved a 1–0 victory for the Pirates, cost Clemente seven stitches in his chest.

Clemente, who was regularly battered in his encounters with walls, was battered after this catch. The UPI man reported that the Pirates star had suffered cuts on his left hip and knee and that "his left ankle and elbow were in packs of ice as a result of the collision with the Dome wall." But it was Clemente himself who put it in perspective.

"A great catch is one that saves a game," he said. "It's just like a home run. It doesn't make any difference if it's a short one or a long one if it wins a game."

In everything he did, Clemente's sense of the game came first. It is hard to appreciate when balanced against the kind of spectacular and risky athleticism he brought to his position, but for anyone who knew him it was this intelligence that distinguished his game.

Bill Virdon, who has been a coach and a manager as well as a player, played alongside Clemente for ten years in the old, gnarled parks. "There was never anybody better at his position than Clemente," he says. "In my tenure playing, managing, watching, he was simply the best in the business, not only because he could catch a ball better than anyone—which he could—or because his arm was so strong, but in every phase of play. He did everything exceptionally well and then his judgment was even better than that. He always threw to the right base, he was always where he was supposed to be, backing up, taking balls off the most difficult fences. His arm was powerful but it was also deadly accurate. Nobody ran on him and when they did run it was from ignorance, not knowledge. Usually, the ones who tried him were the young guys or the guys who were just coming into the league— the rest of the league simply didn't run on him.

"He knew the outfields he played in, he knew the hitters and pitchers, what was going on in a game perfectly. He came in on a ball, went back to the wall, always knowing what he was doing. Once, in the 1960 World Series, because of the noise of the

crowd, we ran together on a fly ball—but in ten years of playing with him, there was never a problem of who should catch a ball. . . . In that whole time, we never collided or lost a ball in confusion."

RIGHT FIELDERS today are better because of Clemente. He was the one player, like Ozzie Smith at short, who simply changed things. And change there was—as profound as that which occurred between 1909 and 1923. From the time Clemente began playing, in the early 1950s, until his last game in 1972, wrecking crews took down seven old ballparks, while builders, seemingly stuck with a single giant cookie cutter, erected twelve new stadiums, eight of them in the National League and five of those with Astroturf. What this produced, among other things, was yet another upheaval in right field. With larger outfields and faster playing surfaces, it was as though athletes were asked to combine running skills suited to open spaces with throwing skills matched to short fields: speed to give all-out pursuit in the far ranges of the field, throwing power to catch runners trying for that extra base. Clemente, who would have been exemplary in any era, was a model for our own.

Ruben Sierra, the young right fielder for the Texas Rangers, happens to be from Puerto Rico, but it is his hitting combined with an unusually aggressive outfield style that evokes memories of Clemente. Bill Mazeroski's *Baseball Annual* for 1988 called Sierra the second-best athlete in the league behind Dave Winfield.

"Sierra is a consistent RBI guy," said Maz's scouting report a year before he won his first RBI title. "[He] does a good job running the bases, and closes on the ball in right as well as any outfielder in the league. His arm is outstanding. The Rangers' precocious Ruben Sierra [is] one of the most exciting players to come along in years."

What is really interesting in this early view of Sierra is that it actually puts a gloss on his fielding skills. Far from having the arm of a Clemente, Kaline, or Furillo, he is one of the many new-

breed right fielders adept at making that crucial first-to-third play with only limited arm strength. Rangers manager Bobby Valentine admits Sierra's arm is only average and Sierra himself says his throwing ability comes from the way he attacks a ball rather than from what he puts behind his throw. He is athletic—and intelligent.

As a teenager, Sierra was tutored in the fine art of right by Rangers scout Luis Rosa. "I learned many things from him," Sierra says, "but first was how to be smart. Balls come off the wall different ways. You have to learn how—the way the ball comes off the bat tells you where it's going, the spin it has on it, do you go back, do you charge? You must know all this so you can be aggressive enough to make the right play."

For Sierra, the big problem was learning how to charge a ball so well that he could compensate for his lack of throwing power. If he got to a ball fast enough and released it quickly enough, he could do what stronger-armed but less aggressive right fielders could not: take away the extra base. By getting to a hit quickly and then by crow-hopping into his throw with no wasted steps, he was able to cut down the time it took to get the ball from the outfield to the far bases. If he threw on a low line, his throw *looked* like it had carry to it—even when it didn't. In his first full season in the majors, he was a co-leader in outfield assists with Jesse Barfield, perhaps the strongest-throwing right fielder in the game. So he left opponents and scouts alike with the impression that his arm was stronger than it actually was.

Tony Gwynn's birthright included an even less-than-average throwing arm. When he began his professional career, he was barely able to reach the edge of the infield on a throw from the outfield.

Gwynn, of course, has been one of the game's great hitters, and so whatever deficiencies he brought with him to the field might seem beside the point. The cliché holds true: Hit .350 and they will find a place for you. But Gwynn is a different sort of player. Over time, he has, almost *because* of his deficiencies, become as exemplary in right field as at bat.

Until he was a pro, he says, he never paid much attention to defense. The joy of the game for him was hitting. And hit he could, like no other schoolboy in the state of California. He also was a standout high school and college basketball player, which suggests that his hand-eye coordination was excellent and also that his arrival for spring baseball practice, with its emphasis on fundamentals, was inevitably delayed.

When he signed a pro contract with the Padres in 1981, he was—because he was fast and a place had to be found for him—assigned to center field. There were two kickers in this first job. The first was that Dave Winfield, the Padres' All-Star right fielder, had jumped to the Yankees, scrambling the team's right-field picture; the other more immediate problem was that Gwynn, by his own admission, felt lost in the field. Though he was fast, he was unable to go back on fly balls very well. He got a slow jump, and he seemed to track trajectories improperly, drifting rather than pursuing balls to a spot, miscalculating angles when he moved into the gaps. Above all, he could not throw, could barely reach second base, no less home or third on a peg from medium outfield depth.

But in his first year in the minors, Gwynn hit .331, and was immediately moved up in class, where he hit .462 through a portion of one season before being called up to the Padres at the end of the '82 season. If Gwynn had signed with an American League team, chances are he would have been a designated hitter. The Padres, having to play him, gave him the phantom's spot in left field.

From day one as a professional, Gwynn was determined to acquire the defensive game he didn't have. He spent hours strengthening his arm with long-toss exercises, improved his outfield tracking and his sense of angles on balls, and took endless numbers of fly balls and grounders. He studied hitters, memorizing their habits till he knew them as well as his own, and he watched his pitchers as if he were their catcher. And then, his world was turned upside down.

Sixto Lezcano, the outfielder the Padres had acquired to re-

place Dave Winfield in right, did not work out. Toward the end of the 1983 season, he was suddenly dealt to Philadelphia, and Gwynn was switched to right field.

"When they put me in right in '83," Gwynn says, "I knew I was in for real trouble. I had never spent a day in right field in my life. For me it was like, 'Look, I was a left fielder—that was what I was supposed to do, that was what I was used to.' "

Gwynn had no confidence as a right fielder. Though he was left-handed and did not have to spin out of the corner, the play there—supposedly easier for a lefty—of reaching across his body with his gloved hand, planting, and throwing was tougher. The angles were all different—and more difficult. And everyone, knowing the weakness of his arm and the tentativeness of his play, ran on him.

"People took all kinds of liberties with me," Gwynn said. "They'd go, they'd test me out, they'd dare me over and over again—and I couldn't answer them. After a while," he added, "you just get tired of it."

Gwynn went to winter ball that year. "My goal," he said, "was to work on all the things I felt deficient in." Everything he had learned about hitters, situations, angles, tracking, he had to learn anew. And even all that was only marginal compared to what he had never had to face in left field: that long throw.

Gwynn could not get a new arm from the gods, but he learned how to play what Dwight Evans called a chess game. Gwynn's single objective was to do with other means what arm strength would not permit. Everything went into cutting down the time it took to make the different plays from right. To overcome the time it took to make the cross-handed catch going to his left followed by the plant and throw, Gwynn learned to slide. He did this by having a fungo coach hit enough balls to him till he got it —till he could slide, catch, and come up throwing, seemingly in a single motion.

In right field, he was unable to compensate for his weak throwing as he had in left, where he had been able to "cheat" in

to a shallower position. The standard in left had been to move in, charge, and make a quick pickup and throw. But in right, especially with men on, cheating was just too risky. With little chance to cheat in, the charge of a right fielder was thus longer and more difficult.

Any outfielder knows that the final steps in charging a ball are slowed so that the pickup can actually be made. Otherwise the fielder may overrun the ball or, even if he picks it up, will take wasted steps before throwing.

Gwynn had practiced charging from his first days in the minors. But as a right fielder, he added a wrinkle: He taught himself to charge full speed right into the throw.

"It took awhile for that to come," he says. Because of the risk, he could not do it on every play. He had to know the parks he played in perfectly so he could pick his moments. In places like Shea Stadium, where the grass is high, the ball would catch and slow without danger of a bad hop. It was different on a turf field or in Los Angeles, where the grass is shorter and finer-textured and the ground harder.

"Eventually I got the hang of it, and once I did . . . things began to fall into place. What I was able to do then," Gwynn said, "was to challenge back." This hard-won ability changed the way Gwynn—and others—thought about his play in right field. It gave him a certain power not only in throwing but in getting into the minds of his opponents.

"I don't know when it first happened, but I know it happens now," Gwynn says. "Guy'll be on first, a ball will be hit through the right side—maybe not so hard—and I'll have gotten not the best jump on the ball, I'll charge thinking, 'Oh, well, now they've got first and third,' I'll pick the ball up, and the runner will be standing there at second looking out at me. He won't have made the move. I can't tell you how good that makes me feel. That's my payoff, because nobody ever had a clue I had that in me."

To anyone not familiar with Gwynn as a right fielder, his physical skills as a defender seem simply natural. But everything

about his game has evolved with time. He made a play in 1984, the year the Padres won the pennant, that people in San Diego still talk about. In a game against the Atlanta Braves that the Padres eventually won 7–6 in extra innings, Gwynn kept his team close with a play he made earlier in the game. On a line drive hit to the right-center-field wall by Brad Komminsk with a runner, speedy Albert Hall, on first, Gwynn, racing at full speed, made an extended, leaping catch against the wall and then, almost in the same motion, made a 360-degree clockwise spin and threw on one bounce to *first base* to get a double play. Gwynn's thinking was as brilliant as his catch. And it was emblematic of an accomplishment he says he values more than his hitting. Three times in the last five years, he has won Gold Gloves in right. "They mean more to me than all of the batting titles and silver bats I've ever won," he says.

Right fielders with big arms, of course, have the opportunity to play the mind game better than anyone. And for years, players like Jesse Barfield, Dave Winfield, Andre Dawson, and Dwight Evans—the game's top guns—have been formidable and intimidating from their corner positions, so much so that it is almost possible to forget that it's the way they *use* what they have that makes them quite so formidable.

Jesse Barfield, like Andre Dawson, was a center fielder before he was a right fielder, and still occasionally plays center. The word Barfield uses to describe center field is "fun," the word for right, never having consulted Tony Gwynn, is "challenge."

"In right field," Barfield says, "what you know is that everyone is going to run on you; the plays you are most often faced with will be challenges to your arm which you just have to answer."

But possessing a late-model howitzer is only incidentally what Barfield's game is all about. He says he learned to be an outfielder under the tutelage of Blue Jays executive Bobby Mattick, one of the game's severest sticklers for fundamentals. During Barfield's first instructional-league season with Toronto in 1977, Mattick

was simply relentless in what he wanted from Barfield. "He worked with me on ground balls, fly balls, throwing to bases, throwing to cutoff men, going left, going right—repetition, repetition, repetition—till I thought I couldn't stand it anymore," Jesse said. "And then I began to enjoy it. All of those chores turned into habits covering a multitude of plays I no longer had to think about. They became part of my routine."

The routine for Barfield to this day is little changed. Like Al Kaline, Dwight Evans, and Tony Gwynn, he is all business in practice. Stadiums may be more uniform today than they used to be, but he goes out early to measure his space. In Kansas City, for example, he makes an inspection of the right-field corner each time he visits.

"A ball going into the corner in Kansas City can kick all the way around to left field if you don't know how to play it," he says. The problem of playing the Kansas City corner is compounded by a four-inch wooden obstruction that juts out deep along the right-field line. If the ball kicks off the wood, it can ricochet unpredictably. The playing method, the practice method, Barfield says, is "getting back to the wall completely relaxed and reactive—like an infielder." Like a left fielder in Fenway Park.

"One of the first times I played Fenway, I went for a ball along the right-field line, but because the stands are so close there, I just stopped. The ball fell in. It was totally embarrassing. I just didn't have enough concentration," Barfield says. Concentration is the key: in Minnesota, with its plastic Glad-bag-style right-field wall; in California, with its collapsible canvas barriers; in Yankee Stadium, with its closer corner. Ground balls move along each turf outfield according to its own carpet, through grass according to its own peculiar cut. "On some fields, the ball gets to you slower; on other fields the ball actually snakes through the grass," says Barfield. "You need to pay attention to all of that because any time, things as small as that can mean the difference."

Over the years, Barfield has learned to make the right-handed counterclockwise spin and throw from the corner a specialty. He

knows that other outfielders, like José Canseco, have a hard time
with the move because it is difficult to pick up a target when
coming out of a full, rapid spin. Al Kaline learned to do it by
pretending second base was a basketball hoop that he had to hit
coming out of the move. Barfield has relied on the momentum of
the spin itself to be the launching mechanism for the throw. But
all of this is utterly dependent on being able to make exactly the
right play. With George Brett the hitter, Willie Wilson the runner
on first in the middle innings of a close game, the spin will target
a throw to second to hold Brett at first. But in another situation
—later in the game, still close, with Brett on first and Bob Boone
hitting—the throw would be launched to third, aimed at the face
of the cutoff man, directly in line with third base. The throw
coming out of that spin would be different—as would a throw
out of the corner to the plate—different sight lines, different
targets, different throws.

Andre Dawson and Dave Winfield also have patented their
moves out of the corner. Dawson often will elect not to spin, not
because he wants to avoid the move but because he has learned
to shorten it so that his throw is made coming out with a single
step, almost flat-footed, with his body already turned at an angle
as he reaches for the ball with his feet nearly planted.

Winfield says the problem of picking up a target out of a spin
is tricky but is overcome by making sure you set your eye on a
fixed spot—not a basketball hoop in his case, but the base being
thrown to or the cutoff man, determined in advance.

Both Winfield and Dawson, perhaps because they are veterans
and refugees from other outfield positions, have come to appreciate what their gifts allow them in right.

Winfield is still remembered for a catch he made as a left
fielder in Yankee Stadium in 1981, when he put his spiked shoe
midway up the padded, ten-foot-high fence, propelling a six-foot-
six frame toward the third deck as he snared a home-run ball
struck by the Orioles' Doug DeCinces. But left was never a place
Winfield preferred. In Yankee Stadium, he says, the field is ugly

and misshapen and he somehow always wound up playing it out of position. And the throwing was limited and cramped—the big throw down the line to the plate came with the base runner's back obstructing him. "But right field is where you put your best guy," he says, "the guy who has the big arm, who keeps things honest, keeps the runner from advancing from first to third, where you can then score nine different ways."

Because third base is so critical for the offense, Winfield says, right field becomes that much more critical for the defense. "People are always trying to advance that runner from first, to get to third," he says, "which means that in right, the action is always going to come your way."

The throw home is easier in right, Winfield says, because the baseline can be used, without obstruction, "like a gunsight." But everything rests on being able to handle the critical first-to-third play, the play that demands the big arm he has.

Winfield says the biggest advantage he has is that people *don't* run on him. That is where something more than arm strength is involved. The key to his game is aggressiveness, something he learned early. "You watch every pitch in the game; you understand sequences, percentages, all those things," Winfield says. "You don't rely on your arm—you learn to take every advantage so you can make best use of your arm." Winfield's positioning is measured and precise so that his outfield setups are rarely extreme. Before a pitch, he will come to his hands-on-knees position facing toward the right-field line with one hitter, toward center field with another—in each case it is so he can get the best push-off toward the most likely direction he feels a ball will be hit. "I know how to cover right field," Winfield says, "which means I know how to make the big play."

Andre Dawson once nailed Steve Sax at home, throwing from the wall in dead center field in Montreal's Olympic Stadium. On another occasion, he took a carom bare-handed off the wall in deepest right center, whirled, and threw out another speedster, Ken Landreaux, at second. He had the arm to make plays like

these in center field, where he won four Gold Gloves, but he prefers to play right field, where he has won an additional four. "Center field was easier," Dawson says. "But right field is just dominant because you have to have a strong throwing arm and the ability—which only comes with work—to use it."

Perhaps because he had a sore arm one year, Dawson has learned to care for his arm as though it were a vital organ. "Not only couldn't I do the same things when my arm wasn't strong," he says, "but it was impossible to be as aggressive as I needed to be. My thinking out there changed."

Aggressiveness, for Dawson, as for Winfield, is the key to what he does in right. Positioning, knowing hitters, pitchers, wind, walls, and field surfaces all are part of it but the ability to make—or threaten to make—the big throws that stop or alter rallies is fundamental. And the throw, as Dawson makes clear, is only the end result of a trained intensity at his position.

Dawson visualizes balls when he chases them. He "breaks down" a play so that he can control his throw. He "attacks" a ball in two stages, he says: in his initial pursuit of it, then again after he has visualized its carom or place of descent and thus where he will throw from. "I want to think of every play I make in the field as a challenge—same as a three-and-two pitch when you're at bat with the game on the line. I don't know how to play right field any other way," Dawson says.

THOUGH INJURY forced him to spend much of 1989 as a designated hitter, Dwight Evans remains the game's senior right fielder. His arm, by his own admission, is not quite what it was when, in his early years, he threw with such force that if a ball was sent just inches over the head of a cutoff man it would continue on a plumb line right over the head of the baseman or catcher beyond. Evans never possessed great speed; in a way, he is a throwback to the days of Kaline, Furillo, even of the Babe. But no right fielder in the game since Clemente has played the position so long and so consistently well. He is an eight-time Gold Glove winner, a perennial All-Star, and, among chess play-

ers, the master. Whatever his age, speed, or strength of arm, no one has so systematically articulated what it is right fielders do.

From the earliest times he can remember, Evans says he always had a ball in his hands. As a schoolboy football player, he was a wide receiver—because, he says, he loved catching the ball. During baseball season, he always walked around with a glove and a ball, even when he was by himself. When he became a professional in 1969, he was still doing this—training himself how to transfer the ball properly from glove to hand before throwing it. The goal was to grab for seams so his outfield throw would be straighter and have the kind of backspin on it that would allow the ball to bounce up rather than skip or hug the ground when it hit. This is fundamental in outfield throwing but many outfielders have a hard time with it. "I've gotten to the point where I think I'm throwing cross-seamed ninety percent of the time," Evans says. "Catch the ball, take it out, catch the ball, take it out—you do it so many times it becomes second nature and you don't need to look for the seams anymore; it's like you train your hand to do its own thinking."

The advantage Evans has over other right fielders is not from his strong, accurate throwing alone, but because he *always* knows what to do with a baseball. "There is a purpose to every ball under the sun," he says.

Evans believes his game always hinged on his ability to anticipate correctly. "Anticipation is the biggest part of playing the outfield," he says. This seems like an easy enough generalization but not when the specifics of how outfielders anticipate are taken into account. Jesse Barfield, for example, prepares himself for every ball to be hit to him, keeping strict mental account of each hitter, pitcher, situation. Then he adds another touch: "I key off the catcher; I watch which way he's moving before I do," he says. "But then I have to disguise the way I'm going to move till the last second. They have guys in the bullpen, in the sky, looking to steal anything. I won't give them that. I cheat, but they won't cheat off me."

Evans also has an overwhelming desire to have every ball hit

to him. His touch, part yearning, part imagination, is a bit more rough-hewn than Barfield's: "I anticipate the worst that could happen and the best that could happen. I prepare for the worst and imagine the best," he says.

For Evans, correct anticipation means moving when he is in the field. "I want to move because I know what I'm doing," he says. Which means that he will be in motion—anywhere from five inches to fifteen feet—with every hitter and sometimes with every pitch. And, nearly always, his momentum, his "jump," toward a ball will be correct.

Evans has learned the mechanics of pursuit as well as anyone. On balls to the gap, he will break backward on an angle, try to circle the ball in order to be lined up, shoulder toward the target, for his throw. He measures walls so he always knows where he is before he goes back, and he will try, when he can, to move laterally along a barrier, gloved hand toward the field, so that he will be better prepared to throw and the ball won't jar loose if he makes hard contact with the wall. All of that became automatic long ago.

What he adds, going backward or coming in after the ball, is a special way of keeping his body in line when he moves from the catch to the throw. He does not catch a ball in an exactly upright position; when he can, he takes the ball in a semicrouch, slightly off to the side. It appears to be no more than a touch of style—like a one-handed catch—but it is something different.

By taking the ball at a lower plane, he then stays lower as he makes his throw, which allows him great driving power off his rear foot and far better control of his body—and the baseball—as he makes his weight shift forward.

Evans uses this low-to-the-ground, in-line movement in every situation he can. In his corner spin, he does not merely whirl 360 degrees and throw, but stays low to the ground, corkscrewing around as he comes into throwing position. When he charges, he makes his pickup, and then instead of coming upright, he drives forward as though he is a pitcher, powering himself off his rear foot in a long, low, fluid movement toward the target.

Actually, it is the pitching image that Evans has kept in mind as he has trained his body through the years to perform this in-line movement naturally.

Each spring training, for years, Evans has gone off with a bucket of baseballs to a far corner of the field. There, with no one looking, he places a line of balls across the grass and then spreads his legs apart, the left forward, the right far behind, over the first ball. Then, in slow motion—so his body can remember, he takes the ball, shifting his weight forward like a pitcher starting his windup, shifts his weight backward to his rear foot, then drives forward low to the ground into a throw, measuring every ripple of his weight shift, movement of his arm, release point, follow-through. He then moves on until he finishes the line of balls.

He extends these slow-motion exercises with a coach fungo-ing to him. He takes balls in the corner, in front of him, wherever he feels the need to work on the in-line throw. There is always fine-tuning that will extend what he can do. On grounders that he will have to charge, Evans prefers to field the ball not in front of the left foot but inside it. His throw will lose some power because the weight shift forward and back will be less extreme, but the release will be quicker and the throw more accurate, he says. On fly balls in front of him, he has taught himself, when wind and weather conditions are just right, to make his crowhop *as he is catching the ball*—not afterward, as every other outfielder who has ever played has done. The goal, always, is to reduce to second nature things that were not first nature to begin with but that, once committed to muscle memory, give him advantages over younger, faster players.

At thirty-eight, Evans may or may not be nearing the end of the line. No one in this age of Nautilus and Neptune keeps him-self in better shape, no one more sedulously studies every aspect of the game, looking so carefully at its machinery, for that extra inch, that one additional turn of the screw. But this man who is endlessly devoted to technique is in the end driven by something deeper. Growing up in California, home of the aerospace and make-believe industries, Evans's boyhood idol was Willie Mays,

who knew more about flying and dreaming than Howard Hughes. Evans is one of a few players today who wears the same uniform number, 24 (Rickey Henderson, Barry Bonds, and Ken Griffey, Jr., are others), and, like his illustrious predecessor, he has always known that the game he plays is powered, before anything else, by what is going on in his mind. He has, like Willie Mays, discovered the secret of inventing the space he occupies. Whether or not he ever plays another game in right field, he leaves that as a standard for the position.

CENTER FIELD

Just now he plays as center field
Sometimes as second base;
We all have proof that merry "Ruf"
Is worthy of the place.

① **ANDY VAN SLYKE** *of the Pirates circles under a fly ball. He's considered by many National Leaguers to be the best defensive center fielder in the game today.*
THE PITTSBURGH PIRATES

② **TRIS SPEAKER'S** *idea of playing shallow was to catch everything in front of him—including pickoff throws at second base. Among other things, Speaker made four unassisted double plays at second, including one in the 1912 World Series.*
UPI/BETTMANN NEWSPHOTOS

③ **KIRBY PUCKETT,** *one of the game's new $3 million men and heir to a tradition of dominant center fielders.*
THE MINNESOTA TWINS

④ **WILLIE MAYS** *and Bobby Bonds collide at the right-center-field fence in a 1970 game at Candlestick Park. Mays was nearly unconscious when he hit the ground afterward, but of course, he held on to the ball for the out.*

⑤ **JOE DIMAGGIO** *makes a trademark catch gliding into deep left-center field in the old Yankee Stadium.*
AP/WIDE WORLD PHOTOS

CHARLIE FOX, the old O.S.S. man who worked behind enemy lines in the war, crossed the border again to spend part of 1989 as a dugout coach for George Steinbrenner's Yankees. Less than a mile away, across the river in Manhattan, were a series of apartment buildings on the site of the Polo Grounds, where Fox had a seven-at-bat major league career and where he located his memories of Willie Mays.

Fox, who had remained in the Giants organization throughout most of Mays's career, managing him for a couple of years in San Francisco, began to explain one evening—as many others had—why the 1954 World Series catch was Mays's best. He stopped in mid-sentence.

"Well, there were others," he said. He mentioned the 1970 catch Mays made in Candlestick Park, crashing into Bobby Bonds three quarters of the way to the top of the chain-link barrier in right-center field. Then there was another, before Mays had ever gotten to the majors. In Jacksonville, playing for the Triple-A Minneapolis Millers, Mays made a play from left center:

"He was just a kid then but that was completely beside the point. Even then there was no one like him. There was a guy on third, one out, and the batter hits this shot to left center, I mean it was a screamer," Fox said. "Willie raced over—how he got even close to the ball I still can't figure—then he leaped, caught the ball bare-handed, came down, and threw—on the fly—to nail the runner trying to score."

Many people around the game, of course, have their Willie Mays stories, but the account of these three catches somehow illustrate perfectly both why Mays was arguably the best center

fielder ever and why center field itself matters quite so much in the defensive scheme of things.

Anyone who takes one of those old high school compasses and draws a circle with the center fielder in his position as the midpoint and the three catches as reference points on the circumference will be well on the way to understanding the importance of center field. Even allowing that it is Mays, not just anyone, who is the circle definer here, any arc roughly approximating the swing from deep left center to deep right center—with the center fielder as the median point—will show that the center fielder's area of coverage takes in one fourth to one half of the entire playing surface of the field! The reason Mays *had* to be among the best ever is also apparent in our geometry exercise: He controlled the ground he covered. He had the title; others had time shares.

What a center fielder is asked to do in an ideal sense is be everywhere and catch everything. He must be able to go back and in on balls equally well—not at all a given. Some very good center fielders, because they are unable to go back quite so well, wind up having to position themselves more deeply than fielders who can move both ways. For the fielder who is adroit going back but a step slow coming in, a more shallow set may be required. In addition, the center fielder has to move laterally. He cannot be slow or imprecise in this because he is responsible for too much ground. He must have his footwork down to second nature so that when he starts for the ball he doesn't have to think about making a crossover step—backward at an angle or forward at an angle—to get started. It must happen simply. Then, too, he must have the quick first steps cornermen have, and the speed to cover all that ground. That is the meaning of the word *range* when it is applied to center fielders. It is a generically different word than when applied anywhere else on the field.

Then there are a center fielder's hands. They must be as soft as an infielder's or as a wide receiver's, so he can make all those catches over his head, over his shoulders, over walls—and some-

times over other fielders. His timing must be perfect so he knows when and when not to leave his feet going for a ball; a miss in center can mean a triple or an inside-the-park home run.

Though he doesn't have to regularly make throws as long as the right fielder's first-to-third throw, the center fielder nevertheless has long throws to make. His first-to-third throw, though a bit shorter, may be more difficult than the right fielder's because when it is made from the right-field side, it is often done (if the thrower is right-handed) with a full spin; if the throw is made from the left-side gap, the ball must be backhanded, momentum brought to a stop, the feet set so that a controlled throw, with something on it, can be made.

The other standard long throw is home—straight over the mound (which can be an obstruction causing the ball to kick to the side if the cutoff man decides to let the throw go through). Even with cutoff help, the throw home can often be the deepest, most difficult made anywhere on the field. It is infrequently made with success from real depth, but when it is—when Willie Mays or Joe D. or Kirby Puckett is the thrower—there is no more exciting play in baseball.

Excitement is a byword of the position because so much happens there, so much that is either spectacular or decisive. Center fielders don't have the wall play of the cornermen but when they do confront walls, the results can be spectacular, sometimes terrible, and sometimes both—as in the case of Pete Reiser, the extraordinarily gifted center fielder for the Dodgers. For those who may not remember, one of Reiser's many collisions with a center-field wall effectively destroyed a career of almost limitless promise.

In a June 1947 game at Ebbets Field against the Pirates, a light-hitting, part-time outfielder named Cully Rikard hit a tremendous drive to almost straightaway center field, far beyond Reiser, who had been playing shallow. Reiser, as only a great outfielder would have, completely turned his back on the ball and sprinted toward the point where he knew he had to make his

catch. The concrete walls in Ebbets Field had been moved in almost forty feet during the war years, when Reiser was in the military. He had apparently remembered the old rather than the new dimensions because he ran straight into the wall without breaking stride, thinking he had an easy catch. The impact, which was literally heard throughout the stadium, knocked him unconscious for ten days. Never mind that when medical personnel, teammates, and umpires rushed to his crumpled form on the field, they found him still clutching the baseball; he was lucky to be alive.

Because of the space they cover, because they are literally in the middle of things, because so much action comes their way, center fielders are generals in the outfield: As they move, so the other outfielders move; they are principally responsible for outfield communication—they have right-of-way on catches to their left and right, forward and back, with their cornermen, and in front of them with any of their infielders.

On balls retrieved in the power alleys by the cornermen, the center fielder invariably becomes a director. He takes a position several feet behind the other outfielder, whose back is to the infield, and tells him where his throw should go. It is the center fielder, in those situations, who determines whether a throw will be made directly to a base or to a cutoff man. He is the seeing eye and often the brains of the play.

Sometimes, depending on his aggressiveness—and his voice —a center fielder with strong ability to communicate can greatly aid his cornermen in pursuit of balls off the bat. "In the corners you can mistake a ball that's been fouled off for a ball that's coming your way," says Dwight Evans. "A center fielder who communicates well just by telling you, 'Back! Back!' or 'In! In!' can mean the difference between plays made or not made."

This ability to communicate is not a given. Some center fielders don't have it or are reluctant to use it. Joe DiMaggio, as much a loner as a legend, apparently kept to himself even when he was playing center field. "Joe was a little rough to play with," remem-

bered Charlie Keller, "because he was just so quiet. He didn't call for the ball very loud when he wanted it." Fred Lynn, Evans's center fielder for many years, was an excellent communicator, but had, Evans says, "a very light, thin voice which you couldn't hear more than twenty feet away."

A center fielder's backup responsibilities guarantee that he will be everywhere in the course of a game. Alone among the outfielders, he backs up two outfield positions; he covers the short field on any throw to second from the catcher or pitcher; when there are runners on first or second or the bases are loaded, he routinely has double coverage on any ordinary hit to right—first backing up the right fielder, then doubling back to be in position for any overthrow at second base. Even if he goes through an entire game without a ball coming his way, the center fielder will have gotten in more running than the average daily jogger and, with all the quick stops and starts, at considerable more peril to his legs. Any center fielder can recall this or that muscle pull or residue of soreness that came as the result of simple backup coverage when nothing seemed to be at stake and no one was looking. And unlike that enjoyed by a casual jogger, all of the running done by a center fielder is strategic—fundamental and critical.

With such a job description, it is small wonder that center field has long been the game's most illustrious position. The dreams of young players always seem to involve center field. A generation of young people growing up imitated Joe DiMaggio —his wide stance at home plate, his equally distinctive manner of loping (hopefully with great grace) after fly balls. Later, kids imitated Willie Mays, Mickey, or the Duke, and if those boosting others have it right, who knows but that on the sandlots today they are imitating Kirby Puckett. A recent edition of the *Minneapolis Review of Baseball* carried this echo of T. S. Eliot:

> *In the dome the people come and go*
> *Talking no more of Joe DiMaggio*
> *But only of Kirby Puckett and his glove*

Center field is an important place and players who are aware of important positions think about it. José Canseco, who has played left, then right, where he had an MVP season in 1988, wants to move on to center because, for him, that is the summit position.

"One day, hopefully, I will be the center fielder of my team," he says. "Of all the outfield positions, it is the one where you should have everything. Center field has a lot more command and a lot more open space. It's four hundred feet and more in center field, three hundred and thirty down the lines. Balls come back at you from the walls in the corner but not really in center. I have the arm and the speed. Center fielders basically will have a better concept of the game because they see so much more. They are the center of things. You must have athletic ability, more of the skills—and then I think a center fielder should hit home runs. That is where I want to be."

As does Bo Jackson, the heir apparent to the center-field job in Kansas City.

Initially, center fielders were not quite so prominent. During the early, slow-pitch years of the game, when most of the action was around toward left, center fielders were usually second leads in the outfield. But Chadwick observed something in the position that survived slow pitching: "The Center Fielder should always be in readiness to back up the second base, and should only go to long field in cases where a hard hitter is at the bat." In other words, center fielders were to play shallow—an easy enough call when balls were not hit for great distances but significant nevertheless because it placed center fielders in the middle of things, behind second base, assigned to work plays involving both infield and outfield.

Center fielders gained stature early. Jim Fogarty, who played for two Philadelphia teams between 1881 and 1890, was known to area fans, said Spink in 1911, "as the greatest outfielder that ever lived." Paul Hines, another outstanding center fielder, was even more impressive to Spink. And Bill Lange, center fielder for

the Chicago White Stockings, was swift, daring, and spectacular enough through his career in the 1890s to get mythmakers working overtime. Lange was involved in one of the game's great catches—or tall tales. Lange, so went a story that appeared in 1903, made a game-saving catch, preserving an eleventh-inning 6–5 Chicago win over Washington. With two out and a man on, a Washington batter whacked a long, high liner to center. "Lange charged from out of nowhere," wrote baseball historian Arthur Ahrens, repeating the 1903 account in an attempt to set the stage for an investigation of what actually happened, "dived, somersaulted, and crashed through the fence. Moments later, he emerged from the splinters, ball in hand, to save the game for Chicago." Ahrens believed the catch never took place, that it was most probably a work of imagination stitched together from disparate yarns involving Lange. But the point is that Lange, a completely forgotten player now, was a dominant player then. The superlatives and the myths went with what he accomplished, apparently in routine fashion. When Alfred Spink wrote about Tris Speaker, he compared him with Lange:

> Speaker is considered by many the greatest of the present-day center fielders, and though past baseball age, there never has been but one man who was his superior. Lange, the famous outfielder of Anson's White Stockings, was a greater player . . .
> Lange excelled him in height and reach; equalled him in speed; hit harder and was infinitely a better man on the bases. This is no criticism of Speaker . . .

Perhaps not, but what is astonishing about his opinion is that it was offered when Speaker was in his prime. No player, before or since—including Lange, Joe D., Willie, Mickey, or the Duke, ever dominated his position as clearly as Speaker did.

From all accounts, though he was only five feet eleven and 180 pounds, Speaker was a physically impressive man.

"He has the rough complexion of one who has spent most of his life in the open air," wrote Spink.

He has heavy, buddy, bloodshot eyes, not the kind one would imagine could pick out a good ball and paste it to the far corner of the field, or could start after the ball at the crack and judge to an inch where that ball is going to land.

He has a voice like rumbling thunder, and his softest words sound like the growl of a mastiff. He has large, powerful hands, freckled.

Speaker's athletic ability, however, was even more impressive. He could run, hit, and throw. "Speaker's tremendous speed and his beautiful judgment on fly balls, his perfect sense of direction and his ability to throw make him the best fielding center fielder in the game," wrote Spink, adding, "he can hit, bunt, push and poke."

What may not have been apparent in 1911 but became clear after Speaker finished playing in 1928 is that he single-handedly revolutionized center field. He was the first true superstar there, and because of that he set a standard that may still be unsurpassed. The first big hitter at the position, he finished his twenty-two-year career with a lifetime .344 average (only six players have done better) and still ranks first in doubles, sixth in triples, fifth in hits, and eighth in runs scored. And while he was not a power hitter as we understand the term, he did lead the American League in homers once (ten in 1912) and RBIs once (130 in 1923), and his career totals for both remain eminently respectable (117 career homers, 1,559 RBIs). But it was as a fielder that Speaker is most remembered—and for good reason. He did things that seem, without any need for embellishment, the stuff of legends and tall tales.

Speaker played a shallow center field, considerably shallower than modern center fielders like Paul Blair and Curt Flood, who were both noted for it. Speaker often took his set twenty to thirty feet from second base and moved toward the base on many plays. He had his imitators then—playing shallow in the dead-ball era was not that uncommon. A contemporary of Speaker's, Clyde Milan, played in—but not ever in the way Speaker did. From in

close, Speaker was actually an additional infielder. He sometimes was able to sneak in behind base runners to take pickoff throws from the catcher or pitcher; on occasion, he threw runners out at first and sometimes was actually the pivotman on double plays. In his career, he made four unassisted double plays at second base, including one in the 1912 World Series, the only such play in Series history. And then, he was able to go back on a ball, as far as the field went, to take outfield flies. Babe Ruth, a Red Sox teammate of Speaker's, remembered him years later, as only a pitcher could. In his autobiography, *The Babe Ruth Story,* he wrote:

> Spoke was something extra special. Only those who played with or against him really appreciated what a great player he was.
> In my Red Sox pitching days I would hear the crack of the bat and say, 'There goes the ball game.' But Tris would turn his back to the plate, race far out to the fences and at the last moment make a diving catch. Not once but a thousand times.
> He was more than a great outfielder; he actually was a fifth infielder. Tris would play close and get many balls in short center or right field and occasionally throw a runner out at first. Maybe with the present lively ball Tris couldn't play that way. But he could still go out for them, and with the modern ball his great hitting would be much greater.

Actually, Speaker did play well into the era of the lively ball —and he continued, with some adjustment, to start from an extremely shallow set. Because his career divides so neatly between the dead- and rabbit-ball eras, his fielding numbers for seven years on each side of the 1920 divide are unusually intriguing. In this one instance, stats show—as fielding numbers, generally so risky, do not—the kind of fielder he was:

YEAR	PO	A	TC/G	DP	E	PCT.
1913	374*	30*	3.1*	7	25*	.942
1914	423*	29	3.0*	12*	15	.968
1915	378*	21	2.7	8*	10	.975
1916	359	25	2.6	10	10	.978
1917	365	23	2.8	5	8	.980
1918	352	15	3.0*	6	10	.973
1919	375*	25	3.0*	6	7	.983
1920	363	24	2.7	8	9	.977
1921	345	15	2.9	2	6	.984*
1922	285	13	2.8	6	5	.983*
1923	369	26	2.7	7	13	.968
1924	323	20	2.8	3	13	.963
1925	311	16	3.1	9	11	.967
1926	394	20	2.8	8	8	.981
1927	278	12	2.5	5	10	.967

* led league

The most obvious feature of this chart is that all of Speaker's league-leading figures—with the exception of fielding percentage—occurred before 1920. Clearly, the dead-ball era provided him with better opportunities playing in close (which included greater opportunity to commit errors; a large number of Speaker's errors came on bad-hop ground balls from in close). But the numbers after 1920 show that Speaker adapted himself to the new game with brilliance. He could not play in as regularly as he did, but it was enough to pile up impressive double-play numbers (he is the all-time leader), as well as those for putouts, assists, and total chances per game (he is among career leaders in all of those categories). To keep some perspective on just what he accomplished after 1920: His 1926 figure on starting double plays—8 —was twice that of any 1988 major league outfielder. Only two outfielders in the National League, Brett Butler and Andy Van

Slyke, and one in the American, Joe Carter, all playing more games, had more putouts than Speaker did in 1926. Speaker was able to adapt because he had the ability, but even more important was that he had—to use José Canseco's words—a better concept of the game in center. Speaker, from the start, had a director's sense—perhaps a bank director's sense of cost-effectiveness—of what was possible in center field. For Speaker, who actually studied to be a banker before he discovered that it might be more profitable to play baseball, it all began with this daringly shallow set.

"I have found in my experience," he said in a 1917 interview, "that not over one in six of the balls that are driven to the outfield go beyond the fielder. The rest strike in front of him. Most fielders seem afraid to play close for fear that the batter will get at least an extra base on a long hit because they were not back there to handle it. This is true. But baseball is a game of risks, and I have found it best to be on hand for the short hits and to take a chance on the long ones."

Speaker was no doubt able to "take a chance on the long ones" because he had such great athletic ability. But it was his sense of the game, his concept of what he could do from his position that made what he did even more daring than cost-effective.

Writing in *Baseball Magazine* in 1917, F. C. Lane described an ordinary game of Speaker's. It is a rare look, decades before videotape, of a great center fielder in action:

> Throughout most of this contest Speaker played well in behind second base. He crossed that intangible border line which separates the infield from the out, and took upon himself much more of the duties which properly pertain to both. The Cleveland pitcher passed a fast base runner. The runner, gaining a long lead, tore madly for second base. The catcher in his eagerness to make a quick throw butterfingered the ball and then threw wild to second. The runner was nearly to second when the throw was made. The second baseman lunged wildly for the ball but couldn't reach it. Speaker sprinting deftly from his position in the near outfield, caught it on the first

bounce and held the runner easily at second base. With an ordinary outfielder the runner . . . would have dashed for third. . . . Had he done so he would have scored, for the next man reached first on an atrocious error. Later in the game with a man on third, Speaker had to run far back for a long fly. But he caught it and threw fast and true . . . straight into the waiting catcher's hand for a put out of the runner who was trying to make home on the play. Still later in the game, a batter hit far out to center field. Speaker had to run back to well nigh the limits of his own skill to head off the ball. It was a tremendously long single. The runner itched to make second on the play. Perhaps he might have done so. But he didn't dare.

This was hardly more than a fair day's work for Speaker. There was nothing extraordinary in this particular game, at least for him. He made no sensational double play as he does sometimes. But he cut off one run at the plate by a throw which not one fielder in ten could approximate. He held another runner at second base who otherwise would have scored . . . and he cut down a double to a single, thus eliminating what would have been a fine prospect for another run. In other words, he cut off two runs and spoiled another, which is a fair day's work, even for a shortstop.

Speaker himself had a superbly simplified sense of what his job was about. First, he said, an outfielder was required to hit. Then, a close second, was fielding, which he had refined to an absolute—"the ability to get to the ball." Then throwing, long, accurate throwing: "I believe an outfielder should not alone be kept for his ability as a batter or to catch a few high flies which any amateur could handle, but to assist the infielders and to cut off runners at the bases," said Speaker. "One of the most important plays in the game is to get the runner who is coming home from third. Whether or not the run will score depends mostly on the strength of arm and the good aim of the outfielder who has the ball. This run decides a good many games in the course of the season."

What Speaker did, almost single-handedly, was elevate the role of the center fielder. At bat and in the field, he amply demonstrated that center field meant center stage. Past center fielders

like Lange, Fielder Jones, Hines, or Fogarty might vanish into
the mists of baseball history, but not Speaker or other center
fielders who emerged while he was playing. Though no one could
field the position quite the way Speaker did, Ty Cobb, Edd
Roush, Max Carey, Earle Combs, all contemporaries, could dominate a game from both sides of the field. Cobb, relatively weak-
armed, started twelve double plays one year, got twenty-three
outfield assists another, was a league leader another time in putouts and total chances per game. One of the things lost in the
wash of the Black Sox scandal was a memorable performance in
the field by Edd Roush in the 1919 World Series. *Spalding's
Official Baseball Guide of 1920,* along with *Reach's Guide,* listed
nine different outstanding center-field plays over four games
made by Roush, the National League's leading hitter that year.
And then, in the Negro Leagues, there was "Cool Papa" Bell and
Oscar Charleston, both Hall of Famers. "Cool Papa," a .400
hitter who was reputedly so fast he could get from the wall switch
to the bed before the lights went out, was known as "the black
Cobb," and Charleston, who some Negro Leaguers said was a
stronger hitter than Josh Gibson, was called by many "the black
Speaker." And, at that, it might have been the other way around.

"[Charleston] played one of the shallowest centerfields ever
seen," wrote historian John B. Holway. "Drake, who played with
Charleston in St. Louis, used to kid him: 'What, are you going
to take the throw from the catcher?'

"Only Tris Speaker played as close. Yet no one remembers
seeing anyone drive a ball over Charleston's head. He turned with
the crack of the bat, literally outraced the ball, whirled at the last
second, and put it away."

IN HISTORICAL TERMS, what Speaker—and Oscar Charleston—
did was usher in a golden age in center field, never to be forgotten, not to be repeated till Willie, Mickey, and the Duke came
along at the same time and in the same city a little over two
decades later (this later list, clearly, also includes Richie Ashburn

and Larry Doby, with Jimmy Piersall and Bill Virdon solid understudies). And within a decade of Speaker's last game, the regular center fielder for the New York Yankees was Joe DiMaggio. With DiMaggio, center field had added to it one last dimension —majesty. Strength up the middle, with DiMaggio in center, came to mean royalty at the top.

The hallmark of DiMaggio's style was ease—ease in everything, from his long fluid swing, launched from a spread, seemingly immobile position, to the way he pursued fly balls across the distant reaches of Yankee Stadium so that it seemed even the most difficult plays required little effort. DiMaggio once made a catch of a ball hit by Hank Greenberg to nearly dead center field in and around the monuments—which were then on the field—after running for it, with his back to the plate, for more than 125 feet. No one, especially Greenberg, who had reached second base by the time the ball came down, believed DiMaggio could reach the ball, no less catch it. He made it look easy. It wasn't, of course —DiMaggio said later that his sunglasses "made it hard to pick up the ball out of light blue sky" and that he picked it up at the end only as he "got a flash of it as it passed into the darkness of the glasses."

But as much ground as DiMaggio was able to convert into his special kingdom of grace, his game did have limitations. For a time, he tried, in the tradition of Speaker, to play a shallow field, apparently with only mixed results. In his book *Baseball's Famous Outfielders,* Ira L. Smith recounted an episode early in DiMaggio's career with the Yankees:

> Joe decided he'd play in closer, somewhat like folks said Speaker had done in the days when his fielding was the talk of the baseball world.
>
> The first day Joe adopted the new technique, Lefty Gomez was on the mound for the Yankees. One of the opposition batters sent the ball streaking toward center field. It was a terrific drive and Joe didn't have a chance to get near it—probably wouldn't have been able to catch it even if he had been playing in his normal position.

On the bench, after the opposing side had been retired, Gomez turned to Joe. In good humor, but with a plaintive tone in his voice, he said something like this: "Forget about Speaker and get your mind on Gomez. Speaker's been out of baseball a long while, but Gomez is right here in this game and is trying awful hard to get along."

A view of DiMaggio's fielding numbers suggests some limitation as well. In nine different fielding categories listed in *The Baseball Encyclopedia*, DiMaggio is among career leaders in only one. He ranks fourteenth overall—tied with Tris Speaker—in total chances per game. And this figure, too, is somewhat weighted because DiMaggio played half his games in the largest outfield in baseball, a definite advantage. Through his entire career as a center fielder DiMaggio was a league leader only once in any fielding category (fielding average in 1947; he led in outfield assists—as a left fielder—during his rookie year in 1936). Even among DiMaggios, Joe is third behind Dom and Vince in most categories.

What all of that proves is probably what Casey Stengel took pains to point out to writers when DiMaggio retired: When it came to DiMaggio, numbers did not tell the whole story. "Joe is far and away the greatest player I have managed," he said. "But that is an understatement. I have to explain what I mean by 'greatest.' I mean that he combined qualities which you will not find recorded in his averages."

Look into every aspect of DiMaggio's game—including baserunning, where he was smart rather than proficient—and the sum is greater than the parts. As a hitter, he ranks near the top of the career lists in only slugging percentage and RBIs per game among twenty-three different offensive categories (while Ted Williams, for example, is among the top fifteen in eleven different categories). But then DiMaggio was a lifetime .325 hitter, and he hit for real power, and there was the matter of fifty-six games and the less noted but equally incredible fact that had it not been for

his last year, he would have finished his career striking out fewer times than he hit home runs. Add a genuine reticence and un-willingness to make large claims about his own abilities—even when he played in pain or overcame injury in heroic fashion (as he did in 1949), and something of the style DiMaggio brought to the position becomes clear. There was no one like him—as there was no one like Speaker. DiMaggio bequeathed to succeeding generations of center fielders a certain obligation of style, which, in baseball terms, meant the ability to do *everything,* and to do it well, to the point of seeming effortlessness.

The closest anyone has come to picking up the challenge left by DiMaggio is Mays. Not Mantle or Snider—that argument, the amusement of many Eisenhower summers, was settled long ago—not Ashburn or Piersall or Virdon, all of whom were far above average at their position but were, at least in one area or another—power hitting, hitting for average, throwing ability, speed—missing something. Mays not only picked up the challenge, but by the time he finished playing, he redefined it.

Whatever contemporaries or modern observers say about him, it is the witness of those who played earlier, teammates and opponents of Speaker and Roush and Cobb—men who might be expected to jealously guard the preserve of their own experience —who acknowledged in Mays what they would grant to no one else, including DiMaggio.

"That Willie Mays, he's one of the greatest center fielders who ever lived," Harry Hooper, an old Red Sox roommate of Speaker's told Lawrence Ritter. "You can go back as far as you want and name all the great ones—Tris Speaker, Eddie Roush, Max Carey, Earle Combs, Joe DiMaggio. I don't care *who* you name, Mays is just as good, maybe better. He's a throwback to the old days. A guy who can do everything, and plays like he loves it."

Al Bridwell, an early World Series opponent of Speaker's, had a similar view. "I've seen Speaker, Cobb, Hooper—oh, all the great outfielders—but I've never seen anyone who was any better than Willie Mays. Maybe just as good, but not better.

"Mays can throw, field, hit, run, anything. He can work a pitcher into losing a ball game any time he gets on base. . . . I don't know, there's just something about him."

Mays played shallow—not as shallow as Speaker, but shallow enough. "Guy'd get a hit, line drive over second and you're already thinking about what you're gonna do with the runner on first, then you look up and Mays is there, he's got the ball," said Charlie Fox.

And Mays could go back.

"Then, all of a sudden, the very next guy puts one against the center-field fence, and Mays is there for that one, too," said Fox, sounding as if Mays were more ghost than ballplayer. Actually, Fox knew better then nearly anyone why Mays was the kind of player he was. It wasn't magic but baseball, a lot of it—thousands of plays, hundreds of games—before he ever got to the big leagues, that enabled Mays to play with such command. By contrast, Mickey Mantle was, according to his team's own scouting reports, a barely adequate minor league shortstop a year before he became a big-league outfielder, shaken by the sense that he barely knew what he was doing when he began playing for the Yankees.

Mays, playing in the Negro Leagues before he signed his first professional contract, was an outfielder, going to outfielders' school. At sixteen, he was a member of the Birmingham Black Barons, managed by Piper Davis, whom Mays referred to as "a second father." Even then, Mays was no ordinary student. He remembers that Davis taught him about throwing. But at this point, four years before he was a "rookie" center fielder in New York, Mays already knew his way around:

> It may seem that everything I did on the field was natural because in so many of the throws I made or the balls I caught I followed my instincts. But I also learned. For example, Piper insisted that I charge a ball hit through the infield, especially with a runner on second base. This way I would be in position to throw the ball home or

discourage the hitter from reaching second. Throwing was important. He didn't want me to throw it all the way on the fly because the ball doesn't pick up any speed. A throw is fastest the moment it leaves your hand. From that point on it slows down. So now, you've got to try to help it pick up speed.

'Bounce it,' Piper said. 'When the ball skips off the ground it picks up speed.' With my big hands, I didn't have any trouble charging the ball at full speed and picking it up with my bare hand. Having big hands made it easier for me than for other outfielders to pick up a ball barehanded, and it allowed me to get rid of it quicker and to throw it harder. Most base runners do what they do as a result of their success in the past against other outfielders. But if they come against a ball player who's got something they haven't seen before . . . well, that's when they get fooled, and that's when they get cut down.

Once in a Barons' game against the Kansas City Monarchs, I threw out two base runners. One was trying to make it from first to third on a single past the shortstop. The other tried to score from second on a hit to right center. The third time, Buck O'Neill, the Monarchs' manager, who was coaching at third, held up a runner there on a hit to center. Buck yelled, 'Whoa, whoa, that man's got a shotgun.'

According to Charlie Fox, Barry Bonds, and just about anyone who knew Mays, what marked him as a player, beyond a set of gifts that simply allowed him to run faster, throw farther, and hit harder than others, was an intensity second to none. Mays burned to win at everything he did, from recreational games of pool and golf to 2,992 professional games of baseball (exclusive of playoffs and World Series) played over twenty-two years. Mays was on a tear from the moment he stepped on a field. Hands, legs, elbows, torso, hat, shoes, and shirt seemed in perpetual motion. Sometimes it appeared as if Mays were consumed by his own energy, worn down in the middle of the season. But it was all fire—and showmanship—and smarts.

Mays believed in showmanship. The trademark losing of his cap, for example, came not from exuberance alone, he said, but

because he regularly wore a hat too large for his head, just so that it would easily take flight when he ran.

Mays was as meticulous, as attentive to learning all the way through his career as he was when he was young. After years of playing in the Polo Grounds, where, Charlie Fox said, "any ball that stayed in the air long enough you knew was automatic because Willie could get it," Mays and the Giants moved to San Francisco, where any ball that stayed in the air long enough could finish any player, including Mays. There never was a book on playing the treacherous wind currents of Candlestick Park, but Mays taught himself how to do it. To be a center fielder, you had to play with absolute certainty, he said, and the first thing that went in the wind was certainty. The way Mays tamed the wind says a lot about the way he saw and played center field.

I had played a shallow centerfield my whole life, in every park, and I wasn't going to change now. Somehow I had to figure out that wind. . . .

It took . . . time to learn how to play the outfield at Candlestick. In all the years in all the ballparks I had played in, I usually had been concerned more with the shape of the park, or the condition of the field. Here I had a whole new situation: a wind I couldn't control. And control had always been one of my strong points. Physically, I could dominate a ballpark in the field. Today's ballplayers play back. They may make a lot of leaping catches against the fences, but they also let a lot of balls drop in front of them. If something dropped in front of me, I felt I let a pitcher down. . . .

There were no enclosed parts behind the stadium, and at times the wind would blow the ball back as if it were a Ping-Pong ball. I remember one ball that I thought was going out of the park—only to land at my feet as it dropped for a single . . .

But I discovered the secret of playing there. I used it my entire career in San Francisco, and never let anyone else know about it.

When a ball was hit, I didn't move. From the moment it was up in the air, I started counting to five: one, two, three, four, five. At "Five" I began to run. I made the catch look easy. Believe me, it was

a science as much as baseball skill. I don't think an airplane engineer could have solved the mystery of Candlestick. But somehow those five seconds gave me a chance to see whether the wind would take the ball, and if it did, where it would go. Every day, I would measure the wind in my mind—how hard it was blowing and in what direction. There were days when it blew exactly the opposite of the way it had the day before, and I'd have to allow for that.

Above all, there was this sense of control. It was as if all of the skills, all the charisma, all the enthusiasm, all the years of experience added up to this incalculable ability to take control.

It was not because of his speed alone, but also because he knew hitters and pitchers and game moments so well, that everyone on his team took advantage of whatever position he took. "When Willie moved, everyone moved in relation to him," Charlie Fox said, "and were better off because of it." Mays put it another way:

The other outfielders would play off me. In that regard, the responsibility was totally on my shoulders. Every inning was different. In a way we played the game backward. If I was playing the outfield one way, the infield was playing the other way. A batter could pull a ground ball—but it would be harder for him to pull a fly ball. So in the late innings, we'd have the infielders play in the holes and leave the middle open. On every pitch, the other players would look at me. I positioned them by raising my hand. The player would move in that direction and stop when I dropped my hand to my side. I made it very clear to the other players. If you want to play, look at me. If you don't, then go home.

Mays meant this literally. By 1965, he was, with the club's encouragement, as much a co-manager from his center-field perch as a player. When Hal Lanier, then a second-year shortstop on the Giants, refused to move to his signals, Mays went to the team's manager, Herman Franks, and had Lanier benched. Lanier

returned to the lineup when he understood that Mays moved people for the sake of the team, not himself.

"Willie was an incredible leader in everything he did," Charlie Fox said, "from the field to the dugout to the clubhouse, everywhere—and the thing was he was so smart about it. If I had a problem with a player, for example, I'd go through Willie. . . . First I'd take Willie aside and tell him I had this problem. Willie'd nod; we had it all worked out. Later, when we had a team meeting, the first thing I'd do is light into Willie—in front of everybody. He'd put on this look, hang his head, go into this whole thing about how really sorry he was . . . it was a performance, believe me . . . then I'd go after the player I really wanted to confront. The player—and everyone else—accepted it because, what the hell, if Willie could take it so could anyone else—and all the while, I'd see Willie out of the corner of my eye, grinning while he kept his head lowered. He'd be biting his tongue to keep from laughing."

Mays played into the age of Astroturf, never the player he was before he hurt his arm in 1965, but still so totally dominant at his position that almost every young outfielder afterward has drawn inspiration from him. Mays set standards of speed, power, throwing ability, intelligence, tremendous athleticism combined with personal command by which center fielders are still judged almost twenty years after his retirement.

We are not yet in the next golden age of center fielders, but we are close. The roster of current stars at the position include Kirby Puckett, Eric Davis, Andy Van Slyke, Willie McGee, Ellis Burks, and Willie Wilson, along with ex–center fielders like Andre Dawson, Fred Lynn, Kevin McReynolds, and Chet Lemon—all players who would have been stars in any generation.

The nearly common denominator among all these players is the ability to simply outrun a ball in the open. "To play center," says Gary Pettis, perhaps the swiftest of these swifties, "all you're asked to do is just catch the ball; catch the ball, be in the right place at the right time, and hit the cutoff man." Nothing to it.

Willie Wilson says, "The center fielder is the guy who goes out there to catch anything he can—and also be smart enough to know that if he can't catch it, let it fall in and not make any bad choices."

"My goal," said Willie McGee, simplifying things almost to an essence, "is to run forever and catch everything they hit."

In the new parks, this kind of speed is indispensable. Balls that would have been singles from the Stone Age through the middle of the twentieth century can turn into triples or worse on turf surfaces if they are not quickly flagged down. Because the new parks, uniform as they are, are also generally more spacious, they also are harder to cover. The gaps are deeper, and balls that reach these areas on a couple of hops, and would slow down on grass, pick up speed as they skip off the turf. Outfielders who could traditionally rely on diving or sliding to gain additional yardage for a catch find those moves problematic on turf. Unless the synthetic stuff is wet, the uniformed body clunks and sticks as it hits: Shoulders are often jammed, bones broken. In lieu of wings, additional speed is the only answer. Balls dumped in front of a fielder may be the most treacherous of all; not only do they demand an all-out sprint and possible dive, but they also pose the risk—if they are handled too aggressively or lazily—of kangarooing all the way to the fence.

No matter how much speed has been incorporated into the position today, it is not enough. The new parks have virtually eliminated shallow positioning. Modern stadium design has interfered with the center fielder as surely as the designated hitter has taken away from the skill of first basemen, and nothing can change that save the wrecking ball—and real grass, which is not likely in the age of water-sucking Zamboni machines. "Anytime we play on a turf field," says Lloyd Moseby of the Blue Jays, who play more than half their games on the artificial surface, "we just bunch up the outfield. We play deeper, move closer together, and we give them the lines—that's all you can do."

The major reason it is so hard to characterize our era of center

fielders is that good as the players are, they no longer can dominate a ballpark as their predecessors did. Yet there are still those men in center who could have played anytime for anyone.

From 1983, when he replaced smooth Amos Otis, through 1989, when Kansas City said it would release him to make way for younger talent, Willie Wilson was the regular center fielder for the Royals. Among those currently playing the position, only Moseby, who began in '81, has played more games there. Given that Kansas City boasts one of the game's most spacious turf fields, Wilson says experience and Amos Otis have been his best teachers.

Wilson came to the position with a liability many of today's center fielders share. His arm, worn and injured, never was strong. "I know I can't throw a guy out from center field," he says. "I have a center fielder's body but a left fielder's arm." He has worked on charging and releasing the ball quickly, of course, but another technique, he says, "is trying to catch 'em all." He plays deep and tries, with his great speed, to outrun—and outwit—whatever is hit to him.

Wilson defines what he can do by what he can't. He says that he must back off certain balls, particularly those he might have to reach with a dive or slide, where the likelihood of extra bases or personal injury is great. He does not like to dive or slide on turf but will do it if it is wet and the moment in the game demands it. He gauges what he can and cannot do by whether he can catch a ball knee-high or above. Above the knees, take it; below the knees, don't let it take you.

Positioning, which Wilson says Otis greatly helped him with, was fundamental. But so, too, did innumerable tricks he acquired over the years help him, fast as he was, to get a better jump on any ball hit his way.

"You get a pretty good view in center field to begin with," he says. "You get to see all of the batter and the location of pitches—but there's a way of looking at that, too." Having been a catcher in high school, Wilson looks in to the plate a little differ-

ently than other center fielders. "A lot of people watch the batter," he explains. "What I do is just watch the bat—just the bat." This enables him to pick up the point of contact. "That's how I get my jump. That way—and by listening." The sound the ball makes hitting the bat—which some center fielders say is an unreliable measure—is helpful for Wilson, depending on the park: different parks, different sounds. "Everything sounds good indoors," Wilson says. "It's hard to discriminate. But Yankee Stadium gives you a really accurate sound; so does Boston. Toronto's okay and Baltimore's really good. Most parks are good—except mine." The most unexpected casualty of turf, it turns out, is in what it does to sound.

"You just can't tell that much in Royals Stadium because of the turf," Wilson says. "The sound kind of sinks into it and gets deadened. You can't really use it." With good sound, though, Wilson says he can discriminate between balls that are well and poorly hit, balls that *look* good coming off the bat but that will die in flight, balls that *don't* look good but that will have greater carry.

Willie Wilson has been sobered by his sense of limitation. He does not talk much about compensating for his weak arm. On balls to right-center field, which normally might be handled by a strong-throwing center fielder, Wilson merely yields to his right fielder, who, he knows, will likely have a better throwing angle and a better chance to make a play. But he is smarter and shrewder for knowing what he can't do.

"You have to go at it play by play," he explains. "If a ball's hit to right center, sometimes you might take it—you might need to spin and throw. Sometimes you give it up. You try to angle at a ball, but sometimes you can't. It all depends on the moment; you have to play the moment."

Early in his career, while still a left fielder, Wilson picked up the most valuable lesson of all from Otis: command. It began with positioning but it had really to do with the ability to inspire confidence. Wilson stormed and fumed when he did not come

through at bat or when he failed to make a play in the field. Otis, he remembers, had a special way of dealing with him.

"He'd come over to me—he'd let me get out all my frustrations," Wilson says. "Then, very calmly, he'd say, 'It's two out, runner on first, so-and-so is pitching—don't let this guy get over here or don't let such-and-such happen.' And he'd say it so calmly to the point where I'd have to stop and think and then realize I was out there not for myself but to win a game." Otis wasn't running a charity, but a game, Wilson realized. The two men actually were in competition for the same position (as, ironically, Bo Jackson then was with Wilson), but a center fielder's job was to take charge of the outfield so games could be won.

When he took over in center, Wilson always tried for that. He talked with his fellow outfielders constantly, ensuring that the lines of communication were open in all game situations.

"You have to know the guys you're playing with, what their personalities are, and then talk to them in their language, actually get into their moods, something that'll make 'em calmer, able to turn their attention back to what has to be done."

Wilson conveys the impression that he has no great affection for this role, but that it goes with the territory. "It's demanding, very demanding, if you really let it get to you," he says. "But you just have to know who to shade, who's the quicker of the two other outfielders, who's the best outfielder to make what play—and then you do it."

Among the younger center fielders, this sort of leadership is not automatic. It comes with time, which, in any baseball life, means games played. "The center fielder's job is to take control," says Eric Davis, the Reds' twenty-seven-year-old comet. He has been a center fielder only since 1986 and an outfielder only since 1981, when he was converted from shortstop at the outset of his professional career. But he already seems to be in the mold of classic center fielders. He has been a prolific home-run hitter, a base stealer, a Gold Glover, all in an exceedingly short period of time. He is flamboyant and daring, a fence crasher with wonder-

fully soft hands. Having been a shortstop, the spins he makes on balls in the gap, the quick moves in on grounders, have come easier than they might, as has his infielder's habit of anticipating that every ball will be hit to him. He already knows that aggressiveness is a key to what he does in center. All that is missing is the number of games he has played. He does not move his outfielders; the bench does. He has not yet taken control in the way older, more experienced center fielders have. "It is something we're working with him on," said Pete Rose, before he was banished from baseball. He had been Davis's manager through his first five major league seasons.

Perhaps the most surprising of the new men in center is the Pirates' Andy Van Slyke. In the two years prior to his injury-plagued season in 1989, the former right fielder for the Cards transformed himself from a very good outfielder to a nearly great one. It was as though center field were waiting for him when he got there. "I was wondering why it took you so long to ask," he said with characteristic brash good humor to his manager, Jim Leyland, who had waited six weeks after the trade with the Cards to propose the position change to him.

The very first thing that Van Slyke talks about when he asked about making the adjustment from right to center is who was playing alongside him. "The biggest thing for me," he says, "was that I was playing with two, not one—knowing what kind of ground they cover, what kind of balls they can and can't get to."

In St. Louis, he had been, in his words, "a small fish in a big pond." But he played alongside Willie McGee, the often injured but still elegant man in center in an outfield that was all speed and open spaces. McGee, like Joe D., was quiet but could travel to places no one had been before. By the time he came to the Pirates, Van Slyke knew all about an outfielder's fundamental instinct to catch any ball hit—and, just because of that, about the advantages of communication.

"I want to know that I have room rather than that I don't," he says, "because I'm always thinking I have a chance to make a

catch." Perhaps because Willie McGee had been as quiet as he was and also because Van Slyke tended to be too aggressive in his pursuit of fly balls, the new man in center for the Pirates needed no prompting to direct traffic with his cornermen. When he became a bigger fish in a smaller pond in Pittsburgh, it was almost a natural progression—and one that allowed him to be an even better player than anyone, probably including the Cards' front office, realized.

Van Slyke came to his job with already proven physical abilities. He was fast (he regularly stole between twenty and thirty bases a year), he could throw (his arm was generally considered strongest among all National League outfielders), and he could hit (.270 with thirteen home runs in his last year with St. Louis). But his physical gifts only partly explain why he became a near franchise player in 1988.

Van Slyke, who is allowed to position himself, plays shallow whenever he can, but there are too many variables to characterize his positioning reliably; he moves according to situation. He will move differently on the same batter depending on whether he is hitting in the first, third, seventh, or last inning; he will move differently when the same hitter is behind or ahead in the count, and will move again depending on who is on base, who may be up next. And then all of that will change depending on the park he is playing in, whether the surface he has to cover is grass or plastic.

"These are all things you have to take into account," he says. "It's not really a question of shallow or deep. I'll move three, four, five, six steps with two strikes on a hitter. I've watched many major league outfielders stand in one position for a whole game, and anytime that happens that means that outfielder just isn't thinking about the situation in the game. The key is being able to move—that's what allows you to take chances, and that can only come from knowing the situation really well. I'll bet you if you ask outfielders what to do in the seventh, eighth, ninth inning with a four-run lead, half of them won't have an answer."

The answer?

"I play four steps shallow because eight out of ten balls are hit in front of you; you have a four-run lead, you want to keep men off base—give 'em doubles, triples, inside-the-park home runs if you want, just take the base hits away from them."

Van Slyke tries to think with his pitchers. In taking a shallow set in a tight game—very daring for most outfielders—he senses, correctly or not, that his pitchers will be less upset about a ball hit over his head than "a bleeder that could have been caught." Then again, when he thinks with his pitchers, he relies greatly on *their* intelligence to aid him.

"Sometimes I'll question some pitches—I question throwing a left-handed leadoff hitter a change or a breaking ball when you're swung over shallow into left center and he then can pull the ball into the right-center-field gap—but over the course of the year, my job is not to question what my pitchers are throwing but to better think along with them. That's how I dictate what I do in center field," he says.

Van Slyke has the arm for the big throws but it is the way he thinks about this part of his game that makes him an intimidating thrower. He is always strategic. Sometimes, depending on his positioning and the moment, he will deliberately throw to the "wrong" base. On a single to center with a runner on second, the throw is either home or back into the infield at second. But if out of the corner of his eye he sees the third-base coach raise his arms to hold the runner, he will suddenly fire to third because of the great likelihood that the runner, under a full head of steam, will make a big turn around the bag before stopping.

Van Slyke has measured every step of the ground he covers in every different park, treating each as a separate environment. There is no simple division for him between playing on turf and playing on grass, for example, something many outfielders accept as a matter of course. In each place he plays, Van Slyke is looking for ways to maintain his aggressiveness. He says he can be more aggressive in playing balls in the air on grass, where he can dive, and on ground balls on turf, where he can charge more confi-

dently. But then again he has spent time learning how to dive on plastic. He is one of the few outfielders in the game who will risk it.

"Not all turf fields are the same," he says. "There are some—like the covering we had in Pittsburgh for years—that are so worn you will slide when you hit the deck, same as when another turf field is wet. But other fields—like Houston—you can't risk diving because you stick." Van Slyke believes that diving, particularly on turf, is almost an art. Like former teammate Ozzie Smith, he has refined it into one. Smith made sure to bend himself backward into a rocking-chair runner as he dove so his gloved hand would not be jolted when he hit, and he could more easily come up throwing. Van Slyke says the key for him is using his right (throwing) arm to both brake and steer himself to a safe stop: "I have to plant my right arm and catch with my left and almost use a pushing motion so the slide becomes something like an airplane landing," he says.

But all of the attention to detail, all of the determination to play aggressively, has in the end this sense of place. As a center fielder, he can do more. Moving there has allowed him to be the leader he always knew he could be. "I'm a selfish outfielder that way because I want to do something to pick up my game and my team's game. And in center field you have to think that way all the time."

KIRBY PUCKETT looks like the unlikeliest center fielder in the game. Though he is as well muscled as bridge cable, he is short (the Twins' media guide lists him as five feet eight—he is shorter than that), and as round, at 210 pounds, as a medicine ball. In addition, he looks as odd at his position as he does in his body. He plays the deepest center field in the game; his Wilson 2000 glove is one of those oversized Venus flytraps that have done more to destroy the fundamental two-handed outfield catch than generations of hotdogging; and when he speaks, his words come out in a rush and stumble all over themselves.

"I try to catch any ball if I can get to it," Puckett says like

other center men, but then tumbles on to his own special place. "The thing that separates me from the rest of the guys is that I don't know how to dive for a ball. Now I love to dive for a ball but I don't know how. Every time I dive, I hurt myself—my face, my nose—I don't think that's the way it's supposed to happen. You're supposed to be graceful—and I don't think I'm like that. I want to be like that but I just don't know how."

But he is, with his funny body and funny way of speaking, very possibly the best all-around center fielder to come along since Willie Mays. In 1988 he hit .356, the highest any right-handed batter in the game has hit since Joe D. hit .357 in 1940; before that he hit .332 and .328. In 1989 he hit .339 and was the American League batting champion. And he has hit for power: 121 RBIs with twenty-four homers in 1988, and then two seasons with just under 100 RBIs with twenty-eight homers one season, thirty-one another. And with all of that, he has given his team defense in center second to none. Puckett has won Gold Gloves in each of the past four seasons. He may not dive but he covers as much ground as anyone (438 putouts, 455 total chances in center field last season), his throwing is powerful and deadly accurate. Whatever he might miss in grace he makes up for in his command of the position. He may control territory more like General Kutuzov than General Patton, but that is only because he knows so well what must be done.

Puckett makes no bones about playing back. It is an either/or choice that must be made and held to. He plays deep, he says, because he wants to take away hits over his head—the big hits. "If you play shallow, you're taking a chance of a ball being hit over your head. If you play deep you're taking a chance of a ball falling in front of you. My theory is that I want to take away balls over the wall so I'll give up the shallow hit to do it."

There are no precise stats for this, but last year Puckett says he took eight or nine balls from the other side of the fence. There were many more made in and around walls that would have been hard or impossible to reach as well. This stat, depending on the situation, should be called "runs saved" or "games saved."

If Puckett were not so fast and did not get the kind of jump on a ball that he does, undoubtedly this kind of positioning would surrender more than it took. But from his deep places, he moves in on balls dumped over the infield as though his positioning were shallow. He is the ideal turf center fielder, the new model. He is Speaker in reverse. And playing as deep as he does, hanging in the walls and alleys like a midnight bat, he does far more than anyone thought possible in those first giddy days of silicone fields, Glad-bag walls, and indoor lighting. Puckett has made the deep field a source of strength. He has tailored his skills to it.

Because his arm is so strong, he is able to take the chance of fielding, retrieving, and throwing from a point farther back than usual. But he also compensates by making sure that his throwing is fundamentally correct. He throws low, flat, and hard. By correctly gripping the ball, releasing it at the same point high above his shoulder, he is able to deliver a throw with very little movement on it. His goal is to hit his cutoff man face-high. Never mind the distraction of the mound when he is coming home— his target is Kent Hrbek's face. Does Hrbek set up in back, on top, in front of the mound? Doesn't matter; ask Hrbek. The job is done when the connection with the cutoff man is made, or the decision is made, improvised in a split second, to go to another base.

Puckett protects his deep set by the way he charges balls, too —as though he had a weak arm. He makes sure that whenever he can he retrieves a ball off his left foot with the right foot coming forward as he makes his scoop: one step, absolute max, and then the throw.

By playing back, Puckett not only protects walls but sometimes also his cornermen. He is able to back up plays more effectively, angling farther into the gap to stop hits that otherwise might go to the wall. One of his more spectacular catches occurred in his rookie year, when he ran a backup route behind left fielder Mickey Hatcher, who lunged for and missed a ball headed for a triple or an inside-the-park homer. The light-hitting Spike

Owen, who thought his ball was going out of the park, was in his home-run trot as he crossed second base, and he looked up to see Puckett, who had been stationed in deep right center, flash in behind Hatcher and impossibly grab the ball backhanded before it hit the fence.

Puckett plays walls differently than most other outfielders, using them as springboards to start his momentum back to the infield for his throw. This was a fundamental he picked up in junior college, one generally taught but rarely perfected. Rather than drift along the base of a wall, content to set his feet for a throw, he uses his right hand, unobtrusively placed against the fence, to propel himself into his throw, much as a swimmer uses his feet making a racing turn at the end of a lap. Puckett has even taught himself to do this full tilt, using the weight of his body to alter his momentum, which would otherwise make a strong throw impossible.

Like any great center fielder, Puckett thinks along with his pitchers. He knows hitters now, knows how and when to take his two or three or four steps within a single at-bat. He doesn't read signals from the catcher, doesn't isolate on zones or on the bat. All he watches is the ball. "The ball is what they hit; that's what I watch," he says. He can tell what kind of spin a ball has when it leaves a pitcher's hand, knows it's a breaking pitch before it breaks —and his hawklike eyes are reliable enough to read balls with precision as they come off the bat. He gets as quick a jump as anyone in the game.

Puckett, despite his own reluctance to see himself that way, is a man who accomplishes what he does with ease. There may not be grace, but there is extraordinary body control that allows him to cover the center-field deeps with sureness. That is the test, the only one: Can a player really cover all that ground, command it, tame it, turn it into his own special territory?

Puckett works hard with his cornermen, talks to them, directs them, makes sure they know what he is doing, because they will have to move as he does. He protects them—tries to play closer

to slower cornermen—and draws on them equally for help when he needs it. He makes sure the lines of priority on balls in the gap or between fielders are understood at all times. "I'm the boss out there; I make all the decisions and I have to live with all the mistakes," he says. But this is not ego. This is the position. "The center fielder is the guy who just goes and gets the ball," says Puckett.

Of course, it is one thing to want to be a guy who "just goes and gets the ball"; it is something else when a player can actually do it. Something happens to him—and because of it, to us—and to the way the position is played.

As a rookie in 1982, Willie McGee made one of the great catches in World Series history. In the eighth inning of the third game between the Brewers and the Cards, with the Series divided at one game apiece and the Cards trying to hold off a big Milwaukee rally, McGee (who homered twice in the game for his team) took a three-run home run away from Gorman Thomas with a leaping, twisting catch against the left-center-field fence. It was an "impossible" catch. Except that it wasn't. It was just a catch that, as McGee describes it, somehow defines what the special magic of center field is all about:

"To start with, I knew who was hitting, what he was capable of, what he was likely to try to do. I knew I had to play deep and, most likely, he was going to pull the ball. If he hit the ball the other way we would be in trouble—I knew that," McGee said. "But that wasn't likely from the scouting reports and because Bruce Sutter was pitching. Sutter wasn't overpowering but he was a great pitcher who put the ball where he wanted.

"At the point of contact I was in the right position—to where I could go back and be under control. Because I was set up right and knew what I was looking for, I saw the ball good all the way. I got a good jump. I knew where the fence was at all times, I knew where I was going, I was in control all the way, and then something amazing happened. I still see it and feel it to this day every time I think about it. The last five steps or so, it seemed like

everything went into slow motion. I have no explanation for why it happened other than that I was under control. It couldn't have happened if I was all out. But there it was. The ball was up there real slow, my body was slowly moving towards it. It was amazing. When the ball was hit, I saw myself breaking, I knew where I had to run to—and when I jumped it was like I was somebody else watching me do this in slow motion. I was this other person who knew exactly when I had to jump, where I had to jump to, where the fence was. I saw it all happen before it actually happened. And then, after I came down with the ball, there was just this total silence. I became aware of the silence only afterwards, when I was walking back to my position and I heard somebody in the stands behind me whack a glove or something on the railing. There may have been a lot of noise then—I don't know. All I know is that I gave myself enough time to calculate what I had to do to catch that ball."

Never mind that he covered the entire left side of center field in doing it.

CATCHER

We used no mattress on our hands,
No cage upon our face;
We stood right up and caught the ball
With courage and with grace.

—George Ellard,
1869 Red Stockings

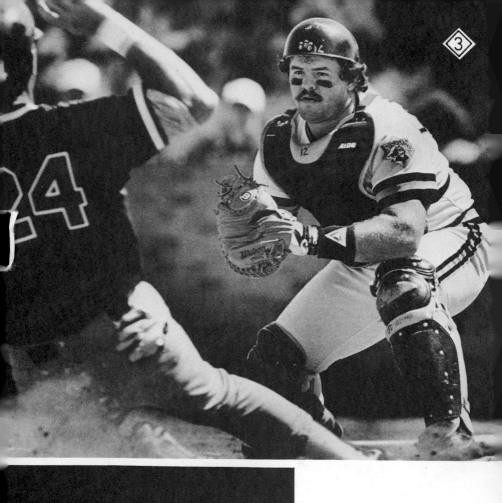

① **JOHNNY BENCH,** *airborne, in a game against the Chicago Cubs. Bench's one-handed catching style, his tremendous athleticism behind the plate, as well as his offense and field leadership made him an automatic Hall of Famer when he became eligible in 1989.*
AP/WIDE WORLD PHOTOS

② **BOB BOONE** *sways toward an incoming outfield throw. The game's top—and senior—catcher is a picture of power, fluidity, and grace.*

③ **MIKE LAVALLIERE** *of the Pirates in position at home plate. He gives the runner a portion of the plate, which he will close off as he applies the tag. Notice the perfect distribution of his weight and the slight forward lean of his body so that he will be better able to absorb the impact of any potential collision.*
PHOTO BY PETE DIANA

EVERYWHERE THEY GO, Bob Boone, age forty-two, and Carlton Fisk, age forty-one, are regarded not so much as longtime members of the dusty trade but as vanishing Americans, the last of a breed. It is as if their enormously successful careers as catchers have shrouded them in celebrity and ambiguity, rendering them like old chieftains at a Wild West show, living embodiment of a culture dying in our midst. They bring us wisdom and sadness, for they will not be in the game much longer.

But both these men seem beyond age, unwilling to accept either the prejudices or the praise heaped on them for having played so long. In their minds they are not there because old is better or because young these days is worse, but because they still can do a job. They may be surprising to others but not to themselves.

FISK: "I know that in 1983 the question arose whether I could play anymore. I didn't play until the end of June that year. Then I played every day and we won the division. Then in '84 I got hurt a little bit, so there it was: He's too old, he can't play. Then '85 was going to be my last year—so they thought—and I ended up playing a hundred and fifty-four games. Then it was '86 and they brought in Joel Skinner because I couldn't play anymore; '87 they brought in Ron Karkovice because I couldn't play anymore, so in '88 and again in '89 I got sidelined by a broken hand, and so now they know I can play, it's just a question of how many more years."

BOONE: "As you get older you start looking for signs that you're getting older. But I haven't really seen it and so I decided

a couple of seasons ago to quit looking for them and to not accept them if I ever did see them. If you get jammed, suddenly it isn't just that, it's also whether or not you've slowed up a hair; if you're in a slump then maybe just maybe it's something more than a slump. Once you give into thinking like that, you're defeated. So I decided a couple of years ago not to accept that, that I would leave it to someone else to tell me I can't play anymore. I just don't and won't think about the age factor. I'll play till someone tells me I don't have a job. And then if they say that, I'd probably apply all over the place to get another job. Yeah, I have an idea of how long I can go on, but I don't share it with anybody because people wouldn't believe it and it would sound outrageous. So my plan remains to do as well as I possibly can every day."

One of the reasons Boone and Fisk have become more or less the Kirk Douglas and Burt Lancaster of batterymen is that there is a rising consensus that catching is a diminishing art. In an April 1989 *Sports Illustrated* article "They Don't Make 'Em Like They Used To," *SI*'s baseball man Peter Gammons wrote,

> Consider this: before 1985, no catcher past the age of 36 had ever caught 100 games in a season. That year, both 37-year-old Bob Boone* and 37-year-old Carlton Fisk passed the 100 mark. Boone, who as a free agent signed with the Kansas City Royals in November for $883,001, and Fisk, who re-signed with the White Sox for $1.2 million in February, are now 41. In a poll of managers, coaches, and scouts, Fisk and Boone are still ranked as the best defensive catchers in the American League. "I respect Boone and Fisk tremendously," says bullpen coach Glenn Ezell of the Royals, "but it's kind of sad that two 41-year-olds are best."

The *SI* article goes on to survey a plethora of reasons, social, commercial, organizational, and personal, for this sad decline.

* The ages given for Boone are in error. Boone, born November 19, 1947, is a year older than Fisk, who was born December 26, 1948.

But in the end the mystery of why these two men have served quite so long and so well remains, as does the larger puzzle of why there seem to be so few good catchers left in the game. The answer, if there is one, may not be so much in our stars as in the position itself. Catching is the most elusive position on the field, its skills, its demands, even its view of the world—looking out from rather than in to home plate—at odds with the other positions. As catchers are hidden from us by mask and armor, so their skills are hidden. The best-caught game is the one least noticed. Catchers move within a circle of space as though at the wrong end of a telescope. The more a catcher can work himself toward invisibility the better. He does not want opponents to see what he is up to; he does not want umpires ever to wonder whether he has or has not stolen a strike or kept a ball in play that might not pass baggage inspection at an airport. The most spectacular thing he does—standing his ground for an incoming throw from the field against the full-bore rush of a base runner—occurs rarely, and his most watched and measured play—attempting to nail a base stealer—is also relatively infrequent. The bulk of a catcher's work takes place on a dime, down in the dirt, behind a mask, with micro rather than macro movements. The old catcher Charlie Fox was a spy. So was another catcher, Moe Berg. Catching *is* intelligence work and, like master spies, good catchers do their chores without anyone quite realizing how they do them.

As unromantic as it sounds, the principal job of a catcher is to catch the ball—not once or twice but every time a pitcher pitches and then a few times more when fielders come to him as well. This business of just catching the ball, something we assume *any catcher* can do, perfectly illustrates why it is so hard to see catching skills. "A good catcher is actually a receiver," Charlie Fox says. "He receives the ball rather than catches it. The good ones always take the ball in; the poorer ones go for it." This seemingly arcane distinction is the difference between holding the hand too far into the mitt (taking away give in the hand) and fitting it so that just the digits are into the mitt (allowing more

catching action in the web of the mitt and more free play in the wrist for the taking in of that ninety-mile-per-hour pitch). It also pertains to the angle at which the glove is held: If it is held straight toward the pitcher, bull's-eye fashion (which is what most of us think we see), the catch will be made with a stiff wrist; conversely, the slight inward tilt of the mitt, placing the outside blade of the hand at an approximate forty-five-degree angle to the pitcher (somewhere between the mound and third base), allows the target to be given while the hand remains relaxed enough so that glove movement left and right and up and down will be easy, permitting the ball to be received rather than caught.

Catchers' footwork is just as hard to pick up. The usual squat (with no runners on base) allows a catcher to comfortably hold a position as low to the ground as possible, glove to the front knee shielding signs from the third-base coach (the right-handed catcher here and elsewhere is assumed). This stance requires good balance so small, swaying movements left and right in the taking in of a pitch can occur with as little fanfare as possible. One of the fundamentals of receiving is catching borderline strikes in such a way that umpires will give the pitcher the benefit of the doubt. If this "framing" of a pitch is done with jerky movements, the frame will be broken, the illusion destroyed. Without the proper setting of his feet, the catcher's body will betray him—he will either lurch for the ball or reach for it too obviously with his hands.

With runners on, footwork becomes even more crucial. The inches given this way or that, the extra step taken or not taken, mean the difference between catching base runners and letting them advance, between being able to block balls in the dirt and having them skip away.

The hidden danger a catcher faces with men on is not the stolen base but the passed ball or wild pitch. More than a pitcher's control is involved. The pitcher may throw one way if he has confidence in his catcher's ability to block balls in the dirt but

another if he does not. Either way the catcher better have his feet right. On an outside pitch to a right-handed batter, the catcher either slides over or steps to the right, possibly turning and dropping the left knee to the ground so more of his body will be in front of the ball (the fundamental in this situation is to block, not catch, the ball). This ensures that the ball remains in front and in play. But if this pitch in the dirt is a breaking ball, the catcher must move his feet slightly differently. And *slightly* here is everything. Instead of making a step to the side, the step, if the pitcher is right-handed, is at an angle toward the field, about forty-five degrees, with the right shoulder more or less lined up with the place the ball hits. The spin of a right-hander's curve will cause the ball to kick back the other way, in toward the plate, into rather than away from the catcher's body. This "simple" move at an angle by the catcher takes inches off the hop of the ball coming out of the dirt and substitutes inches of blocking surface instead. The footwork is reversed going left. The veteran catcher Gary Carter has, for years, been an acknowledged master at this.

Throwing against attempted steals requires trickier but still barely noticeable dance steps. Most catchers are taught one of several ways to move the feet in a throw. For years, the standard was simply to move forward into the pitch, taking one step with the right foot, pivoting so that the left shoulder and arm were aimed at the target as the left foot came forward with the throw.

In recent decades, things have changed. For most of baseball history, catchers wore round, stiff mitts that resembled pillows. Beginning with Randy Hundley, a Cubs catcher in the late sixties, catchers began to use lightweight, hinged gloves that resembled first baseman's mitts. The old gloves required that catches be made with two hands so the ball could be held in the pocket. Techniques in footwork and throwing followed accordingly. But the new mitt allowed for one-handed catching and far more flexibility in footwork and throwing. Instead of the old catch-step-throw, catchers were able to throw staying closer to the ground by doing a jump-pivot from the crouch itself, the feet coming

quickly to the side in throwing position as the ball was received, the throw following instantly on a flowing movement out of the crouch. And then some catchers with strong enough legs and balance moved into the throw with less footwork than that—with just a preparatory weight shift to the right foot and then from the right to the forward-striding left foot with the throw. (Benito Santiago, the young Padres catcher, has at times dispensed with footwork in throwing altogether—his arm is so strong that he was able, in 1988, to nail seven base stealers with throws from his knees!)

When a catcher lines up for an incoming throw with a base runner hurtling toward him, we are reasonably sure of what we see—or are we? If the catcher is Mike Scioscia of the Dodgers what we see is a collision that more or less approximates a one-ton safe hitting the sidewalk. Scioscia takes a stance that covers all of home plate; he plants his feet and turns himself into concrete for the incoming runner. Only he is *not* concrete, and he has paid for the imitation with broken bones and surgery.

The standard for covering a play at the plate calls for avoiding heavy contact when possible: The feet should be firmly planted but only partially in the way of the plate. By placing himself this way, the catcher gives the base runner a portion of the plate as the rules (never strictly enforced) require. Then, with the throw, the rest, even with the catcher blind to the runner, is ballet—or bullfighting. Even if he doesn't see him, the catcher knows where the runner is. He takes the throw with his mitt coming up from the ground—like an infielder—to protect against the ball skipping between his legs. He turns his left leg toward the runner, shin guard facing any possible contact with spikes, drops his right knee to the ground, and makes his tag downward against the sliding or charging runner, with the glove turned so that contact will be made with the back rather than the front of the mitt. If there is no time, if ball and runner arrive at the same moment, then the catch, tag, and collision may be almost—but not quite —simultaneous. The catcher will have to make sure that he se-

cures the ball first, then try, if he can, to shift his weight slightly forward so that when contact occurs, he can pitch forward and allow his body to go out from under him rather than setting it immovably against the force of the runner.

The smart catchers do little things we never see that make all the difference. They "deke" runners approaching the plate, making it appear that a catch and tag are not imminent. Or they will offer portions of the plate to the runner, then close the plate off altogether as the runner begins his slide. The Dodgers' Roy Campanella, a Hall of Famer, was particularly adept at this. He would open a side of the plate to the runner, then as he took the throw in that kneeling position, he would simply roll his forward left foot and knee to the side, forcing the already sliding runner away from the plate. The tag would be applied with the runner skidding toward no-man's-land. Yogi Berra had another method: He offered a runner his side, then sidestepped him— -as in Madrid or those old Saturday-morning Road Runner cartoons.

Watch a catcher on a high pop foul behind the plate. The ball has more English on it than pop-ups anywhere else. Unlike other position players, the catcher's natural movement is not toward but with the ball. His effort appears to be a near-comic pantomime in which he gropes, staggers, circles, and then holds out his mitt much as if it were a portable basket into which the erratically-moving ball will finally plop. But then take another look, watching the catcher's free hand—he is carrying his mask with him and then, at an exactly appropriate moment, early or late, he casts the mask away from him so he can make his catch without risk of tripping over it.* All the while we imagine him to be in a stagger, the catcher is relentlessly keeping an invisible plumb line between the ball and his own forehead. As the ball

---

* The 1924 World Series was actually decided by a catcher tripping over his mask. With the Giants and Senators tied at three games apiece and locked in an extra-inning tie in the deciding game, the Senators' Muddy Ruel lofted a pop fly behind the plate. Hank Gowdy, the Giants' catcher, missed the catch when he stumbled over his mask. Ruel, given new life, doubled and then scored the winning run.

moves he moves his forehead, until the ball is securely in line for the catch. In the stands, we appreciate a catcher's skill—and courage—when he snares a ball from the first row of seats or at the top step of a dugout, but at the same time we probably don't quite appreciate the skill required to take a ball that rises and descends straight over the plate; most catchers consider that the toughest of flies to handle.

We again can barely appreciate just how much the catcher is up to on bunt plays. On a bunt down the third-base line, he will make his pickup with his back to first base, the position of his hands, his shoulder, his feet needing to be exact, so he can pivot on his right foot, spinning left and stepping toward first for the throw. If the throw is to go to second, he will make his pickup head-on, facing toward third, pivoting on his right foot, stepping with his left toward second for the throw. If he fields bunts on the first-base side and his throw is to first, he will have to do a little arabesque toward the infield after he picks up the ball so he will have a clear throwing lane to the inside of the base. Finally, the catcher, because he is the only one looking out at the bunt play as it develops, is the director. It will be his decision who fields the ball and to which base a throw will be made.

And then, after all this, there is the game we *never* see. Almost every catcher in the game plays with pain. By midseason, the accumulation of foul tips off body parts, of collisions, of ordinary wear and tear from the daily round of deep knee bends and other torso twists, force catchers to depend on mental toughness to make it through. Pain simply goes with the territory, but the ability to play through it requires a vibration as high—and as invisible—as bliss or martyrdom.

Neither do we see how a catcher handles his pitching staff or calls a game. "This is the most important part of what catchers do," says Tim McCarver, the broadcaster and ex-catcher. "It's at least as important as throwing or blocking balls in the dirt. It's the game only a handful of people know anything about—namely other catchers—and there's a mystique about it for good reason:

It's hard to explain because each case is so individual. A pitcher usually deals with the same catcher, but a catcher deals with many different pitchers." The catcher's wisdom and sometimes his psychological acumen are as much tools of the trade as mask and chest protector, but they are simply not discernible. We expect the catcher to call a game that will ensure his team's victory and to shepherd his pitching staff, but we are able, in the end, to evaluate only things like his hitting, throwing, and ability to block balls in the dirt. It is little wonder that catching is so easily misjudged and opinions about it so questionable.

It might be supposed that catching was easier in the beginning, before the game went into its overhand, fast-pitch mode. It was not. Catchers—without protection of any sort—took their bases-empty stance well back of the plate, retrieving pitches on the bounce. With runners aboard, however, they were expected to move up behind the plate and to catch pitches directly. If Chadwick has it right, catchers had to live behind enemy lines:

> This player is expected to catch or stop all balls pitched or thrown to the home base. He must be fully prepared to catch all foul balls, especially tips, and be able to throw the ball swiftly and accurately to the bases and also keep a bright outlook over the whole field. When a player has made his first base, the Catcher should take a position nearer the striker, in order to take the ball from the pitcher before it bounds; and the moment the ball is delivered by the pitcher, and the player runs from the first to the second base, the Catcher should take the ball before bounding and send it to the second base as swiftly as possible, in time to cut off the player before he can touch the base; in the latter case it would be as well, in the majority of cases, to send the ball a little to the right of the base. The same advice holds good in reference to a player running from the second base to the third. As the position occupied by the Catcher affords him the best view of the field, the person filling it is generally chosen captain, although the pitcher is sometimes chosen for that honor. We would suggest, however, that some other player be selected as captain, from the fact that the physical labor attached to that position tends to increase the

player's excitement, especially if the contest is a close one, and it is requisite that the captain should be as cool and as collected as possible.

Equipment for catchers was introduced piecemeal and with only gradual acceptance. The first catcher's mask appeared only in the mid-1870s. Long after catchers started taking foul tips off the face, the standard protective device was a rubber mouthpiece. Anything more, said Albert G. Spalding, was considered unmanly. Catching gloves were also reluctantly accepted, and it took more than a quarter of a century for chest protectors and shin guards to become standard items (the latter was said, probably mistakenly, to have been introduced by Hall of Famer Roger Bresnahan around 1908).

What can be inferred from these beginnings is clear enough: Catchers were both under the gun and strong of heart. It took a peculiar blend of stolid courage and swift intelligence to play the position well. Good mechanics were essential. And long before Tim McCarver was born, the hidden game was even more so.

"[A catcher] must first be able to catch and throw," said Billy Sullivan, a defensive star for the White Stockings in the early 1900s. "But that is only the mechanical basis for work in a position which many spectators largely think is a mechanical one." He was just as concerned with how the catcher ran the game before him. Interviewed for *The National Game*, he noted:

> Thus the catcher has to watch the pitcher and the baseman in addition to the purely mechanical work of his position. This is to say nothing of old and experienced men in steadying young pitchers and in indicating to them what balls to try on batsmen with whose weakness they are familiar. Headwork and coolness count as much behind the bat as anywhere except in the pitcher's box.
>
> My method of steadying a pitcher is to first try to slow him up and let him get his bearings again. Walk down with the ball and hand it to him, say something encouraging or offer advice if he seems

to need any. Stop to fasten your chest protector, adjust your mask, or tie your shoe, anything to gain time if the situation is critical and the pitcher's wildness only temporary.

Bob O'Farrell learned his game from Roger Bresnahan. It was inconceivable to him that Bresnahan—or anyone else—ever caught a game without shin guards. But O'Farrell, catching in the 1920s, used equipment barely out of the Kitty Hawk era. "In 1924, a foul tip came back, crashed through my mask, and fractured my skull," he told Lawrence Ritter. Nothing special. "Those were the days when catching was really tough. There were so many offbeat pitches then, you know. Like the spitball, the emery ball, the shine ball. You name it, somebody threw it." And somebody caught it, knew what to do with it, and played minister to all those pitchers who threw all those pitches. O'Farrell remembered the seventh game of the 1926 World Series. His team, the St. Louis Cardinals, led the Murderer's Row Yankees 3–2 in the late innings at the Stadium. As the Yankees mounted a bases-loaded, two-out rally, O'Farrell and Cards manager Rogers Hornsby conferred at the mound, and after a visual inspection of the pitcher's throwing hand—bloody from too many knuckle balls—Hornsby sent for Grover Cleveland Alexander, the team's and possibly the game's best pitcher. Alexander had pitched the day before and, worse, not expecting to pitch again, had spent the previous night carousing. O'Farrell, in that moment, knew two things about his pitcher: He was the best in the game and he was clearly in need of sleep.

"I can try," was all Alexander could say when Hornsby asked him if he could pitch. With Tony Lazzeri coming up, the agreed-upon strategy was to keep the ball low and away—nothing up high. The first pitch Alexander threw was on target but the second was not. Lazzeri lit into a lazy, high pitch and launched it into the left-field seats—foul by about ten feet. O'Farrell immediately saw that the ball would be foul but still went into a melodramatic rain dance. Then he marched to the mound.

"I thought we were going to pitch him low and outside," he said.

"He'll never get another one like that," replied the chastened Great One.

"And," O'Farrell told Ritter, "he never did." Lazzeri struck out, and Alexander, free of his cobwebs, set the Yankees down easily the rest of the way. Nothing special.

All of the great catchers from that era and those immediately following were personalities and skilled laborers hiding in a deceptively ungainly-looking trade. Gabby Hartnett caught more games than anyone until Al Lopez. He led the National League in fielding his position seven times, had possibly the strongest arm ever among catchers, and in twenty big-league seasons, playing at a time when two-handed catching was universal, *never* had a finger mashed from a foul tip—partly the result of luck but also of the particularly relaxed way he had taught himself to hold his hands.

Through his seventeen-year career, Bill Dickey was elegant, reserved, and deadly—rather like Gary Cooper at high noon. Rogers Hornsby, in his autobiography, remembered the one big shoot-out in Dickey's career:

"Dickey, who batted .313 and hit 202 home runs in 17 seasons with the Yankees, had one of the strongest arms I ever saw. He blocked the plate with the best. He wasn't dirty, but he didn't let anyone run over him," the Rajah said. "One day Carl Reynolds, a Washington outfielder, had the play at the plate beat easy, but clobbered Dickey, knocking him about 15 feet. Dickey walked straight for the dugout and hit Reynolds so hard in the jaw that nurses had to feed him through a tube for the next month. Dickey was suspended for a month and fined $1000. That was his only fight."

Mickey Cochrane, Hall of Famer with the Athletics and later the Tigers, had a legendary temper and an incendiary obsession with winning. Inner fires seemed to consume him—but also to define his skills. He was not an adroit catcher at first. The word

his first major league manager, Connie Mack, used was "crude." Mack, who prized Cochrane's reputation as a minor leaguer and who "liked him on the train because he listened so eagerly," was shocked by Cochrane's lack of defensive ability when he first saw him play.

"He was crude at receiving the ball," Mack told a reporter at the time. "His stance and crouch were both wrong. And on foul balls he was simply pathetic . . .

" 'What can I do with that boy?' I wondered. 'He's trying his heart out but he doesn't even look like a catcher. Outfielder, maybe?'

"I was so disappointed, and worked harder with him. He was that eager you couldn't hurt him if you had a heart. One morning I found him catching flies knocked out to him; after practice he had rookies hitting them. That night he was in my room asking questions.

"By the time we left camp, I knew my worries were over. A misfit in February, he was a star in April. Player and manager these fifty years, I've seen hundreds of men but none ever made such a quick and complete job of correcting weaknesses."

Cochrane did more than correct weaknesses; he transformed them. He became the best in his era in taking foul pops. He learned to come out of a low crouch throwing as well as anyone. Cy Perkins, a veteran catcher on the A's who worked with Cochrane, remembered how inept this part of his game was.

"It's no wonder Mike didn't know how to catch," he told Bob Broeg of *The Sporting News.* "He didn't know how to stand or to shift . . . He was too high behind the plate, an easier stance from which to throw, but not a good enough target for pitchers who want to keep the ball down.

"It's tougher throwing from back there when the ball is down and especially if the catcher's knee is down, but Mike worked on throwing them out from down low until he was blue in that tomato face instead of red. He was great at it."

He was even better at handling his staff. He let his fire and

temper guide him. In one game, early in his career, when an A's pitcher, Rube Walberg, was experiencing wildness, Cochrane came to the mound, grabbed the young pitcher, spun him around, and then, in full view of everyone, kicked him solidly in the rump. The startled pitcher laughed, somehow aware of the absurdity of what Cochrane had done, and, more relaxed, was actually able to resume pitching.

"Many times in my career I asked pitchers whether they did not think they needed a little help, [only] to get the surprised look of an insulted artist," he wrote in *Baseball—The Fan's Game.* "Once I asked it of Lefty Grove when we were kids breaking in:

" 'Get back there and do the catching. I'll do the pitching,' he snapped.

"I went back and he nearly tore my hand off with fireballs that the hitter still hasn't seen. Lefty had been unconsciously letting up, and when he got sore at me he wanted to knock me out of the park with every pitch.

"I used to do that with [George] Earnshaw all the time. He'd get so sore at me that he'd try to knock me down with a fast ball," Cochrane wrote. Strategy was never far from anything he did.

CATCHERS IN OUR TIME, with one glaring difference, are up against the same complex set of challenges that the game's older catchers faced. The one difference, of course, is Astroturf, but the ways in which the surface changed what catchers do—and perhaps what they have become—is not quite so obvious.

On the surface, the major change is in base stealing. In the decades prior to turf, the average number of stolen bases each season, per league, had dropped to less than 500. By the fifties it was under 400. But toward the end of the sixties—exactly when Astroturf was introduced, the totals rose dramatically. Even allowing for expansion and division play, which increased the number of teams in both leagues from sixteen to twenty-six, stolen-base totals grew disproportionately. In 1989, there were 3,116 total stolen bases, up from a combined total of 923 in 1960 (the

last sixteen-team year) and from 1,515 in 1968 (the last year prior to divisional play).

While base-stealing totals were higher at the turn of the century and before, their more recent revival in the age of Astroturf introduced an unprecedented challenge to catchers. Where formerly catchers threw out around 50 percent of all runners, the number has been steadily declining to where today anything over 30 to 35 percent (the recent average figure in both leagues) is considered excellent.

Part of the difficulty may be because catchers really don't throw as well as they used to. But other factors are involved as well. Scouting today emphasizes speed as never before (to the point where teams today will actually scout potential talent at track meets). Also, base stealers these days are decked out in featherweight running shoes, which help them fly from base to base. Add turf and the result makes the job of contemporary catchers an ever tougher challenge. Increasingly, their performance is measured not only against living opponents but against stopwatches and computer printouts. A catcher is expected to get a ball to second base in under 2 seconds. If he gets it there in 1.9, he is said to have an unusually quick release. If he gets it there, as does Benito Santiago of the Padres, in 1.8, dip his arm in gold and preserve the mold.

What this has done is subtly change things behind the plate, deemphasizing some possibly more important skills—like blocking balls or handling pitchers—for the sake of others—like throwing. The catchers who get the ball down there in 1.8 will always be employed, while those who don't will be living proof (regardless of how much time it takes pitchers to come to the plate) of a general decline in standards at the position.

The first catcher who was a match for the revolution was Johnny Bench. Bench would have been a prototype in any age. With his low-to-the-ground build, quick reflexes, massive but soft hands, powerful throwing arm, and first-rate baseball mind to go with his best-ever bat, he was simply an ideal catcher, one in a

million. But playing on turf, he was even better. He knew how to attack speed.

Bench, following Randy Hundley, first stripped his big catcher's mitt of padding, then redesigned it altogether so that it would allow him added flexibility in taking balls left and right and in scooping them from the dirt.

"My glove," he says, "automatically squeezed the ball—you had to squeeze with the old mitt. You became another infielder in the sense that the glove just closed around the ball if it hit in there."

Because of this and because his hands were so good, Bench could do things, against all conventional teaching, that other catchers couldn't.

"I used to catch balls backhanded," he said. "I could pick balls out of the dirt that way—I became as known for that as anyone. You couldn't do that before."

Bench geared everything to the new Astroturf challenge, which he seemed to understand better than others. He needed the freedom of one-handed catching, of greater range behind the plate, because he saw what kind of athletes were out there on the new, pool-top-fast surfaces.

"Since the advent of Astroturf you just had to have faster players to cope with it—we got them—and of course they had more ability to steal bases, and these players were all wearing lighter uniforms and lightweight shoes. It just inevitably meant more pressure on catchers—you had to be up on your legs more, you had to be over your legs more than in the past, so you could move all the time."

Movement, razoring mitts, and razoring time to win a war waged in tenths of seconds—that is what the position seemed suddenly to be about. "I was doing all my movements to get into the cock positon to throw as the ball was coming," Bench says. "I didn't have to go out, play the ball, turn around, and get an extra step."

Bench's arm was strong enough to allow him a different kind

of release, quicker than the catch-step-throw or even the newer jump-pivot, where the catcher literally leaped up into throwing position as he took the ball. Bench's throwing stance allowed him an unusually secure base from which he could execute the most difficult part of the throw for one-handed catchers—the transfer from glove to hand. This move must be lightning-fast and absolutely sure. Either the ball is there or it isn't. The transfer is one discrete component in a seemingly seamless movement.

"I had to make the transfer between hand and glove second nature. And the transfer finally came around," Bench says, "because I was always in position to throw."

Since he was so flexible, Bench's movements oddly seemed held to a minimum. And limited movement meant that he could do more in less time.

"The one thing coaches are always working on is the setup behind the plate and the transfer. You know a lot of guys have this unconscious worry about transferring," he said, "and they rush. So many base runners are stealing eighty percent of the bases they attempt and it puts so much pressure on the catchers. . . ."

Bench's way around this pressure was to see through it. He seemed not as interested in actual kill ratios (he regularly had about 50 percent) but in the *threat* posed to would-be base stealers—an intangible for which no percentages exist.

"The thing that isn't looked at," Bench said, "is how many do you deter from running. The great base runners are going to steal bases, but you eliminate the other guys from even attempting to steal." The few tenths of a second that Bench saved in the way he set up, caught, and released a ball did not affect the Lou Brocks of the game so much as base runners in the middle to lower parts of the batting order—and the pitchers on Bench's own team, who knew that with this extra sliver of time, they could concentrate more on getting hitters out without having to alter their mechanics.

Above all, the changes in catching style by Bench allowed him

to preserve the traditional role of catchers—that of running the game. When he talks about what he accomplished as a catcher, Bench keeps returning to what he was able to do with his pitching staff. The pitchers themselves determined what he did or did not do. If Gary Nolan was pitching, there was little chance base stealers would be caught—his delivery was too slow. The goal, then was not to change his delivery but to have him make the most of what he could do: hold the runners as close as possible, throw to the base often, let the catcher snap a throw or two. On the other hand, if Don Gullett was pitching, much more was possible. "But the whole thing is that pitchers have to feel comfortable with what they do on the mound," Bench says. "They have to feel comfortable in their kick; you never want a situation where they wind up saying, 'I've shortened my kick and my stride but I've given up three runs and five hits.' So your goal is always to make them comfortable as possible; you won't do anything more important as a catcher. The number one goal is to keep guys off the bases—that comes before throwing out base runners."

In watching and talking with young catchers making their way in the game today, it is clear that the ability to catch base runners is overemphasized. Some of the young catchers like Benito Santiago, Joel Skinner, and Ron Karkovice have extremely powerful and accurate arms. (Others, like Mike LaValliere and B. J. Surhoff, have less powerful arms but still have had some success in throwing out runners.) Santiago and Karkovice, in particular, have attracted attention because of the high percentage of base stealers they have caught. And if throwing alone were the standard, these catchers would be as representative of the position as any at any time. But they are not, at least not yet.

The most significant common attribute among these batterymen is youth. The decline and fall of catching rests not so much on the relative strength of their arms but on whether or not, over time, they will actually catch enough. They are young, and their personalities as catchers are not yet fully defined. The relentless

pressure to guard against base stealers may, as Johnny Bench and others suggest, have seriously cut into their offensive abilities, but even beyond that there remains this nearly immeasurable matter of inexperience.

Benny Santiago, the Padres' twenty-five-year-old catcher, won his first Gold Glove at his position in only his second year in the majors. Because he has developed the ability to throw from his knees and has bagged elite runners like Vince Coleman and Otis Nixon among the 45 percent he has caught stealing in the last two seasons, it is easy to misread his game.

Santiago is a technically superior, if unfinished, catcher. He tends to use his quickness and soft hands to reach one-handed for balls in the dirt rather than shifting his body over to block them. He makes errors (twenty-two in 1987, eleven in 1988, and twenty-two in 1989, all league-leading for the position) and is likely to use his arm more than he should. He *knows* how to throw; the business of unloading from his knees, generally assumed to be the good result of simple brute strength, is actually something more. The throw, Santiago says, comes from properly aligning his body prior to a pitch. "I already have shifted my weight so when I come forward on my knees I am ready to throw. It is easier for me to throw from that position." How easy? In the past two seasons, apart from cutting down base stealers, he has picked off twenty-five runners, including nine at second base—all from his knees!

What Santiago has not yet proven he can do is just what other young catchers find most difficult—control his pitching staff. Beginning in the minors, when he was not yet fluent in English, through his most recent sojourn in the majors, he has not been allowed to call his own game. The bench or his pitchers have determined what is to be thrown and when. This fairly widespread practice, which any veteran receiver knows is wrongheaded (no one on the bench sees as much as the man closest to the plate and to the innumerable small, moment-to-moment adjustments of the batter), can hinder a catcher's development and

damage his self-esteem. It is something that Santiago is well aware of. Accused of being "moody," his moods often flow from this not-so-subtle emasculation of his game.

"Tonight I called only a couple of pitches; I don't know who was calling the pitches," he said after catching a shutout one night in 1988. "I'm gonna be here twenty years—twenty years it's gonna be like that? How am I gonna improve?"

As eager as Santiago is to take control of his staff, the problem is different for B. J. Surhoff of the Milwaukee Brewers. Far from being "moody," Surhoff is quiet to the point of reticence. He is allowed to call more pitches in a game than Santiago is but that still, at times, presents a problem. In college, where he was an All-American his freshman year, he was newly recruited to catching (from third base) and thereafter, through his senior year, his coach permitted him to call his own game—to a point. "On oh-and-two, the coach called every pitch," Surhoff says.

In the pros, playing for Tom Treblehorn, a manager well matched to a young team, Surhoff has been encouraged to take as much initiative as he can. Because he is quiet and intense and constantly up against a standard of near perfection that he has set for himself, Surhoff sometimes looks to the bench for help. He will not always know when a pitcher is tired or what pitch he is looking to throw. He acknowledges that the complexity of managing pitch-to-pitch situations is sometimes more than he can handle. It is possible to be mentally tired behind the plate, which for Surhoff means losing the ability to think ahead.

Even with his manager's encouragement, he has a hard time going to the mound. In one game last season he went out to talk with pitcher Bill Wegman, who is also a friend. Wegman was having difficulty closing a game in which the team had a big lead. "I went out and said, 'Hey, does your arm hurt or what?' He said, 'No.' I said, 'Well, throw the damn ball, willya!' He called me a name—and laughed."

Surhoff, acutely conscious of his inability to speak confidently, sometimes rehearses when he is by himself. "I don't get

in front of the mirror or anything, but it's like I'm just trying to think—'You piece of blank,' you know, you know—'We gotta get some damn innings out of you'—or if the guy shows you up or something. I've heard of catchers meeting pitchers in the locker room afterwards."

But above all, Surhoff measures this against the job he has to do and his own years. He knows he is young. Treblehorn, himself a former catcher, and Brewers catching coach Andy Etchebarren, who handled the great Orioles pitching staff of the sixties and seventies, both say that no catcher begins to learn his trade until he has about 600 major league games under his belt. At the end of the 1989 season, Surhoff, highly intelligent and motivated, had caught barely over half that number.

Mike LaValliere, like Surhoff a converted infielder, has caught 437 major league games. Of the current crop of younger catchers, he is the least imposing physically. LaValliere is listed as five feet ten in the Pirates' media guide but is probably an inch or two shorter than that and, in addition, his hands and feet are unusually small, almost dainty. His arm, by his own admission, is not nearly as strong as those of some other catchers, but he has piled up better throwing numbers with an extraordinarily quick release and solid fundamentals. His fireplug body is set low to the ground, perfectly balanced behind the plate, and with his quick feet, he moves to block balls as well as anyone. As a rookie in 1986, a year prior to his Gold Glove season with the Pirates, he allowed just one passed ball in 827 innings, the best rate in the majors.

"I know I'm not as physically gifted as others but I use what I have and I work hard," LaValliere says. In a way, this too is a catcher's deception. His short body is actually an advantage. Because he is so low to the ground, he does not have to uncoil in order to throw, but can come straight up through his crouch to get his throw off. Taller catchers like Fisk and Boone have to worry more about getting all of themselves, segment by segment, aligned for the throw. But LaValliere has used his low build

productively. It took him two to three years to get down the mechanics of throwing correctly, he says, but he has it now. "When I come up to throw, it's all one motion—I don't catch-step-throw. I'm already stepping and catching at the same time. Because of my arm, I have no choice but to do it this way."

The part of his game in which he takes most pride, however, is his signal calling. That, too, came slowly.

"I call every pitch—I don't get any from the dugout. I call pitch by pitch; each pitch dictates the next. We have a general game plan and it's my job to vary from it as the need arises," he says.

This ability to adjust from pitch to pitch, to think in sequences of pitches and then change as the moment and situation dictate, is the heart of signal calling. Intuition as much as experience is required, as is the particular ability to watch every muscle and twitch of the batter, every slight alteration of motion in any pitch that is thrown, any untoward movement by base runners or position players in the field—and then make something of that.

At twenty-nine, LaValliere is the oldest of the young catchers as well as the one with the most game experience. He already knows that good mechanics and sound signal calling are part of a larger objective: gaining the confidence of a pitching staff. They also serve who squat and wait:

"It's important to block the ball, it's important to throw the runner out, but the most important thing is to get the most you can from your pitching staff," LaValliere says. "That means taking the time to learn everything that can be learned about different pitchers. That means using every situation, whether it's spring training, batting practice, or back at the hotel having a beer— you sit with ten different guys, and pick their brains a little bit, seeing how they act in every conceivable situation on the field."

It also means having authority going to the mound, knowing when to challenge a pitcher, when to back off, when to encourage, when to wheedle. The psychology is important, but having the pitcher throw the pitch he has most confidence in is more

important. "If I call a pitch and my pitcher shakes me off, I'll usually go with what he wants, unless I really think it's wrong—then I'll go out," LaValliere says. He then asks why the pitcher wants to throw that particular pitch. "If he gives me a good answer, I turn around and go back to the plate. If he has no answer or no good answer then I'll tell him he needs to rethink it. We'll talk about it."

LaValliere works with a young staff, still unproven, still likely to undergo significant personnel changes. The confidence he gains from this year's crop of pitchers may not hold with next year's any more than his own tenure with any one team. Once traded, once injured, the future, as any young player knows, is always uncertain—with catchers even more so. Endurance and duration always stand between the masters and those who would succeed them.

IT IS JUST these two qualities that finally separate the game's two geriatric masked marvels, Fisk and Boone, from their catching brethren. Coming into the 1989 season, Boone had caught a major-league-record 2,056 games, Fisk 1,838—fourth on the all-time list (Al Lopez, with 1,950, is second, Jim Sundberg, recently retired, third). Both Fisk and Boone have no business being at the plateaus they have reached. Both have injury profiles fit for the files of *M*A*S*H*. In addition to twice breaking his hand, Fisk has been sidelined with a broken leg, broken ribs, ligaments separated from his pelvic bone, cartilage frayed and broken in his knee joints. One of his knees has been surgically repaired. Boone's medical dossier includes four different knee operations: He has had cartilage removed from his left and right knees, and had torn ligaments surgically repaired in his left knee. In addition, both men have endured the yearly battering all catchers endure, the usual collection of contusions, lacerations, sprains, strains, swellings, lumps, and bumps—only for many more seasons than most.

The two men have different attitudes about having played so many games. Fisk, more expansive and more easily given to

laughter than Boone, enjoys playing Father Time with players half his age—players he successfully competes against. Ask him about his age and he will not only call the roll of younger catchers brought in—unsuccessfully—to replace him, but he likely will summon their genealogies to enliven things:

"Do you know Matt Merullo, the newest kid they've brought in?" he asked in 1988. "This kid's grandfather scouted me when I was playing high school. Yeah. His grandfather, Lennie Merullo —played for the Cubs. Hey, just look around now: You've got Roberto Alomar, Barry Bonds, Dick Ellsworth's kid, Ken Griffey. It's amazing. Can a player play in an old-timers' game and then in the regular game? You think that's funny—I played against half those guys."

Boone seems less willing to linger over the years and games he has accumulated. He says he is lucky to have been given a body that has worn better than most and that his record for longevity is something others—fans and media—have been more impressed with than is warranted. It is as though even thinking about age is just not on his agenda.

Neither of these men has continued at the top by accident. Following very different mind sets, each has maintained himself with punishing training programs that others—at any age— would be hard-pressed to keep up with.

Despite his patrician looks, Fisk has always been more like a New England woodsman. He has lived—and exulted—in the outdoors. Long before running became popular, he ran—to the ballpark from the hotel, around and around the warning tracks of ballparks—anywhere and everywhere he could, miles at a time, just because he enjoyed it. In addition, in the off-season, he played racquetball and basketball, chopped wood, ran some more.

But following his pelvic injury in 1984, Fisk says he undertook training with "a purpose." Working with a chiropractor, Phil Crossen, he started a grueling weight-and-aerobics regimen that he has continued to this day—one and a half to two hours a

day, four times a week during the season, more in the off season. What the guru did, Fisk says, was "basically pound the crap out of me." But the purpose of the labor was to focus on that area of the body most crucial to catching—between the knees and the chest. "That is where your strength as a catcher comes from," Fisk points out. Strength in the trunk, as opposed to the extremities, specifically builds endurance over the long haul and even game by game, when catchers commonly experience fatigue in the late innings. In addition, there is a mental payoff. "You get the feeling of being solid," Fisk says. "You draw on that in everything you do behind the plate." In practical terms, what this allows Fisk is a much enhanced ability to "glide" in his movements—going out to block balls, coming up out of the chute to throw—not merely to endure in terms of years, but to prevail in terms of skill.

Bob Boone has been conditioning himself "with a purpose" ever since the mid-1970s, when he began working with the Phillies' trainer, Gus Hoefling. Hoefling, an expert in Japanese and Chinese martial arts, runs a program harder on body and mind than the Spanish Inquisition. Hoefling has only limited belief in weights. The key to the physical side of his program is "natural resistance" (i.e., if you stand in a pit of sand and try to work your feet down through to the bottom, the strength needed is matched by the resistance of the sand, rather than by the preset calibrations of a machine). The other essential to Hoefling's program is the trainee's sense that he has more in him than he—or anyone else —knew.

Boone's regimen is similar to Fisk's in terms of hours, and also in its sense of punishment (it is never "fun") and reward: He feels better at forty-two than he did at twenty-one.

Since he left the Phillies in 1981, Boone, with the help of another trainer, has refined the "program." Four to six times a week he does variations of the kung-fu katas he has learned, now streamlined into catcher-related work. Watch the old men of China in their ritual outdoor movements—they are able to trans-

fer weight seamlessly from crouched positions with impressive fluidity and strength. The remnants of old warriors' moves—"Mind of Moon," "Elephant Walks on Lily Pads"—are in his swaying catcher's executions.

But enough. Let us go down to the old rag-and-bone shop of the field and see just what it is about catching that can rouse professional observers to wonder about the future of the craft.

For convenience's sake (and because injury has kept Fisk from television), I have run three games of Boone's together. They show him with two different teams, California and Kansas City, over two years, against a single opponent, the Yankees. There are no real catcher's "highlights" in any of the games (although there is a throwing error and wild pitch that might have been a passed ball in one of the games), yet the composite picture, coherent as any, is a catcher at his everyday work. A word about television, too. In this one regard, the tube beats the ballpark because all of the minute and usually undetectable moves a catcher makes are vivified by the camera to a degree not available from any perch in the stands. It is even possible, with a good videotape machine, to study some of the unseen game—pitching sequences and strategy —that cannot be measured in the stadium.

The first of the games, in 1988, was a late-August 7–6 extra-inning victory by the Angels over the Yankees in Anaheim. In this game, the Yankees jumped out to an early 6–0 lead only to see the Angels come all the way back, tying the game on a homer in the ninth, winning it in the twelfth. The Angels' starter was a young pitcher named Willie Fraser, who was subsequently replaced by a string of even more inexperienced pitchers, one of whom, Bryan Harvey, pitched the last three innings for the win.

The second game, in the early part of the 1989 season, was a 5–3 Royals win over the Yankees in Kansas City. In this game, a veteran pitcher, Bret Saberhagen, went the route for the victory. The last game, in New York, was again won by the Royals, 5–3, with Mark Gubicza pitching a complete game.

In a technical sense, it is easy to see why Boone, at forty-two,

is still a superior catcher. His moves are precise and smooth, full of extraordinary subtlety and deception. Begin with his crouch: All catchers are taught the imperative of forming a low, wide base from which a good target, down in the strike zone, can be given and from which blocking movements will better be accomplished.

Most catchers in this ordinary set get down and flash their sign deep in their crotch, out of sight of the coaches, but then will usually give something away as they set their target. Because it is so hard to stay balanced in a deep crouch, catchers usually sway left or right depending on the location of the pitch they call. An astute batter, even a spy in the stands, will sometimes have enough time to process this slight betrayal of information. This is not the case with Boone.

Because he has become so strong in the middle of his body, precisely because he has learned how to generate enough power and lightness to walk like an elephant on lily pads, he shifts for location at the last split second, too late for anyone to pick up. He barely holds up his glove (incredibly, a palm-sized model, the smallest in use by any catcher) and then it is not a real target—pitchers tend to use parts of Boone's very reliably, very precisely held body for that.

When Boone shifts his body to receive a ball, it is done with an economy of movement, the sway left or right accomplished by maintaining a martial artist's center of gravity in the middle of the body so that movement to the side involves almost no surrender of balance. It *seems* as if he takes every ball not egregiously wide of the mark or in the dirt straight on—which, of course, is not the case. It is this sense of exquisite balance that enables him both to disguise the location of pitches and then to "frame" borderline pitches as well as he does.

In the seventh inning of the Yankee Stadium game, after the Royals, trailing 3–2, had rallied for three runs, Boone stole an important pitch. The Yankees' Mike Pagliarulo led off the inning with a single. Boone framed a 2-and-2 strikeout pitch on the next hitter, Don Slaught. The pitch was clearly outside—at least from

the vantage point of the center-field camera (and also in the mind of Don Slaught, who argued the call with the umpire).

What Boone did to secure the call, which was a turning point in the inning, was position his body with an absolute minimum of movement. The sway to the outside corner was just prior to the release of the pitch and was done in seeming slow motion. There appeared to be no movement of the hands—though there was. Boone took the ball in the middle of his body as though it were a strike down the pipe, turning his glove slightly downward into the strike zone. It was almost impossible to tell that his hands had done anything because his body—immobile above, in slow sway below—permitted this one quick, almost invisible sleight-of-hand.

"The key," Boone says, "is that movement of your body in front of the ball, giving the illusion that your hands are not moving." The mistake that many catchers make is pulling the ball back toward the plate, which gives the deception away. Also, unless a catcher has Boone's tremendous strength from the quadriceps to the upper abdomen, it is simply not possible, with all the good intention in the world, to shift the body into position smoothly enough to disguise the framing.

In that same at-bat, Boone blocked a pitch in the dirt and came out of it throwing—a pickoff attempt at first that came close but did not succeed. The blocked pitch was more important in that situation than the missed pickoff, but both were done in exemplary fashion.

Because Boone is so agile and has such good, soft hands, he will sometimes try to pick up balls in the dirt rather than block them. By his own admission it is an occasional lapse in his game (but one even more frequently seen in younger catchers who use one hand and a flexible mitt). But this time, Boone used his body. The pitch was a right-hander's slider low and away to a right-handed batter. With a runner on first, Boone had slightly altered his deep, low set. Still down, he had rolled forward, almost onto his toes, the usual adjustment that allowed him to spring from the box to block, field, or throw with runners on base.

Knowing the likely location of the pitch, he had already anticipated the possibility of a ball in the dirt. (Many catchers say that
it is prudent to anticipate a wild pitch on every pitch with runners
on). But when Boone went for the ball, he did things a little
differently. He turned his left knee three quarters of the way in
and down to the ground, offering his left side and front from
knee to shoulder as a blocking wedge. At the same time, having
angled out to cut down the inward kick of a breaking pitch, he
dropped his mitt backhanded, like a second baseman, to short-
hop the ball cleanly from the dirt. This motion simultaneously
allowed Boone to shift his weight to his right leg, which then
became a loaded catapult for a snap throw. With his weight back,
he simply took a short step forward with his left foot and brought
his arm up, simultaneously transferring the ball from mitt to
hand, for the throw—which he got off with a minimum of arc.
The arm came back at about shoulder level, not all the way back,
but enough so that, driving forward off his rear foot, he had
good snap on the ball.

The throw was exactly where it should have been, slightly
forward of the first-base bag and knee-high, but late by just a
whisker.

Earlier in the game Boone had a throwing error on another
pickoff attempt, this time at third. In that instance, with Rickey
Henderson hitting, Roberto Kelly the runner at first, and Slaught
leading down from third, Boone had to create more arc in order
to get his throw over the right-handed batter partially obstructing
his view. The throw hit Slaught in the back and bounded away,
permitting a run to score.

Both plays revealed the quickness of Boone's release, but also
why accurate throwing from behind the plate is so difficult. In
the one instance, Boone's body was in proper position to come
up throwing. In the other it was not.

"My throwing is a little unorthodox in that I have almost no
stride," Boone says. "All my movements are made prior to the
pitch. And I don't really come up from the crouch when I throw."

The preferred method for accuracy, Boone says, is to be rid

of the ball before you come up, to go "through" the target at a rising angle. The drive off the rear foot opens the shoulder at precisely the right moment and the body comes forward with the arm—exactly what happened on the snap throw to first.

On the throw to third, however, Boone—all six feet, two inches of him—had to come almost straight up to get throwing room past the hitter. There was more arm than weight shift in the throw, and hence greater risk of inaccuracy. (The key to accurate throwing, Boone stresses, is not arm strength, or cocking the ball by the ear or snapping the wrist or in any of the hundred misconceptions traditionally absorbed by sandlot catchers, but in the driving power of the rear foot. Even the usual helpmate in straight throwing—grabbing a ball across rather than with the seams—can be eliminated without affecting the flight path of the ball if the weight shift is properly executed off the drive of the rear foot.) Here, throwing from an upright position rather than at a rising angle, Boone could not properly power off his rear foot. The ball struck the base runner in the back and skipped away.

But the error, the result of calculated risk, only pointed up just how precise Boone usually is behind the plate. He is as finicky about the small details of his position as a bomb maker. From the way he has razored down his glove so that his hands can work as fast as a middle infielder's, to the positioning of his body on bunts (always so that he will be able to pivot or drive on his rear foot as he picks up the ball), on throws, on blocking balls in the dirt or runners from the plate (give them the plate, give with them when you can, bail out when you have no chance, stand in when there is no other choice), he has a reasoned explanation for every move he makes. His technique, though not necessarily suited to all other catchers, is complete and perfect for him.

Yet a description of Boone's mechanics no more explains him than old Billy Sullivan's mechanics would explain him. Boone has mastered technique only to get past it. He is an artist—or warrior—at his position. It is his intelligence and spirit that make him as good as he still is.

The heart of his game, he says, is signal calling. "You can do everything wrong—they can steal five bases, you can fail to block three or four balls, you can go oh for four and strike out three times, and yet if you called a good game, you can still win. If you don't call a good game, chances are you won't win no matter what everybody else does."

Boone's signal calling inevitably involves the relationship he has with his pitchers. Though a psychology major in college, whatever psychology he uses as a catcher is focused always on the game, on getting pitchers to have confidence in what he calls "the plan" and in their own ability.

Boone's job begins not with pitchers but with hitters—knowing exactly who they are, what their strengths, their weaknesses, and their most recent tendencies at the plate are. When he has to, he consults scouting reports and videotape, but he does other things as well.

He regularly watches the other team's batting practice. "You see what guys are working on, what they're trying to do, what kind of trouble they may be having," he says. And then he watches hitters constantly during their at-bats. "I work until I get an image of a hitter in my mind; then I work from that."

Boone also pays minute attention to every other participant on both sides of the lines: coaches, base runners, pitchers, catchers, his own position players. It is a catcher's way of seeing, indicative, perhaps, of why catchers seem so often to be drawn to managing. In order to call a game well, you have to be into *all* of the game; "your powers of observation can be trained like a painter's," Boone says. "Painters will look at a picture and just see more in it than the average person ever imagined was there.

"I was always pretty observant," Boone acknowledges, "but in teaching, when I don't have time to teach all the mechanics, I stress this. My biggest statement to kids is: Watch. If you really watch, everybody'll tell you what they're doing." Boone means this even down to sign stealing—something he is as good at as anyone—and it all goes into calling a game.

Boone does not like verbalizing much. He doesn't sit down

with pitchers and go over scouting reports or the opposing team's batting order. He has an exact game plan but a keen sense of its limitation. Pitchers cannot throw the pitch he wants in the place he wants it every time he puts down a sign. He thinks in sequences of pitches but changes according to what is going on. "The plan," he says, "is actually three or four different plans."

His goal is to give his pitchers maximum confidence in their own ability. More: to sometimes coax from them things they never imagined they had—to throw a breaking pitch in a bases-loaded, two-out, three-and-two-count situation with the game on the line—and succeed. "When that happens," Boone says, "a pitcher can go to a whole new level of belief in himself. He'll see that he really can do things he didn't believe he could. He'll think of himself differently than he did before."

Boone, like Mike LaValliere and many other catchers, will "reason" with his pitchers when they shake him off, generally letting them throw what they want. But he has his own approach. In the end, he is no democrat.

"There are only about five or six pitches in a game that I think are crucial," Boone says, "so most of the other times, when I'm putting down fingers, I'm just suggesting a pitch. If a pitcher has a feel in his hand for something else, if he prefers something else, fine—I don't consider myself a know-it-all. It's in those five or six pitches that I do know this is exactly the wrong pitch to throw.

"When that happens, I'll call time and go out and say, 'Look, this is why I think you shouldn't throw that pitch—because of this, this, this, and that.' I'll give him a couple of options. I'll tell him, 'I think you can throw a fastball away or a slider away but I don't want you coming in because I think this guy might be looking for that pitch and he has the power to jerk it out.' I may not be exactly right but I know I'm gonna keep the ball in the park in that situation. In most cases, the pitcher usually says, 'Fine,' and goes along." No strong-arming, but no real voting rights either.

In the three different Boone games I taped, he worked with

very different sets of pitchers. In the 1988 game in California, he worked mainly with young, not yet established pitchers. In the games from 1989, he worked with a two-time Cy Young Award winner, Bret Saberhagen, and an emerging star, Mark Gubicza.

Boone says that there is absolutely no magic to calling a game for a top pitcher. A Roger Clemens or a Steve Carlton, whom Boone caught for eight years in Philadelphia, put the ball basically where they want with overpowering stuff. There is little need to improvise on the basic game plan. With younger, less talented pitchers, the task is more challenging, and patience, improvisation, and much more exact knowledge are mandatory.

"With younger pitchers, I've got to know what pitches he can throw—accurately—in what situations," Boone says. "So I may know a change-up outside is the pitch to call but I also know this guy will only have a twenty-percent success rate throwing that pitch, and I can't afford to waste a pitch here so I'm going to have to go with something different."

All of the specifics of calling three different games with different pitchers and essentially different lineups, are just too much to cover. But it is possible to see how Boone's "plan" and its intricate sense of adjustment work by looking at two hitters who normally do well against *all* pitchers—Rickey Henderson and Don Mattingly.

In the opening inning of the 7–6 game in California, Willie Fraser, who featured a good fork ball to go with an adequate fastball, faced Henderson leading off. Boone called for two sharp breaking balls (for strikes), the first inside, the second down and out. Henderson then fouled off an inside fastball, and Boone called for another, even though the breaking pitch away would have seemed more logical. But Henderson's one vulnerability as a hitter has always been inside fastballs, particularly up in the strike zone. He protects himself against the pitch with his extreme crouch, but good location with some velocity can get him. With Henderson looking for Fraser's best pitch outside, the inside fastball worked—almost. Henderson muscled the ball weakly the

other way, and it had just enough to carry beyond the reach of the second baseman for a single.

Fraser successfully held Henderson at first as Claudell Washington struck out and then, with the threat of a steal still outstanding, Boone started Mattingly with three outside fastballs—even though Mattingly cannot be overpowered and is particularly deft at flicking outside pitches the opposite way. There was nothing fancy in Boone's reasoning. Anyone batting with a base burner like Rickey Henderson on first will see fastballs. But Fraser's 2-and-0 fastball was a balk, and Henderson moved to second. Fraser threw a breaking ball for 3-and-0, then a fastball down the middle with Mattingly taking all the way. On the next pitch, Boone had Fraser come down and in with his fork ball and Mattingly bounced it routinely to the right side—with Henderson taking third.

In the third inning, Henderson came up with a runner on second, none out, and the Yanks leading 1–0. Fraser missed with a high inside fastball, got a strike on the fastball away, missed with an inside breaking pitch, had an inside fastball fouled away. At 2-and-2, Boone, knowing that Henderson had been fooled on the last inside fastball his first time up, went for two fork balls, Fraser's strong suit. One missed inside, the second outside: a walk. After Washington doubled home two runs, Mattingly got an RBI single to center on a fastball that stayed in the center of the plate.

Against a new pitcher, Jack Lazorko, in the fourth, Rickey Henderson, with no one on and no one out, struck out on a 1-and-2 fastball high and inside. The two previous pitches that set up the strikeout were breaking balls, one outside, one in. The routine fastball looked faster following the breaking pitches. In the same inning, with one on and one out, Mattingly tapped out to short on an outside fastball following a breaking pitch down and in.

Thus, within a few innings, even with the Angels getting battered, Boone's "plan," it was clear, was to work sequences that

would expose Henderson to high inside fastballs, Mattingly to fastballs away. "You don't get major league hitters out on the same pitch from one at-bat to the next," Boone says. "That is why they're major league hitters. You must disguise what you're doing, change what you're doing, even if you know what you're after."

In the sixth, with one on and none out, Henderson, on an 0-and-1 fastball that probably missed its outside target, flied easily to center. Mattingly, one out later, facing a new pitcher, left-hander Sherman Corbett, took two breaking pitches, one inside, one outside, then got under an outside fastball that came back in toward the middle of the plate, and flied to right.

In the eighth inning, with veteran righty Greg Minton pitching and the Angels trailing 6–3, Boone kept everything away from Henderson. Two fastballs, a slider, a curve, another fastball —all outside—the last, at 2-and-2, all were designed to keep Henderson "in the park," but also to keep him looking for the inside pitch that never came. He bounced weakly to Minton. Mattingly, on the other hand, with a man aboard, had to have been looking for that outside fastball. Because Boone knew Minton had excellent command of his breaking pitch, he had him come down and in with a slider—home-run territory if the slightest error was made in location. But Mattingly, a shade off stride, bounced wide to the first baseman, who flipped to the covering Minton for the final out of the inning.

In the games the following season when he was with the Royals, Boone, working with experienced pitchers, attacked Henderson and Mattingly more directly. In the 5–3 game at Kansas City pitched by Saberhagen, an excellent control pitcher, Henderson and Mattingly both got first-inning hits to right field on fastballs that missed their targets inside and out. In the third, though, with Henderson batting with one out and no one on, Boone worked him high and in with a fastball, possibly a "purpose" pitch, setting up the next pitch—a fastball on the outside part of the plate. Saberhagen threw a sharp slider low and outside

for a second strike, and then struck Henderson out with the inside fastball. Mattingly was retired in the next inning on four fastballs, low and in, high and out, outside again, then up and in. Mattingly, ready to go the other way on another outside pitch, lifted a harmless fly to center.

In Henderson's next at-bat, Boone again went to all fastballs —high and outside for a swinging strike, a ball high and in, a swinging strike high and outside, a grounder tapped weakly to second base on an inside, belt-high fastball.

Mattingly, in his last two at-bats in the game, flied to left, swinging behind outside fastballs early in the count. Henderson, also not wanting to fall behind, impatiently bounced a first-pitch outside fastball off Frank White's glove for an infield single (at first ruled an error) in his last at-bat.

Back in New York, with Gubicza beating the Yankees by the same 5–3 score, Henderson and Mattingly were again closed down, Henderson on patterns leading to inside fastballs, Mattingly somewhat differently. Boone chose to use Gubicza's outstanding slider to work Mattingly. He induced a grounder to the first baseman in the opening inning on a ball down and in; then a grounder to the second baseman on a slider low and outside, following a slider low and inside; he got him next on a bouncer to the first baseman unassisted—on a first-pitch slider, down and in, which Mattingly decided to offer at.

In all, through the three games, Henderson and Mattingly combined had five hits, in twenty-six at-bats with one extra-base hit (a double) and one walk—a .192 average. Even accepting an element of happenstance in calculating these particular three games, it is clear that whatever was being called against these hitters worked. Boone knew what he was doing, both with younger pitchers and with the veterans. He worked from a plan at all times, but the plan worked because of the skilled ways in which he departed from it. The "book" on these hitters was a text, and the departures upon which success depended poetry.

"Signal calling is more an art form than a science," Boone

says. "You can say, 'Okay, throw a curveball out here, then a fastball in off the plate,' and then that gives you that outside corner. Well, not always—I can't tell you when it does and when it doesn't. You just have to know it. You watch. You watch every hitter, everything he does. If he moves his feet, what's he trying to do? Where's his weight when the ball gets in the hitting zone? Then what does your pitcher have? Where is he at? Then, what's the exact situation we're facing—it's *everything* that determines what you do."

To master signal calling means that a catcher must be able to bring out the best in his pitchers. He must be consistently right and only occasionally wrong—that is his ultimate psychology. To accomplish this he must, obviously, have a strong and supple intelligence. But something else is required. Early in his career, before anyone knew much about him, Boone became Steve Carlton's catcher. Aside from being a great pitcher, Carlton was notoriously high-strung. For years he had insisted that Tim McCarver, a familiar veteran, catch him whenever he pitched. Boone did not have the luxury of reputation to guide him. He had to prove himself as a signal caller. He found something within himself that perhaps he had been forced to find:

"There's nothing I've really done except that over time it's turned out that I've been right more than I've been wrong. With that," he explains, remembering the evolution of his career, "you get a reputation, and it's easier to set up a game plan. Rookie players in general, catchers in particular, have a tougher time imparting to older players what they think is right—it's something you have to earn. A manager can't give it to you—signals from the bench won't do it—you have to find it in yourself. You have to think with your pitcher, really be one with him. That takes something. And it's amazing what happens when all of a sudden you call for an exotic pitch that the pitcher hadn't been using and it's exactly right; it was what he was thinking at the same time—you put down a change-up inside to a power hitter and this pitcher says, 'That's unbelievable—that's what I was

thinking,' and then he'll throw you an unbelievably great pitch." It takes audacity and imagination to believe that what you think is what others think—even on a ball field.

Boone doesn't believe that there is a crisis at the position today; in his mind the game has simply filled up with many young catchers all at once who need experience to get better. But there are others who disagree, including Carlton Fisk, who feels that what is missing from today's young catchers is a sense of strong personality that was present in a number of earlier catchers.

"Whether you like it or not, you are the front of the boat; everyone on the field keys off you," Fisk says. "They look to you to be a catalyst, a leader, to be the director; they look to you for stability, confidence, everything. That's why catchers are usually strong personalities—most of the time very opinionated, sometimes hard-headed, but that's their personality. Catchers' skills are developed, but not their personalities, because you can't develop that—you have to have it.

"In the mid-seventies, there were a lot of good catchers coming up and they all had strong personalities—the Benches, the Carters, the Parrishes, Sundberg, Munson—all these people were very strong characters as catchers.

"Now there are only a few of us left—you've got Parrish, Carter, myself. Sundberg's retired, Dempsey is still playing and, of course, Boone: all the guys who prepared to play. They're motivated; they have a passion for the game—they have a passion as a leader."

PITCHER

Our Captain is a goodly man,
And Harry is his name;
What'er he does, 'tis always "Wright,"
So says the voice of fame.
And as the Pitcher of our nine,
We think he can't be beat;
In many a fight, old Harry Wright
Has saved us from defeat.

① **JIM ABBOTT** *of the California Angels, one-handed but never short-handed as a defender. Because of his handicap, Abbott has actually mastered the fundamentals of pitching defense far more thoroughly than others.*

THE CALIFORNIA ANGELS

② **JIM KAAT** *was as large as Shantz was small, but Shantz was his boyhood idol. Here Kaat shows his amazing quickness by covering first in time to take a throw and make a play on the Royals' Cookie Rojas during a 1974 game at Comiskey Park. When he played for his last team, the Cardinals, Kaat was used as a relief pitcher—primarily because of his fielding ability.*

UPI/BETTMANN NEWSPHOTOS

③ *During the fifties, in the prime of his career,* **BOBBY SHANTZ,** *at five feet six and 139 pounds, looked more like a jockey than a major league pitcher. By nearly all accounts, he was one of the best fielding pitchers ever.*

AP/WIDE WORLD PHOTOS

④ **RON GUIDRY'S** *concentration is all toward home plate as he prepares to release a pitch. As soon as the ball leaves his fingertips, however, he will take a little hop into position as a fifth infielder.*

THE NEW YORK YANKEES

I N A REDS-PIRATES GAME during the 1989 season, Cincinnati pitcher José Rijo saved a run and possibly the game when he threw a gloved hand behind his back to improbably snare a hit up the middle and turn it into an easy out at first. Rijo's spectacular play made all the highlight films but has been duplicated enough times by other pitchers in other situations for observers to recognize the play when they see it. Though catches like these can never really be planned for, split-second reactions—or failures to react—to balls smoked at the pitcher have always been a part of pitching defense and, according to Jim Kaat, the sixteen-time Gold Glove winner at the position, the most fundamental part.

"Most of fielding for the pitcher is reflexes," Kaat says. "The rest, like getting over to cover the base or backing up on plays, is what you learn to do."

There have been some notable and frightening reminders of just how critical this ability to react can be:

- In a 1957 game between the Yankees and Indians, Herb Score, the Indians' left-handed pitcher, considered by many to have had raw talent equal to that of Sandy Koufax, was struck in the eye by a line drive off the bat of Gil McDougald. Score's career was effectively ended.
- Bib Gibson, an otherwise superlative fielding pitcher, used to fall off balance to the first-base side in his follow-through to the plate. In one game, he was unable to recover quickly enough, and a line drive off the bat of Roberto Clemente shattered his leg. Gibson still had enough presence of mind

—and heart—to pursue the ball, pick it up, and make the play at first.

Excellent reflexes, along with a throwing motion that leaves a pitcher in a balanced position, ready to field, are not only good for body and soul, they are also enormously helpful to a team's defense. A pitcher who is quick off the mound, who can cover more ground to his left and right, who can catch or knock balls down that might otherwise go through into center field, is really an extra infielder, creating run- and game-saving opportunities that otherwise would not be there:

- In a 1988 game, Minnesota pitcher Allan Anderson, unobserved as one of the two ERA leaders in the American League that season, also fielded his position brilliantly. In one game, reacting to a foul bunt with a runner on first, he sprinted from the mound, dove into foul territory to make the catch, turned over, and managed, in one continuous motion, to flip the ball to first for the double play.
- Mets pitcher Bob Ojeda saved a 1–0 shutout early in the 1988 season by making a diving, single-motion pickup and shovel scoop on a ball topped in front of the plate in time to cut down a tying run coming in from third base.

Both of these latter plays, though many pitchers would not have been able to make them, *are* plays good fielding pitchers make—and in making them, change the nature of a team's inner defense.

In a curious way, a pitcher's good reflexes, especially when they are on display in life-threatening situations, make us see less and perhaps value less of what pitchers can do as defenders. The rocket off a pitcher's body, the taking of a hot shot behind the back or between the legs or in the webbing of a glove, are all spectacular but exceptional plays. It is possible for even the best fielding pitcher to go through many games without having to

defend his honor or his team in that fashion. Most fans and even a large number of professional people simply don't pay that much attention to pitching defense. Pitching, we all know, is 75 to 90 percent of the game, and in that regard a ninety-five-mile-per-hour fastball is the best defense there is. Except pitchers—even Nolan Ryan—know that is not enough. It is pitching *and* defense that is 75 to 90 percent of the game, and pitchers who are fielders give their teams that much more.

AT A RECENT coaches' convention and clinic, Andy Baylock, the head baseball coach at the University of Connecticut, distributed a work sheet he had prepared on pitching defense. It wasn't about fielding skills but about the different fielding situations pitchers regularly face. This was the sheet:

PITCHERS—Defense After the Pitch Is Delivered

BASES EMPTY: Ball right side . . . Comebacker . . . Dribbler . . . Bunt . . . Single . . . Double . . . Triple.

RUNNER ON FIRST: Ball right side . . . Comebacker . . . Dribbler . . . Bunt (regular 50–50* situation) . . . Wild pitch (cutoff to 3B) . . . Delayed steal on pitcher . . . Single . . . Double . . . Triple.

RUNNERS ON FIRST AND SECOND: Ball right side . . . Comebacker . . . Dribbler . . . Bunt (regular 50–50 situation) . . . Wild pitch . . . Single . . . Double . . . Triple.

BASES LOADED: Ball right side . . . Comebacker . . . Dribbler . . . Squeeze . . . Wild pitch . . . Single . . . Double . . . Triple.

RUNNER ON SECOND: Ball right side . . . Comebacker . . . Dribbler . . . Bunt (regular 50–50 situation) . . . Wild pitch . . . Single . . . Double . . . Triple.

* meaning infield is halfway

PITCHERS—Defense After the Pitch Is Delivered (*cont.*)

RUNNER ON THIRD: Ball right side . . . Comebacker . . . Dribbler . . . Squeeze . . . Wild pitch . . . Single . . . Double . . . Triple.

RUNNERS ON SECOND AND THIRD: Ball right side . . . Comebacker . . . Dribbler . . . Squeeze . . . Wild pitch . . . Single . . . Double . . . Triple.

RUNNERS ON FIRST AND THIRD: Ball right side . . . Comebacker . . . Dribbler . . . Squeeze . . . Catcher's throw to second base . . . Delayed steal on pticher . . . Single . . . Double . . . Triple.

There are really only two matters of canon on the work sheet: On any ball to the right side, a pitcher must start for first base. That is as close to an absolute in the fielding of any position there is. As Baylock puts it: "Ball to the right side, bell goes off like Pavlov's dog, *bing*, break to first base!" The other absolute involves backing up: The instruction on any single, double, or triple is to move from the mound into position. Jim Kaat puts the two absolutes in another way:

"The number one thing to train yourself to do is break towards every ball hit to the right side because—I've seen it so often—a ball's hit between first and second, the first baseman makes a great play, and the pitcher says, 'Oh!'—and it's too late. So every ball that's hit that way, you go—you take three or four steps and if they don't need you, fine. Then the other thing is to discipline yourself so that you always have a place to go and know where you're going."

The play covering first is routine, so routine that pitchers, doing it hundreds of times in spring-training drills, will do it lazily. Instead of approaching the bag coming up the first-base line so they can hit the side of the bag with their foot, they will amble directly across the base itself—no harm in a spring-training drill but disaster if done in a game with a live runner coming down the line to the base.

But on Andy Baylock's chart, a perfectly standard checklist for pitcher's field work, the plays, beyond the absolutes, are not only many, but each requires varied responses to the point where one play is really many plays within a play. Take the comebacker. With no one on, the pitcher is to be mindful of the first baseman, who may be playing back. Give him time to get to the bag, take a couple of crowhops into the throw rather than throwing on the run or flat-footed, which more easily precipitates throwing errors. Keep the elbow up and the ball exposed so the first baseman can see it well. With a runner on first and less than two out, though, the comebacker is often the beginning of a double play. If the ball is fielded to the shortstop side, that means a lead throw, chest-high, tied to the arrival of the second baseman at the bag; if the ball is fielded on the right side, the lead throw is to the shortstop. The throw, in either case, for both left-handed and right-handed pitchers, is done with a pivot or spin, and must be practiced.

"That throw to second is the toughest play I make as a fielder," says Rick Reuschel, Big Daddy, the Giants' Gold Glove right-hander. The reason, Reuschel says, is that "a pitcher's repetitive throwing is all platewards and this spin and throw the other way is a severe break in rhythm and mechanics." He is forty years old, a veteran of seventeen major league seasons, a spinner of hundreds of double plays, and he is still not comfortable with the play.

The comebacker with a runner on third is different again. The pitcher must check the runner before making his play to first. A head motion or a look is what we notice, but the key to the play is the pitcher's quick feet: The look from a set position followed by a quick stutter-step movement into the throw. And then, with runners on second and third, the comebacker is handled with yet another variation. Some pitchers simply look the runner back to third, but Baylock, along with many major league managers, has his pitchers do something else: "If you check third and go to first, good. But who's always twenty-five feet off second base? So we run what we call 'lighthouse'—check three, check two, then go to first. To do it you've got to really have quick feet."

Through all of these plays the mechanical task for the pitcher is really only half of what he is doing; the other half is his thinking. He *must* be in the game, pitch to pitch, as much as the catcher. On dribblers and bunts, for example, he must keep in mind not only who is hitting but how his fielders are playing. The pitcher will react differently if his infielders are back (he will have to go all out to reach bunts and swinging bunts then) or if they are in, or if they are halfway (the pitcher lays back in one, charges on the other), and each of these setups may change with a single at-bat and thus change what it is the pitcher will have to do.

On wild pitches, again the pitcher's work involves not one but several tasks. We are all familiar with the sight of a pitcher rushing to cover the plate on a ball that has gotten through to the backstop. It is a difficult, often dangerous play, made nearly always with no time to get set. The pitcher must get to his spot to receive the throw, his back to the runner, who is given one half of the plate in order to avoid a collision. Straddling the inside or outside corner of the plate, depending where the catcher's throw is coming from, the pitcher then takes the throw, still blind to the runner, and sweeps his tag down, making sure he uses the back of his glove so that the ball is less likely to be kicked free. If there is no time to set up or the pitcher miscalculates, the results can be scarifying—as they were one year for pitcher Al Nipper, who was run over at the plate and suffered a nearly career-ending gash in the muscles and tendons just below his knee.

In everything he does, the pitcher must be alert to the moment-by-moment adjustments of his position. He has different backup responsibilities anytime there is a hit and different communication responsibilities on bunts, pop-ups, and slow choppers.

On a hit to left field with no one on, he usually backs up the first baseman; on an extra-base hit to the outfield with runners on, he will almost certainly back up any play at the plate or at third. Then again, if there is a hit through the infield on the right

side and the first baseman is sprawled in the dirt, the pitcher will in some situations act as a cutoff man; in other situations, when a first baseman fields a double-play grounder wide of the bag, the pitcher suddenly becomes an auxiliary first baseman, covering the base for the throw that completes the double play.

Pitchers obviously play a significant role in keeping runners from stealing. Perhaps even more important is one aspect of this, the ability to hold runners close. A runner who is checked at three to five feet from the base rather than seven to ten can mean the difference in an advance of one rather than two bases on a hit, which in turn might mean a run not scored, which in turn might mean the outcome of a game.

Through his many years as a pitching coach and manager, Ray Miller, currently the pitching coach of the Pirates, has annually distributed slogan-emblazoned T-shirts to his pitchers. The slogan, contained within a design of home plate, counsels:

Work Fast
Throw Strikes
Change Speeds
Hold 'Em Close

Miller believes that pitching effectiveness and awareness of defense go hand in hand. By working fast, a pitcher not only is more apt to keep his rhythm or "groove," he also makes it easier for the players behind him to stay alert. Throwing strikes and changing speeds (rather than just powering the ball to the plate) is a smarter way to attack hitters as well as guaranteeing that the ball will more often be put in play, the defense more consistently engaged. And as runners are held close, they steal fewer bases, advance less often, and more consistently engage the pitcher in defensive play. A pitcher with a good pickoff move can win a game for his team; a pitching staff that leads the league in pickoffs —like some of those Miller coached in Baltimore—can help its team win pennants.

If the notion of pitchers as defenders seems unusual, the very first pitchers were probably more unusual than anyone. Standing on flat ground forty-five feet from the batter, they pitched underhanded with considerably less velocity than pitchers later used. Clearly, any defensive accomplishments from these first pitchers must have been astonishing. But Pud Galvin won 361 games between 1879 and 1892 and was a top fielder, the National League's best in the nineteenth century, according to a survey taken by the Society for American Baseball Research. (Among other things, Galvin had a pickoff move. In one game in 1886 he picked three men off base in one inning—and none at first base. Ninety-seven years later, Tippy Martinez of the Orioles picked off three in an inning—all at first.) And then there were Tommy Bond and John Clarkson and Guy Hecker and Ted Breitenstein, stars from an age that only winks at us from afar.

What these early pitchers had in common was versatility. They were not just pitchers, but *athletes*. Pud Galvin played the outfield fifty-one times in his career and shortstop a couple of times as well; Tommy Bond was an outfielder, third baseman, and first baseman; Guy Hecker split his time among the mound, the outfield, and first base, leading all first basemen in the American Association in starting double plays one year.

With such defensive experience a regular part of their play, these early pitchers would not have been fazed by Andy Baylock's work sheet and even Ray Miller's T-shirt. Our old friend Chadwick appreciated a pitcher who "can combine a high degree of speed with an even delivery and, at the same time, can, at pleasure, impart a bias or twist to the ball," but he counseled would-be mid-nineteenth-century pitchers to do more:

> When a player attempts to run to the home base while he is pitching, [the pitcher] should follow the ball to the home base as soon as it leaves his hand, and be ready at the base to take it from the catcher. The pitcher will frequently have to occupy the bases on occasions when the proper guardian has left it to field the ball. And

in cases where a foul ball has been struck, and the player running a base endeavors to return to the one he has left, he should be ready to receive the ball at the point nearest the base in question.

In Harry Ellard's remembrance *Baseball in Cincinnati,* there is this picture of Asa Brainard, one of the 1869 Red Stockings' pitchers:

> He delivered a swift, twisting sort of ball, and combined a good deal of head work with his physical exertions. He very rarely pitched a ball where the batter expected it, but sent them in too high, or too low, or too close to the striker, until the latter became nervous or irritated, struck at a ball not fairly within his reach, and "Foul, out," was the usual result. He played his position very neatly, wasting very little time in contemplating the ball (as a great many pitchers did at that time). He watched the bases very carefully, and was a very plucky fielder in his position, and was generally sure of all sorts of high fly balls.

Cy Young, not usually remembered for his fielding, in *The National Game* talked about his approach to both pitching and longevity:

> In the every day run of games, it is not a bad idea to remember that seven other men are behind you on the field, ready to handle the ball if it comes their way, and with plenty of room. I believe in putting the ball over the plate for hitting, trusting to the fielders, in this way saving your arm, for, after all, a pitcher amounts to but very little unless his pitching arm is strong.
>
> Pitchers should practice getting back into position after delivering the ball to the bat, for nothing looks worse than to see a weak grounder go bounding through the box, with the pitcher out of form, after losing his balance.

It is hard for us to imagine that our legendary pitchers were also top fielders. Christy Mathewson's fadeaway was matched by

his pickoff move and general quickness around the mound; Walter Johnson and Herb Pennock were superb defenders.

If he could have, Ray Miller would surely have hired Mathewson's catcher, Chief Meyers, to advise his players. This was how Meyers recalled Mathewson to Lawrence Ritter in 1965:

> How we loved to play for him! We'd break our necks for that guy. If you made an error behind him, or anything of that sort, he'd never get mad or sulk. He'd come over and pat you on the back. He had the sweetest and most gentle nature. . . . He was a great checker player, too. . . . Actually that's what made him a great pitcher. His wonderful retentive memory. Any time you hit a ball hard off him, you never got another pitch in that spot again.
>
> You know, those fellows back there, they *thought,* they used their head in baseball a whole lot. They talked baseball morning, noon, and night. Baseball was their whole life. . . .
>
> Nowadays, the pitcher wastes so much time out there it's ridiculous—fixing his cap . . . pulling up his pants . . . rubbing his chin . . . wiping his brow . . . pulling his nose . . . scratching the ground with his feet. And after he does all that and he looks all around at the outfield, and then he st-a-a-res in at the catcher giving the sign. . . .
>
> They waste an hour or so every day that way. We *always* played a game in less than two hours. Never longer. Two hours used to be considered a long game, really a long game.

The average length of games today is an hour longer than in 1950 and almost two hours more than in 1910. Matty may or may not have belonged to a better time in the ballpark but he almost certainly belonged to a quicker one. And if Ray Miller is any help, that means defense, starting with the pitcher, had inevitably to have been more at the ready.

ACCORDING TO MOST OBSERVERS, the best fielding pitcher in the past forty years or so was Bobby Shantz, who played for several teams between 1949 and 1964. Shantz began in one era,

playing for Connie Mack, ending in another, playing for Gene Mauch. Shantz was hardly alone as a defender of the hill. Harry "The Cat" Brecheen and Harvey "The Kitten" Haddix were around when he began, and Bob Gibson and Jim Kaat were pitching when he finished up. What characterized Shantz—and perhaps the age that ended with him—was just how much pitchers were able to project themselves into games as defenders.

In his salad days with the Athletics and Yankees, Shantz never weighed more than 139 pounds to go with his dripping-wet five-foot-six-inch frame. He delivered a ball to home plate quickly, with a minimum kick and a short, fluid stride that left him, always, in a balanced position, ready to field. He says his size was probably a factor in his quickness. "Because I was so small, I had to put everything into every pitch and because of that I had to be doubly sure that I was ready to field."

Sometimes he wasn't. A line drive off the bat of Nellie Fox once caught him in the pit of the stomach. Shantz says he never really saw the ball before it hit him. Just before the World Series in 1958, Shantz instinctively put out a bare hand to catch a line drive. He caught a couple of broken fingers instead, forcing him to miss the Series. In a spring-training game against the Pirates early in his career, a line drive tore the top of one ear from his head. The blows he took never made him afraid, he says, "just readier to field my position and smarter about how I pitched batters." (He was doubly vigilant whenever he had to pitch outside to strong hitters like Frank Howard and Mickey Mantle, "who could put me clear through the center-field wall with a ball up the middle.")

Shantz's quickness got him from line to line, literally from dugout to dugout, faster than anyone. He remembers a play from his days with the Yankees:

"We were playing Kansas City at the Stadium once and Bob Cerv hit this pop-up over near the Yankee dugout. Yogi went for it and the ball jumped out of his glove and hit Bill Skowron right

in the hand, but it bounced off him, too, so I caught the god-damned thing."

Then Shantz was able to cover ground behind him just as well:

"I couldn't go up the ladder to get a ball the way taller guys could, but sometimes I would go back," he says. "I had this ability to make a quick turn. I remember one time in Detroit, there was a guy on first and I thought there would be a bunt, but there wasn't. The batter was Harvey Kuenn, and he hit away. He hit a ball that bounced on the plate and over the mound. I caught that thing running full steam towards second base with my back completely to the plate. I took the ball halfway between the mound and second, didn't have time to get the runner at second, but because I was left-handed I just planted and threw to first—I got the out there."

Shantz grew up in Pottstown, Pennsylvania, a couple of hours' drive from Philadelphia. He had a child's—and a captain's—love of fielding. Shantz's father regularly took his young sons Bobby and Billy to games at Shibe Park. Their routine, scrupulously adhered to, included a stop at a ball field on the way so the father could hit ground balls to the sons.

Later, Bobby organized his own sandlot team, named himself captain, pitcher, and shortstop ("because I had the bats and balls and they had to let me do what I wanted," he said with a laugh). Shantz's father then regularly hit ground balls to the whole team.

Whether it was because he was quick and owned the bats or because pitchers then were taught to involve themselves in more plays, Shantz, with his shortstop's hands and captain's sense of things, wanted to play every ball he could reach from the mound —line drives, bouncers, bunts, pop-ups, anything. Shantz told his cornermen they could play back and encouraged his middle infielders to shade more to the holes—clear out, make room for him to help the team. It was a habit of mind he took with him when he got older.

During one of his first seasons, Shantz's first baseman was

Ferris Fain, an aggressive and smooth fielder who, having seen George Sisler play, often charged the length of the infield grass to field bunts, regardless of who was pitching. "I used to have to call him off on bunts up the third-base line," Shantz said, "and then one time, in a game in Detroit, with two men on, he cut in front of me and heaved the ball into the left-field stands. Mr. Mack gave him hell, told him after the inning was over to let me take those balls."

Shantz often improvised his own coverage. On hits to the outfield with runners on, he would not, as the book mandated, go directly to a set position behind home or third. "I'd wait," Shantz said. "I'd lay right in the middle between home and third till I knew where the throw was going and then I'd run like hell to get behind one base or the other."

On one occasion, rather than uselessly backing up, Shantz went directly to an empty base and became its defender. "I remember getting a putout at third in one game against the Senators in Washington," he recalls. "Eddie Yost slid into me and I got him. There was no one there to cover third, so I was there."

In the days before stopwatches and unpronounceable Eastern European training programs, Shantz constantly worked to improve his game. As though he were a middle infielder, he practiced the way in which he angled and threw—accuracy and smarts were acquired, not given.

And along with other top-fielding Yankees pitchers like Whitey Ford, Ed Lopat, and Tommy Byrne, he lured Mickey Mantle into pepper games. "I don't know what it was about Mickey," said Shantz, "but he liked to see if he could hit us in the shins. He would really whack the ball. But, I tell you, we got faster because of it."

In a career full of best plays, the one that stands out for Shantz was not a line drive back at him, a shot to his left or right, or a pop fly impossibly far away, but a bunt.

"It happened when I was with Philadelphia. Rizzuto laid down one of the best bunts I've ever seen in my life—and some-

how I got to it and threw him out at first. Remember the way he used to bunt?" Shantz asked, then answered himself: "Rizzuto would wait till the last second, tuck the bat behind his front shoulder so you couldn't see it from out front, and then just drop the bat on the ball. This one dropped down the third-base line and stopped dead. I got to it, could only pick it up bare-handed, whirled, and threw him out. It was the best fielding play I ever made."

Shantz believes bunting as an art—and therefore bunting defense—has faded in recent years. "I don't understand it," he says. "There are so many guys who just don't know how to bunt anymore. Maybe it's that Astroturf stuff—its harder to bunt on that—but there are just so many who can't even square around and bunt. It's like a part of the game that's missing."

For Shantz, clearly, it was a part of the game that allowed him, as a pitcher, to use his quickness. But it was also a part of the game that challenged him most, highlighted the thinking side of what he did, the side that allowed him, even as a grizzled veteran, to have some sense that he still owned the bats.

Jim Kaat, six feet five, quick as a cat, had a hero growing up: five-foot-six-inch Bobby Shantz. Why Shantz rather than other, more obviously heroic types? "I never liked the knock that pitchers weren't good athletes," Kaat explained, "and I wanted to be good at hitting, fielding, in all phases of the game, so I worked at it. I started working at it as a kid, throwing balls off the garage, and I kept at it through my whole career."

Kaat believes that his height and weight (his playing weight was about 235 pounds) made his quickness deceptive and surprising to others—to the point, he says, where surprise itself may have been a factor in his winning a major-league-record sixteen Gold Gloves (tied with Roberto Clemente). He moved from the mound into a balanced position and then could go left or right to the foul lines in just two or three steps. If he was quick as a cat, it was a big cat, and if he had never done more with his game than simply allow his reflexes to take over, he would have been

among the game's better fielding pitchers. But he did more. Almost from the start, he had a coach's sense of his position. By the time his twenty-five-year playing career came to an end in 1983, no one had so clearly elaborated the practice and understanding of pitching defense.

When Kaat talks about the importance of reflexes he is talking about art as much as nature. Quickness is only the clay a pitcher works with, not the finished work. Everything he does, from outsmarting a hitter to somehow flagging down a ball he never quite saw, goes to the single end of keeping the other team from scoring—first getting batters out, then, if they do reach base, keeping them there, limiting their advance, eliminating them if they try to steal.

With the pitcher finishing his delivery about fifty-five feet from the plate, balls rocketing back through the middle are a matter of bodily—and strategic—concern. "Quickness helps you knock a ball down," Kaat says. "What you want to do is not necessarily to try to catch the ball cleanly but just knock it down—you'll have a good chance of making a play then. That's using your quickness."

Using his quickness also determines how the pitcher will approach different batters. Just because he is in so close, his anticipation is critical, and knowing batters well helps establish not only pitch selection but that extra split second of response time that can be both play-saving and life-saving.

"You learn different hitters from both a pitching and a fielding standpoint—it's part of the same thing," Kaat says. "You know the guys who are likely to bunt; you're conscious of pull hitters, guys who aren't likely to hit the ball through the box. But then you pay even more attention to the contact hitters—they're the ones who are most likely to come up the middle."

Because it was defense and not quickness in itself he had in mind, Kaat's radar screen was far-flung. He paid as much attention to the game behind him as that in front of him: who was running, who and where the position players were, what their

strengths and weaknesses were. Kaat played with a first baseman at Minnesota, Don Mincher, who went particularly far to his right in fielding ground balls. In any situation with a likely right-side grounder, Kaat, in addition to anticipating his own moves, anticipated Mincher's as well!

On bunt and double-play coverage, Kaat's quickness got him into plays, and his quickness of mind kept him one step ahead. On double plays, for example, he made sure he knew which of the two middle infielders was covering at second base. That determined the kind of throw he made. "Throwing to second requires that you lead the fielder. If you throw to the base instead of the man you'll mess up the play," Kaat says, "but the throw to the second baseman is a little different than the throw to the shortstop—like the difference in throwing to a wide receiver on one side of the field or the other." And knowledge of who is covering changes within the count on a single batter. "You might start off with the shortstop covering with a right-handed hitter because you know that batter in that situation is going to try to go the other way. But then you fall behind two-and-oh, and you know the guy has the ability to pull the ball, and you're gonna want him to put it in play on the ground. Now you look around and your shortstop lets you know that he's going to hold his ground; the second baseman goes into coverage. You need to know that," says Kaat, "because you need every split second to make that play when it develops."

Kaat eventually learned to take as much advantage of his intelligence as of his quickness. He was a pitcher first, but he was also a defender in the middle of the field. When he played for the Cardinals at the end of his career, Whitey Herzog used him as a relief pitcher, not because Kaat had overpowering stuff (he did not) but because he fielded his position so well. In this role, he invariably came into games with men on base. A sharp fielding pitcher, like Kaat, Herzog reasoned, would be particularly useful in situations where the sacrifice bunt, the stolen base, or the hit-and-run play were so obviously in order.

Kaat paid as much attention to how he held runners on as to how he threw them out. When he took his stretch position with a runner on first, he automatically stood on the edge of the rubber nearest first base because it gave him an extra fraction of a second in throwing time. He fixed base runners in invisible planes or zones. If a runner, taking a lead, passed the boundary line of that zone, Kaat threw over. He would step off or throw until the runner consistently held his lead within the zone. When he could hold a runner close at second base in a place like Fenway Park, with its handball-court wall in left, he surmised, it was the difference between a runner being able to score on a hit off the wall and one having to hold up at third.

On all hits to the outfield, Kaat always knew where to go and, like Bobby Shantz, created opportunities beyond the book. On high, short flies down the right-field line with runners on first and third, instead of taking a backup position behind the plate, Kaat planted himself in cutoff position between home and first. If a ball was hoisted into the middle of the infield, Kaat, as any pitcher should, took charge of traffic. "The pitcher's job on pop-ups in the middle of the field is to look up and locate the ball, quickly look at your third baseman and catcher, you listen to hear if any of them had hollered for the ball—if none of them have, you make a quick judgment who has the best shot and you call it," Kaat said. But then, because he was so actively responsible for the middle of the field, he went one step further. To reduce the chance of a collision, Kaat walked over and put a restraining hand on one of the fielders called off the play, usually the catcher, as the ball was coming down through the air.

In the aftermath of his career, Kaat remains uncertain about the meaning of all the fielding awards he received, but he is clear about what he did. "Whenever I made a play in the field," he says, "I could look back after the game and say, 'I saved some runs with that play.'" For Kaat it was a matter of pride—and had been ever since the age of eight, when he first understood why Bobby Shantz was his hero.

IT IS NOT surprising that some of the game's seniors are still among the game's best fielding pitchers. It is as though the habit of mind required to field the position well went with the territory when they were growing up, whereas for younger pitchers, learning the game in somewhat different circumstances, that has not always been the case.

Rick Reuschel, at six feet three and 240 pounds, will never win many foot races, but he moves off the mound with the agility of a smaller, faster man.

"I think all pitchers take fielding seriously but they don't necessarily think like fielders," Reuschel says. "It isn't so much about physical ability—it's something in the pitcher's mind at the moment he releases the ball. Most guys are thinking about where the ball is going—will the batter swing or miss, was the pitch a ball or strike—and by then it's too late. The second I release a pitch, my mind's in a defensive mode; I'm looking for the ball to be hit to me. Especially when I'm going good, that's what I'm thinking —I'm trying to make a pitch that the batter's going to hit back to me, the shortstop, or the second baseman for a double play. A lot of guys can make up for ability . . . just by being extra quick reactively when they release a pitch."

This habit of mind, which any sensible coach hopes his pitchers will have, developed in the way Reuschel learned the position and the game as an Illinois farmboy. Playing in open fields without fences, the emphasis was on learning how to catch a ball. "If you missed one, you chased it," he says, "as far as it rolled." As a pitcher, he learned "the second or third time a ball was hit back at me that I had better be prepared." But then there was something else. "Back then, it was just absolutely automatic that the best player on the team was your pitcher. So any kind of pop-up in the infield he's going to try and catch, he's gonna call the other kids off, he's gonna be the cutoff man if the ball's hit to the outfield. You didn't back up at home plate because the backstop was right there—you looked to make any play you could."

By the time he became a big leaguer, Reuschel was no longer the best athlete on the field, but that way of thinking was ingrained; he still wanted to be in on everything. When a pitch left his hand, his mind automatically switched into the mode of a defender.

Perhaps because he was large and, in his mind, a little slower than others, perhaps because his style of pitching featured control and an excellent sinker guaranteed to keep the ball in play and usually on the ground, he worked hard at refining his game in the field.

When he was in the minors, he worked regularly on snagging comebackers. He and fellow pitchers in Huron and San Antonio played a game of "Hit the Hat," where one player fired a ball at a hat on the ground, with a partner fielding the ball on short and in-between hops each time the hat was missed. If the hat was struck, points for the thrower, but each time one of the pitchers snagged a short hop, points for the fielder.

In Chicago, Reuschel's first and longest stop in the big leagues, he played a daily pepper game in the left-field corner during each day's batting practice. But his approach was broader, a holdover from his farmboy days, when every chore in the field was his responsibility. In watching fellow pitchers like Ferguson Jenkins, he realized there were additional ways he could help himself as a fielding pitcher.

Simply throwing strikes was a tremendous help; then he taught himself to work quickly. These skills, Reuschel saw when Jenkins pitched, had an immediate effect on the whole team.

"I learned most about pitching from Fergie," Reuschel says, "how pitching and fielding were really one: When he finished a pitch, he was always in a squared position, ready to make a play. I watched the way he threw strikes consistently, how fast he worked, how much he kept his team in the game by doing all that."

From early on, Reuschel worked on the way he held runners. It was his view that trying to pick runners off was basically a

waste of time for himself and his fielders but that holding them close was essential. He spent an entire six-week period during one Instructional League season throwing exclusively from the stretch so that he could learn to deliver a ball to home plate comfortably without any leg kick—just a slide step forward, then the pitch. The goal was not only quickness to the plate, but incorporating the move, bringing it into his natural pitching delivery. It was not as easy as it sounds. Any tampering with a pitcher's natural motion for the sake of his fielding (getting him to square around rather than fall off to the side of the mound after a pitch, for example) is usually not encouraged for fear of reducing pitching effectiveness. But Reuschel made this defensive maneuver part of his pitching style.

When Reuschel wound up spending a couple of seasons with the Yankees, he marveled at the quickness of Ron Guidry. "I just watched him and wished I could do that," Big Daddy says. But with his "slowness," he still managed to get to places that younger, faster men did not. In a 1989 game against the Phils, Reuschel, a week past his fortieth birthday, saved a run, an inning, and possibly a game on a play he had no business making. Giants second baseman Robby Thompson fielded a smash in the hole between first and second. At the same time, the first baseman, Will Clark, shaded right on a right-handed batter, even though he had no chance on the ball, impulsively sprawled after it at the last second, taking himself out of the play and leaving first base unguarded. But there was Big Daddy. Somehow, as rapidly as the play developed and with as little initial likelihood that coverage from him would be needed, he was there to make the putout. As he did on all such plays, Reuschel had instinctively broken for the bag. Running against someone faster than himself, he had no chance to make the play. And then, suddenly, the lead throw to the bag was hurried, too far out front, headed for no-man's-land. Reuschel, all 240 pounds of him, took off through the air like a flying whale. His body stretched horizontally to the ground, he snared the ball in the tip of his glove and fell thunderously to earth, tagging the base as he landed.

It's possible that Ron Guidry would have made such a play more easily. Certainly no one was quicker off the mound in recent years. When he released a pitch, his follow-through ended with a small, idiosyncratic leap on the balls of his feet (Guidry, in his soft Cajun accent, refers to it as his "little iddy-biddy hop," and says that he had it from the time he first began pitching, around the age of ten or eleven). This hop or leap left Guidry not only in a balanced fielding position, but already in motion toward any ball that might be hit his way. It allowed him to attack a ball actively before it was hit—no matter where it was hit. He was as quick and as comfortable going left as right. This was his secret —or rather his body's secret—because, as Rick Reuschel knows, it really cannot be acquired or taught.

From his squared-but-forward-moving position after he released the ball, Guidry was able to push powerfully off either leg going to either side. His legs were as coordinated as a pianist's hands; left and right were never tangled in different impulses running at different speeds through his nervous system.

Guidry's hands were always "soft," and almost from the time he sensed, early in childhood, that there was some relationship between this strange, inborn gift of quickness and what he could do with his hands, he worked at his fielding. He says, recalling not pain but private joy, that he was in constant trouble at home, whanging balls off the sides of the family house. "I used to break windows, I used to break the sides of the stucco house, I used to break the sheets. *Boom! Boom! Boom!* Like in tennis when you're sittin' at the net and no one can hit it by you."

Guidry continued this habit of almost obsessive boomerang catching throughout his youth. When his family moved from a stucco to a brick house, he went after the brick; when he went to college, he went after dormitory walls. He organized games with friends where they would, hour after hour, spike balls at each other. And then, when he turned professional, Guidry continued to work at retrieving as though it were a high Louisiana hunt.

Each spring training from his first to his most recent, Guidry went one-on-one with a coach on a backfield diamond, taking

ground balls every day. He had the balls hit at him left and right, hard and soft, liners and bounders, testing his impulses against every conceivable type of play he might have in a game.

Though "old" Rick Reuschel thought of "young" Ron Guidry as an example of the current quality of fielding pitchers, Guidry is no longer an active player. His incomparable, youthful 25-3 season more than a decade ago only reminds us today of a pitcher whose ability and accomplishments were special.

Guidry changed the game for his teammates when he played. He told his cornermen to play back, his middle infielders to swing toward the holes. He guarded his space as jealously as a mating wolf. "If you look at a mound," he said, "it's got five or six feet of raised dirt—in diameter—and that's what you have to cover. If the ball's hit on the grass, you probably won't get to it, even if it's hit with average velocity—that's where your shortstop and second baseman come in. But what about the ball that's hit fairly hard right over the mound or two to three feet to either side of it? That's the one the middle infielders just barely miss—but that's my territory."

On soft hits as well, his territory was from the mound to the lines. Guidry had his cornermen play back because he had told himself—and them—"If I can't get to it, no one else is going to get to it either." His teammates, he said once, "are out there to play hard defense, and so am I. I'm never going to forget my part because it's an instrumental part. I play the middle. When you think about it, I have a bigger field than anyone to cover."

Guidry was taut-wired to every situation he faced, to every pitch he threw. He anticipated differently if he threw a fastball from the middle of the plate out than if he pitched inside or went to his downboring slider. Here he was in a bunting situation:

"You go into a stretch with a guy on first or a guy on second. You might try a pickoff play to see what the guy at the plate is going to do. If he squares around or his hands start to slide on the bat, he's probably going to bunt. If he doesn't commit himself, it's still in your mind they might bunt. Okay, you're in your

windup, you're up here and start to deliver the ball—sometimes I'll do this purposely: If I'm not sure the guy's bunting, I'll take a little more time in the delivery to see what the hitter is doing, because just about every successful bunter nowadays has to square around to do it. Okay, I'm up here, I see the guy start—*boom*, I'm going. When he's squaring around, I'm already moving, and because I'm moving forward I can start in one direction and go in another without losing anything if I have to."

Guidry made his plays. He once got from the mound to first base on a line drive caught by his first baseman in a bases-loaded situation against the Royals—in time to double up Willie Wilson, one of the fastest runners in baseball. In a 1988 game against the White Sox, Guidry turned a certain two-run single up the middle into a game-saving backhanded stab and force-out at second base. But he doesn't remember plays, "certainly none that ever directly, bottom-of-the-ninth, won a game outright or anything." He remembers the nuances of the position, its everyday music.

So quick was Guidry that he cannot recall ever being hit hard by a ball back at him. He said his toughest play was handling a line drive five to six feet over his head, where he had to go up in the air off the slope of the mound. That slope is another kind of problem, another puzzle to piece together. Any ball that hits it tends to stay down. Guidry tutored his own quickness—seemingly against the laws of optics—to cope with even these sorts of "smart" bullets.

"The ball that takes one hop off the dirt part of the mound very seldom comes up," said Guidry. "But your reflexes tend to get like this: You don't want to get hit by the ball. Now your brain tells you, 'Don't get hurt,' but your reflexes are faster than your brain. As a pitcher you learn over time how to judge a ball, any ball that you see enough. Your reflexes take over; they are going to take over before your brain transmits the message 'Okay, react,' and somehow you will have made the play."

The game's good fielding younger pitchers range in age and experience from rookies to veterans, from the long and lean to

the short and burly. But what unites them all is this trained sort of quickness. Nearly all of the game's most recent best are former infielders, usually cornermen, who brought their fielding skills with them to the mound. Bret Saberhagen, Mark Langston, and Ron Darling were shortstops; Bobby Ojeda was a first baseman, Mike Boddicker a third baseman, Fernando Valenzuela a left-handed third baseman, Jim Abbott a Little League third baseman, outfielder, and pitcher (as well as a lettered high school basketball player). Jack Lazorko, the California pitcher who has moved up from and down to the minors over several seasons, was actually a hockey goalie in high school and quite consciously transferred shot-blocking skills to the mound, using splits to throw shins, feet, anything in the way of passing baseballs.

But it is their habit of mind that makes these pitchers something more than merely good or even skilled athletes who happen to fill a position. All of them seem to share that twin-signal concentration described by Rick Reuschel, being able to release a pitch and then, immediately, being ready to field.

"The second the ball leaves my hand," Mike Boddicker says, "I'm a third baseman."

"As soon as I release the ball, I think, 'Self-protection and field the ball,' " Bob Ojeda says.

"You are part of the guys out there," Mark Langston said. "I'm an infielder just as soon as that pitch is off my fingertips on the way to the plate."

There are variations in the way these pitchers think, of course. Ron Darling, a Yale graduate but, more significant, a longtime teammate of Keith Hernandez's, anticipates almost like a computer programmer. "I know what my options are, one, two, and three, in every situation," he says. "It's just what you're taught as an infielder—know what you're going to do before a ball is hit. That's one of my real strengths."

On the other hand, Bret Saberhagen says he really doesn't anticipate as such. "For me, the big thing is being in ready position after a pitch and then being quick." He recounts a bunt

ituation in a game against the White Sox at the end of the 1988 season where lack of anticipation might actually have cost him a triple play: "There were runners on first and second, guy bunts to me on the fly. I dropped it and went to second, then it was on to first for the double play. If I had been just a little quicker-thinking, I would have gone to third—and we would have had time for a triple play."

All of the pitchers take pride in being fifth infielders, approaching their work routines with some sense that they add more to their teams than people usually look for.

Langston takes daily infield practice with his team's infielders. Saberhagen continues spring-training drills in handling come-backers and throwing to different bases through the regular season.

He and Darling also have worked hard to refine excellent pickoff moves. "I have about six or seven different types of throws to the base," Saberhagen says. "I'll throw in sequences, knowing which throw will be the one I want to use to get the runner. The key is varying your motion." Most important, he adds, never having seen Ray Miller's T-shirt, is holding runners close. "The best way to hold a runner on is to just hold the ball. The longer you hold it, the more impatient he gets, and then he'll have a hard time getting a good jump. There are no statistics for that, but that really counts over a full season of games."

The incalculable quality that any great fielding pitcher begins with, even more than other position players, is daring. It is not quite reasonable for someone standing at firing-squad distance from home plate to think of being more than a sitting duck. If a pitcher throws well and manages to protect himself, that is usually considered enough by most teams and their fans. But when he actually challenges dangers over which he has only limited control, protected only by the layered shield of his mitt—and by his own courage—he becomes another kind of player entirely.

At first glance, Jim Abbott, the one-handed rookie pitcher with the California Angels who achieved national prominence as a member of the U.S. Pan American and Olympic teams in 1988, is more a potential victim than a likely defender in the middle of the field.

Jim Kaat, when asked to name the game's top fielding pitchers, mentions Allan Anderson and then Jim Abbott. Kaat's judgment, without sentiment, is professional and clinical and is based on the narrowest and keenest of standards: athletic ability. "Abbott has good, quick reactions," he says, "and because he has to use one hand, he's probably more conscious of the ball hit back at him than most; he's just one heck of an athlete."

On his first tour of the majors in 1989, Abbott played with more than the usual load of rookie pressure on him. Everywhere he went, there were press conferences with the same questions asked, the same unsolicited sympathy and admiration extended, all centering around the fact that he was born with one hand. At each stop along the way, Abbott handled himself in a manner that made clear why Doug Rader, his manager, thought he was ready for the majors now rather than later: He was not only greatly talented but also mature enough to deal with extraordinary pressures that went far beyond baseball.

Abbott, not surprisingly, seemed leery about the fuss being made over him. Invariably, questions that began with baseball ended with ones about his hand. He has been asked over and over again about Pete Gray, the one-armed outfielder who played for the St. Louis Browns during World War II. He has been besieged in locker rooms, hotel lobbies, airport terminals. Television and movie producers, book and magazine publishers have fought to get the exclusive rights to his story, the story that out-Strattons Monty Stratton, that out-Grays Pete Gray. So far he has seemed to manage this part of his career as though it were an inconvenience rather than a burden.

It is not that Abbott is unmindful of or ungrateful for the attention he has received. Modest in manner to the point of

feeling some embarrassment for being such a clubhouse focus in the midst of more established players, he is uncannily patient with those whose curiosity seemingly cannot be satisfied. "I know that I have a responsibility beyond myself, so I won't turn away even though I look forward to the day when I will be seen for just the player I am," he says.

Abbott thinks of himself as a ballplayer. That is his defining term. He abjures the word *handicapped* because he says it doesn't describe him. "*Handicap* means limitation, and I've never felt limited in what I can do," he says.

More than in any other area of his game, this refusal to accept limitation shows up in his fielding. It takes only one hand to throw a ball ninety miles an hour, but something more is required before the firing squad.

Anyone who has seen him pitch knows that he negotiates his one-handedness with uncanny agility. Abbott bristles over continuing references to his being one-armed because, in reality, he makes significant use of his malformed limb. "I am one-handed, not one-armed," he says. Before each pitch, he balances his glove on his withered right stump, wedging the baseball between the back of the glove and his body. With the ball hidden from the batter, he takes it in his hand as he goes into his leg kick and then, as he releases his pitch, he immediately transfers the glove to his throwing hand, ready to field as he comes around in a perfectly squared position. The transfer of glove to hand is done so smoothly, so quickly, that even someone watching for it cannot quite tell how it is done. Abbott began practicing the move —and the more complex one of getting the ball from his glove, placed under his handless arm after a catch—so that it was second nature by the time he began playing Little League. Whatever physical moves were involved, there were mental ones too. The transfer of glove to hand immediately following the release of a ~h exactly parallels a transfer of thinking from a pitching to a ~g mode. If any coach wanted a visual representation of this ~of mental gears, Abbot's routine delivery shows it. What

is a sometime proposition with two-handed pitchers has always been mandatory for him. And because of who he is, he has never been content with stopping there.

In one of Abbott's early games, a ball was spiked back at him with a runner on first. He turned it—easily—into a double play.

"You could see how well he handled himself up till then—you knew he was a really good athlete," Lance Parrish, his catcher, said. "But even so, there was always this one little area of doubt—what would happen if . . . you know. He handled this ball better than most pitchers with two hands. It was hit, he had it, it was gone. You never even knew he was one-handed."

The "book" on Abbott, quoted by Kaat and others, is that he is a good and aggressive fielder. That is what advance scouts for the Yankees passed on to the team's brain trust before one mid-season game in 1989. "He fields the ball properly, he's quick with his hand, he makes the plays," said Charlie Fox. "The people who've talked to me all say, 'Don't try to bunt on him,' " then manager Dallas Green said.

The Yankees spiked balls, topped them—and bunted them—in this game, won by the Angels and Abbott 6–4. In the first inning, Rickey Henderson whistled a shot past Abbott's ear into center field that the pitcher did well to avoid. Then Abbott proceeded to hold Henderson at first until a Don Mattingly single advanced but did not score him.

In the second inning, the catcher Bob Geren bounced a sharp one-hopper over Abbott's right shoulder. But he had made his glove-to-hand transfer so quickly he reached across his body, over his right shoulder, and snared the ball, turning a single up the middle into a routine 1-3 putout.

In the third inning, Henderson topped a ball between the mound and the third-base line. Abbott was on it before Henderson had even lit his jets, fielding the ball with the glove on his le hand, transferring mitt and ball under his opposite arm, tran ring the ball to his hand—all faster than the eye could follo nipped Henderson at first.

The very next batter, Steve Sax, hit another topper, a ball that died in the grass down the third-base line, which Abbott retrieved bare-handed but chose not to throw, seeing he had no play.

In the fourth, with the Angels leading 3–1, there was a complication: rain. The rain had started in the top of the inning and continued so that the ground was slick and the footing treacherous. The lead batter in the inning, Bob Geren again, slipped a bunt wide of the mound and beyond it, toward third. Abbott moved for the ball quickly but could not reach it. Then, the light-hitting Alvaro Espinoza dropped a sacrifice bunt in front of the mound. Abbott charged, but fell coming off the mound. The play was the catcher's anyway, and the out was easily made at first.

Abbott left the game in the sixth inning with his team leading 5–2 and the Yankees threatening to move closer. He had given up ten hits in five and one third innings, not one of his best outings, but the fans in Yankee Stadium, never distinguished for their civility, rose to their feet and cheered him. They cheered him possibly for his being there in the first place but also because they were seeing him for the first time as he had wanted them to see him—as a "good ballplayer."

Abbott downplays his accomplishments and in doing so is even more impressive. He learned to handle himself in the field, he says, not because he was one-handed but because there were certain ways you were taught to do things in baseball and therefore you learned them. All pitchers are taught to finish their delivery in a squared position, ready to field; all pitchers are taught to think as fielders once they release a ball to the plate; all pitchers are taught to anticipate and to hold runners close, to back up bases and to communicate with other fielders on different plays. "I tried to do all that not thinking about having one hand so much as learning to do things all players are supposed to learn."

But Abbott has had to learn to do things differently. Just because nature tied one hand behind his back, he has had to be doubly determined. To overcome limitation, to put himself in a

position to aspire to everything he wanted, he has had to risk more in a few years of life than most people do in a lifetime. That is what he carries with him around the league and that is also what he brings with him to the field.

Abbott knows he fields his position well and also that he is still young and learning. The sheer number of games and plays are simply not there yet.

"I don't try for more than I can. If someone hits a shot at me, most times I'm going to try to get out of the way," he says. He knows that balls that hit the dirt part of the mound tend to explode and stay down. His reflexes are still faster than his mind. But he knows, as do many of the great-fielding pitchers, that the game begins with reflexes, and that reflexes can be tutored.

When his team is at home, Abbott works every day with the Angels' eighty-three-year-old conditioning coach, Jimmy Reese. Reese, who was once Babe Ruth's roommate, had a heart attack several years ago and is not allowed to travel with the team. Yet he remains one of the supreme fungo hitters, perhaps from the dawn of sticks and stones to the present. So accurate are his self-generated hits that he once stood on a mound and pitched batting practice by fungoing balls to the plate. He has played rounds of golf using his fungo bat. Gene Mauch, the former Angels manager, has referred to him for years simply, as "a Russian violinist."

Reese still works his players. Because he can place a ball on a dime, he can stretch out a body to its limit, test a player's reflexes to a hair trigger. Everyone loves Jimmy Reese, but few really have the legs or the energy to take advantage of him. He is a person, like Abbott, who generates enormous sympathy just by showing up. But, like Abbott, he is disguised by who he is. Perhaps that is why the two men have become so close. Jim Abbott works, and craves work, with Jimmy Reese. He takes him for who he is and knows, perhaps better than anyone, that Reese's age is no handicap—just as Reese takes Abbott for who he is and knows better than anyone that he is not handicapped.

The two men pair off in the outfield. "He gets twenty feet

away and hits a lot of balls back at me," Abbott says. "I take off the glove and pantomime a pitch, and he hits it at me. I put the glove on and field it. He's got the timing down perfectly about when the ball would be coming back at me."

Reese hits the ball directly at him, to his left, to his right, over his head, at his feet, at his shins, slower, quicker, hard, soft, spinning, straight.

"I miss a few here and there and he laughs if he hits me in the shins," says the young pitcher. Early in the year, Abbott made a throwing error during a home game. "I missed one ball, threw it away," Abbott said. "He looked a little disappointed when I got back to the bench. He said to me, 'That means extra work.'"

In his career, stretching from Little League through his first year in the majors, Abbott, like Ron Guidry, has never been injured by a ball hit back at him. He says he has been lucky. But also, he has made himself the player he is. That is his gift to himself and to us. He got there the old-fashioned way—by learning his position.

Acknowledgments

A NUMBER OF PEOPLE contributed to this book in ways that no standard page of credits can account for. I received research help and guidance from the staff at the Baseball Hall of Fame Library. I owe particular thanks to Tom Heitz and Bill Deane for leading me through a maze of historical material and for being there to answer endless numbers of questions. Bill Guilfoile generously shared with me his stunning collection of anecdotal accounts of outstanding defensive plays, gathered from generations of fans, writers, and participants.

Several people read and reread my manuscript through its different stages and alerted me to what strengthening steps still could be taken. John Thorn, whose desk was surely full enough, had time to make countless helpful suggestions; Jon Segal, my friend and original editor at Times Books, made me think, re-think, and then rewrite what I was doing; Andrew Siff spotted any number of omissions, errors, questionable judgments that I had made along the way. And though it was her job, Amy Edelman, a senior copy editor at Random House, gave my manuscript the sort of intelligent and dedicated going-over that a writer prays for.

There are others to thank: Larry Ritter, Lee Lowenfish, the different teams as well as Pat Kelly at the Hall of Fame for providing photographs, and then all the players, managers, and coaches gathered here who, individually and collectively, made me see the game as I had not seen it before.

Index

Permissions Acknowledgments

Grateful acknowledgment is made to the following for permission to reprint previously published material:

E. P. DUTTON: Excerpts from *The Babe Ruth Story* by Babe Ruth, as told to Bob Considine. Copyright 1948 by George Herman Ruth. Copyright renewed 1976 by Mildred Considine. Reprinted by permission of the publisher, E. P. Dutton, an imprint of New American Library, a division of Penguin Books USA, Inc.

GROSSET AND DUNLAP: Excerpts from *Lou Gehrig: Pride of the Yankees* by Paul Gallico. Copyright 1942, 1969 by Paul Gallico. Reprinted by permission of Grosset and Dunlap.

DAVID MCKAY CO., A DIVISION OF RANDOM HOUSE, INC.: Excerpts from *On Baseball* by George Sisler. Copyright 1954 by George Sisler. Reprinted by permission of David McKay Co., a Division of Random House, Inc.

THE PUTNAM PUBLISHING GROUP AND STERLING LORD LITERISTIC, INC.: Excerpts from *Bums: An Oral History of the Brooklyn Dodgers* by Peter Golenbock. Copyright © 1984 by Peter Golenbock. Rights in the British Commonwealth and open market administered by Sterling Lord Literistic, Inc. Reprinted by permission of The Putnam Publishing Group and Sterling Lord Literistic, Inc.

LAWRENCE RITTER: Excerpts from *The Glory of Their Times* by Lawrence Ritter (William Morrow and Company, 1984). Reprinted by permission of the author.

SIMON AND SCHUSTER, INC.: Excerpts from *Say Hey!* by Willie Mays with Lou Sahadi. Copyright © 1988 by Willie Mays. Reprinted by permission of Simon and Schuster, Inc.

SPORTS ILLUSTRATED: Excerpts from "They Don't Make 'Em Like They Used To" by Pete Gammons from the April 1989 issue of *Sports Illustrated*. Copyright © 1989 by The Time Magazine Company. All Rights Reserved. Reprinted courtesy of *Sports Illustrated*.

SOCIETY FOR AMERICAN BASEBALL RESEARCH: Excerpts from "Bare Hands and Kid Gloves: The Best Fielders 1880–1899" by William Akin from *Baseball Research Journal*, 1981, and excerpts from an essay by John Holway from *Baseball Research Journal*, 1986. Reprinted by permission of Society for American Baseball Research.

GEORGE SULLIVAN: Excerpt from *The Picture History of the Boston Red Sox* by George Sullivan. Copyright © 1980 by George Sullivan. Reprinted by permission of the author.

UNITED PRESS INTERNATIONAL: Excerpt from an article by Darrell Mack relating to Roberto Clemente from June 6, 1971. Copyright © 1971. Reprinted by permission of United Press International.

PROFESSOR DAVID L. WEE: Excerpt from "The Glove Song of Our Kirby Puckett" by David L. Wee. Reprinted by permission of the author.